T0372229

MOTORCYCLE GRAND PRIX

MOTORCYCLE GRAND PRIX

Insider Stories from World Championship Racing

ADAM WHEELER

Michael O'Mara Books Limited

First published in Great Britain in 2025 by
Michael O'Mara Books Limited
9 Lion Yard
Tremadoc Road
London SW4 7NQ

A CIP catalogue record for this book is available from the British Library.

This product is made of material from well-managed, FSC®-certified forests and other controlled sources. The manufacturing processes conform to the environmental regulations of the country of origin.

ISBN: 978-1-78929-677-8 in hardback print format
ISBN: 978-1-78929-761-4 in trade paperback print format
ISBN: 978-1-78929-678-5 in ebook format

1 2 3 4 5 6 7 8 9 10

Cover photographs: Rob Gray/Polarity Photo
Cover design: Ana Bjezancevic
Designed and typeset: D23
Printed and bound by CPI Group (UK) Ltd, Croydon, CR0 4YY

MIX
Paper | Supporting responsible forestry
FSC www.fsc.org FSC® C013604

www.mombooks.com

For Nuria, who has my heart and is the mate of my soul.

To Alex and to Jordi, do what you really want to do.
Be special.

To Mum, for her patience and support of a small, dreamy boy.

And to Dad: I never got the chance to tell you,
but I think you did everything right.

Contents

Warm-up . . .   9

ONE   Entering the Hive   13

TWO   The Red   48

THREE   The Gift   93

FOUR   The Layer   124

FIVE   Orange Spirit and the
           Hardline and Hope   156

SIX   The Salsa   218

SEVEN   The Reason   249

EIGHT   Riders   292

           Acknowledgements   328

           Index   331

Warm-up . . .

F abio Quartararo is late, but my cappuccino is warm and the Monster Energy Yamaha hospitality area in the paddock at Misano, San Marino, is quiet, almost deserted. Somewhere in the side offices, someone is tapping a keyboard. A large glass jar of marshmallows stares at me. A nearby TV beams images of MotoGP World Champion Pecco Bagnaia and his principal rival Jorge Martin, the two Ducati references of the moment in the FIM World Championship, talking in the official press conference a hundred metres or so away at the Emilia Romagna Grand Prix. It is September 2024 and a hesitant Thursday ahead of round 14 of 20. MotoGP will race, then pack and hustle to the other side of the world on Sunday evening for a six-week rush through events in Indonesia, Japan, Australia, Thailand and Malaysia.

Yamaha's corporate bolthole at grands prix is a grey and blue, low ceilinged compact box with natural light fighting to enter one side of the structure through thick frosted windows. A microwave oven. Valentino Rossi used to hold his media debrief/ press conferences in one corner of this space, the collection of dining tables and chairs turned around, converting it into a mini auditorium. Another age.

Finally, I hear an electric scooter whine to a halt outside.

The 2021 MotoGP world champ bounds in, dressed in non-descript sweats (no cap or corporatism yet), fresh-faced and with tufts of mousey hair. He offers a firm handshake and a short apology. While a member of the hospitality staff saunters over to offer Fabio a drink, I quickly calculate that this is the fifth or sixth one-to-one interview we've done together since he entered Grand Prix racing ten seasons ago with a wave of hype barely seen in MotoGP.

Why all the 'rage'? Firstly, there was the onslaught of results in the key feeder series to the world championship. Then there was the outrageous natural motorcycling technique and speed, followed by the boyish good looks, the loose and likeable character, and the nationality. In Misano only three years ago, Quartararo was the celebrated new champion and the first ever for France in the premier class. Tellingly, he was also the third winner from the last four years, when, prior to 2020, there had been only four champions from the previous twelve seasons.

The 25-year-old from Nice unscrews a cap from a bottle of water and nestles into the chair. Quartararo might just be MotoGP's most stylish racer – both atop the 220mph factory Yamaha M1 and away from the circuit, where his life centres around running, friends (some very famous ones), eyebrow-raising fashion and other distractions that would appeal to outstanding sportsmen and multimillionaires in their mid-twenties. Fabio's skill, openness and vigour might make him MotoGP's most accessible 'totem'. His pathway to the top has been long but predestined.

'Every Saturday and Sunday with my dad, we went to the same place, the same circuit. It was the only one and the closest one, but it was a two-hour trip each way,' he recounts of his origins in the sport. 'I was riding a 50cc bike, with older and bigger guys, and I was faster than them. I already had this mentality of "I don't want to lose". I can remember how fast I was. I thought it was really cool but, of course, you then go faster, faster and faster and maybe I crashed once from every three attempts because I was pushing the limits. It was at that moment I decided: "I want to do this; I want it as a job."'

We talk about extremes of MotoGP riding and how he was the 'offspring' of Jorge Lorenzo and Stefan Bradl with the breathtaking shoulder scrape at the Circuit de Barcelona-Catalunya's Turn 5. 'When you see the pictures you think, "F**k, I'm really low ..." and I have a photo of me when I am maybe ten years old at the same corner and I am trying to put my elbow out to touch the ground. Now I just have to tip-out and I have the shoulder there!' he laughs.

We touch on his six years with Yamaha, his ability to focus ('like most people I worry about stupid stuff, but the moment I put the helmet on I forget about everything') and how he fixates on running to help him prepare. 'I recently had a target of 10 kilometres in 35 minutes; my trainer was unsure because my best had been 37 but I explained it to him in a way where I felt if I didn't do a 35 then I would not win in MotoGP again,' he reveals. 'When you get to the fourth or fifth kilometre, then you think about that. Mental strength is much bigger than the physical. You might arrive somewhere very tired but it's only the half of your possibilities. I think your brain can give you much more than what you expect. I like to put myself into the red zone.'

Later in the weekend, I will watch from behind the infield fence as the number 20 Yamaha howls, bends and commits to Misano's Turn 11 kink, 'Curvone'. It is one of the fastest and most illustrative corners in MotoGP, taken at 155mph and with 55 degrees of lean angle. It sums up the splendour and the disbelief of this riveting sport. Underneath the competition and the rabid commitment of Quartararo and his rivals to rule the track, there is a miraculous swirl of forces and dynamism, coupled with the rush of wind and sound. It never gets dull.

I bring up the subject of Curvone. 'On the bike, you don't feel that fast because you get used to it super-easy,' he claims. 'I asked the team what the speed was at the lowest point going in and they said, "238" [kmph]. Try doing that in a car! Now imagine on a bike and with only a few centimetres of the wheels touching the track, sliding; it is totally ridiculous.'

Quartararo is slated for the second press conference slot in San Marino and has to go. Before he departs, I ask him whether his elite status in the sport sometimes makes him feel more like an artist as much as a racer. He pauses. 'I think we are both,' he compromises. 'We do things that 0.0001 per cent of people in the world can do. If you see in detail just one corner: the way we brake, downshift, we turn, we lean, we push the handlebars, we push with the footpeg. We do many things in just a few seconds and it feels very natural. We all want to finish first, so we are all racers, but we are also doing art with the bikes.'

ONE

Entering the Hive

Turning the handle of the door is a brave step into one of the most exclusive and secretive areas of MotoGP. Entry into a pitbox means invasion of a race team's compact and claustrophobic workspace. Here, stealthy prototype machinery is laid bare, organization is (normally) at a premium and activity never stops. The pitbox is an environment of high functionality and rhythm. It's an often dark and – for the uninitiated – intimidating warren of passages, parts and protrusions. It costs around 10 million euros per year to put a rider on the track. The pitbox is where this is stuffed into a cohesive state that is unpacked and packed on a bi-weekly basis.

I shouldn't be here. I don't have a colourful uniform covered by logos. I don't have a headset and a radio. I'm not holding a tool or a clipboard or tablet. I have an orange media pass and, regardless of the permission I have been given to hover, that usually comes with a little glance of suspicion from those who spend the better part of a week in this burrow. Two nine-person 'front-of-house' crews busily service a racer each, as well as an angular motorcycle designed for a singular purpose. At various times during a grand prix weekend, visitors and VIPs will be granted brief access for a swift tour, but only when the bikes and the tech are 'dressed', lest any sensitive or secretive innards are too revealing. Like I do, these guests have to weave through the structure that is erected in an otherwise stony vacuum. It is an impermeable buffer between the activity of the paddock and the business end on the track. The hinge of racing's existential soul.

There are layers to MotoGP. The paddock itself is the domain of pristine and polished trucks, all backed-up meticulously to the rear of the pitboxes. Other large trailers serve as offices and meeting rooms. Multi-level hospitality units fold up and down like a complex Ikea flat-pack of windows and walls. In one corner of the paddock is a rank of expensive and sometimes customized motorhomes – the riders' refuge from the gaze of privileged public with a pass and the revolving beads of pressure – and the comfy line of 'GP rooms': premium rented mobile accommodation for athletes who have no interest in their own fancy vehicle. MotoGP assembles around several thousand workers per grand prix, not counting the staff employed for almost a week by the facility the championship invades for set-up and the three-day event itself. The inner sanctum of this world is organized by the International Race Teams Association (IRTA) in conjunction with promoters Dorna Sports – who, from 1992 to April 2024, were the majority owners of MotoGP until the 4.2 billion dollar, 86 per cent acquisition by Liberty Media Corp left the championship on the cusp of change as it heads into its seventy-sixth year (of which Dorna had been the guiding force for thirty-two) for 2025.

MotoGP hovers in an endless adaption process.

Brands tweak and customize the current season's motorcycles to different tracks, climates and conditions, as well as the annual characteristics of the controlled Michelin race rubber allocation: those who best harness the grip and the longevity of the slick tyres usually prevail over the course of the campaign that runs from March to November, in fifteen or sixteen different countries spread over five continents. Riders continually search for peak feeling, confidence and a performance 'window' each race weekend. Championship management attempt to conjure new initiatives and attractions at the events to entertain spectators and ensure their enthusiasm to return the following year or to travel and watch MotoGP in another territory.

Teams arrive at circuits on Tuesdays. They will either find large, fit-for-purpose garages at modern facilities, like the Algarve International Circuit in Portugal (built in 2007/2008) or the Lusail International Circuit in Qatar (in 2004 but upgraded in 2023) or the Red Bull Ring in Austria, as well Silverstone's F1-orientated 'wing', or they will have to squeeze and bend into archaic 'shoe boxes' found in venues like the Misano World Circuit Marco Simoncelli on Italy's Adriatic coast or Phillip Island, mere metres from Australia's southern Bass Strait. In places like Le Mans, where the battered and dented steel pitbox doors convey a quaint sense of history, the metal monolith of the grandstand above reverberates engine noise around the interiors and exteriors so it becomes impossible to think, let alone communicate. The teams adapt to each environment.

Red Bull KTM Factory Racing are the 'rookies' in the pitlane, following their full-time introduction to MotoGP in 2017 on the winged heels of victory in almost every other motorcycle racing discipline. They have filled a pitbox with at least two slots of the twenty-two-rider grid since that tricky debut in Qatar when they were more than two seconds a lap off the pace. By 2018, they were on the podium. By 2020, they were winning grands prix. Most of their team staff were recruited and picked from other squads and boast decades of experience. On Wednesdays, they will click together the panels, the tubes, the light racks and holders for at least eight LED monitors, stick down the dark blue carpet and distribute the other components of the pitbox set-up. Then the bikes roll out of the trucks.

Entering the completed Red Bull KTM pitbox usually involves the sight of an orange wall: the labyrinth starts. In a cubby hole to the left or the right will be an imposing tyre rack. The Michelins are wrapped in dark blankets, lights blinking away to show their temperature status as they are gently baked for abuse. Fuel cannisters, boxes and other storage give way to the first small work desks containing laptops of data and telemetry. The 'backstage' group of three to four engineers and strategists monitor information from upwards of six kilograms of wiring and roughly sixty sensors on the motorcycle. They watch, they analyse, and they plan: operating ahead and troubleshooting the present.

The narrow, blue-and-orange-screened corridor funnels to an opening and the main workspace of the pitbox. This nerve hub is only part of the 'brain', however; the main office truck housing the management figures of Red Bull KTM Factory Racing (a soft-toned, wood-panelled interior with at least eight workstations, a Red Bull fridge and a meeting room) sits outside in the paddock, emitting the signals that direct the urgency and activities of the pitbox bustle.

The atrium of the pitbox splits left and right for Brad Binder and Jack Miller, the riders entrusted to represent the company both in 2023 and 2024. There is usually a symmetry with the positioning of the motorcycles in these spaces. The solitary, flanking workbench against the wall contains layers of thin drawers housing spotless tools. Overhead, piping and cables drop down and plug into the stationary and hoisted RC16s. Technicians from Michelin and WP Suspension mingle with the mechanics that are endlessly moving around the small footprint, preparing and maintaining the bikes, often in a silent, balletic way, when the increased tension of a live session is ominously close to happening on track. During these critical times, MotoGP cameramen will add to the congestion and cross the fat, painted border line on the floor that separates the pitbox limit from the din of the pitlane itself.

This state of flux is hypnotic to watch, and even more so when a rider swooshes to a stop outside (the engine is cut metres in advance) and enters the box. The bike is turned and pushed backwards. While a mini debrief is going on, the mechanics are on the move around the RC16. They make changes, swapping wheels or tyres or brakes wordlessly, in a well-established routine. Wrenches click, metal clangs. A rider's shouts can be heard through the helmet, occasionally with expletives, as the MotoGP squall continues in the background. There is a faint smell of cleaning product and fuel. Sometimes sweat.

Passing through these confines and into the pitlane requires a shrewd timing. Dodging between bodies and bits of bike as tyres are wrapped and exchanged, the refuelling container harried back and forth.

The pitlane is another hallowed zone of MotoGP. Access is strictly administered by Dorna personnel, rather sensibly in the name of safety. It is the domain of team staff, TV broadcasters and select media, as well as the odd escorted VIP. Once Saturday's qualification schedule begins and the stakes are raised, helmets (mainly bicycle or trial lids) become compulsory and most press are booted out. After a few years of tolerance against the 127-decibel howl (the same as your average rock or music concert, but close enough to feel the thick air on your face), my hearing has dulled ever so slightly to the point where I struggle to differentiate foreground and background noise. Earplugs have become essential. MotoGP bikes do not use silencers and the gleaming Akrapovic titanium exhausts jut from under the engines of models like explicit sawn-off shotguns, prepped to perforate an eardrum from five paces. A rider will leave the apron of a pitbox after his bike has been fired up by a portable chainsaw-esque starter that plugs straight into the crank. He first rasps the throttle to get going and to manage a first gear so tall that many others would probably stall and drop the thing. Over the other side of the pitwall, motorcycles are at full scream down the straight.

The pitlane is a cauldron of coming-and-going of power and awe, and barely suppressed violence emanating from the engine tone of 220mph motorcycles, caged by a 45mph pitlane 'limiter'. To stand among it is a humbling, intimidating and very visceral, sensory experience of MotoGP. The first time it really struck me was during a pre-season test at the Lusail, around the mid-2010s. I was positioned outside Ducati's pitbox and watched as Andrea Dovizioso approached very quickly, scythed into inertia and jumped off the blood-red factory Desmosedici. Within a moment, the Italian was in the box but the engineers hesitated with the bike, checking an area of its metallic anatomy. Stood close by, I could connect with the smouldering mass of a machine that had just been overworked. The main straight at Lusail alone hits well over 200mph. The stilled vehicle let out crangs and pings, and a burning odour. There was an unmistakable aura of mechanical stress. I remember thinking, 'The thing is alive …' The Ducati was so beefy, muscular and jutted; equipped with those vast, melting, slick tyres it resembled a vibrating, potentially explosive mass. No comfort, no pleasure, just pure performance. Just one resolve. The simmering number 4 – easily the fastest motorcycle in MotoGP at the time – was then turned away for further dissection.

The bikes are stripped, assembled, crashed and rejuvenated race by race, sometimes day by day. There is very little time to get spiritual about these conduits of speed in a grand prix. When the fairing and the bodywork is clipped off, a 1000cc beast like the KTM RC16 is an intricate amalgamation of parts, bits, cables, guards, carbon. Shiny stuff. It looks like a squashed assortment of tech. A manual doesn't exist, but if it did it would be bible thick. For all the mindboggling convolution, MotoGP bikes have to have a minimum weight of 157kg. Standing next to one reveals just how flimsy and bespoke they are. At the test after the 2024 Grand Prix of Spain, I watched Binder's crew almost 'will' a new prototype fairing into place as the fixings and positioning wouldn't quite align. Sometimes the bike shakes as it's prodded and worked on. The fragility is evident. When in the saddle, the power to weight must be daunting. Pick up a piece of the upper fairing and it feels like holding a thick lifestyle magazine – it's almost nothing.

The Red Bull KTM team is surrounded by all these puzzle pieces. They carry enough of them to rebuild another three KTM RC16s if necessary. Crashed parts are binned or recycled where possible. Studied if required and stored for future repair if salvageable. The materials and the tools are the substance of the pitbox but it is the working system, the team's interaction and the atmosphere that instil their success. The environment is one of routine and familiarity, and that extends to the people as well: senior professionals with thousands of race miles and countless hours in a grand prix pitbox behind them, whether they are the hands-on mechanics, the data engineers, the tyre and wheel technicians (Red Bull KTM's Craig Burton is a large, sturdy chap who looks like he could spin the 12kg wheels like plates), Team Manager Francesco Guidotti, the constantly alert public face or those responsible for general logistics.

I find people like the ever-friendly truck driver Robby Gregor, Team Co-Ordinator Bea Garcia or Team Logistics Co-Ordinator Jeremy Wilson, or 'Jez', in the back of one of KTM's two race trucks that are stationed a few metres away from the rear door of the pitboxes. Jez has a chair, laptop and a small desk at one end of the galley. He's in his late fifties, tall and well built, his notebook open in from of him. He fixes me with a blank, studious look through his glasses. I pull up the only chair available and look around. 'I'd say there is 50-odd million worth of equipment on these trucks,' he says, following my inquisitive scope.

A former racer himself, competing in the British Championship and the Isle of Man TT, it seems he used to be something of a 'wild one' in his 'salad days'. Jeremy is one of those versatile figures in the pitbox, who has filled a number of duties in grand prix teams since the 1990s – from a mechanic to tyre man, general assistant, truck driver and now the general planner, after joining KTM right at the beginning of their MotoGP plan in 2015.

'We have three 40-foot containers plus the [pitbox] set-up here, which we call the "European set",' he explains. 'If one of the mechanics wants another tool or a component, then I make sure we have it.'

People come in and out of the truck. Near my head is a ladder that allows access to the upper section. One of Binder's mechanics, another Brit, John Eyre, climbs down and sees us talking. 'He'll have some stories,' he grins, nodding at my interviewee. Wilson gives him a deadpan look. 'I first met Jez in 2001, in Welkom, South Africa, and he was in the bar. I was at Shell Advance Honda and he was with Red Bull Yamaha. It was "buy one, get one free" and I remember him saying to me: "The more you drink, the more you save!"'

'I was out of control,' Wilson admits.

Jez seems very much in control when it comes to the layout of the Red Bull KTM operation. While Bea moves the squad of 50–60 people around the world, Jez makes sure all the equipment and, of course, the motorcycles are there. It's an intricate and detailed procedure of organization, efficiency and delivery. Wilson is constantly stocking, sending and compiling, but, like the rest of the team, his season starts back at the KTM Motorsports HQ in Munderfing, Austria, in January, when the new racebikes are built and all the new parts are labelled and recorded. To see this is like viewing a massive modelling kit laid out on benches as the technical crews note fresh fragments, prototypes and variations from the previous year. KTM also relies on a decent amount of 3D printing, so many items are bespoke and have their own little bags. For techies, it's the definitive build project. Wilson's role includes formulating a checklist: 'Eight bikes need to be built between the two teams and all the new parts have to be boxed. It's a busy time,' he admits.

At the circuits, Wilson's knowledge of the pitlanes, the pitboxes and, in particular, of what KTM has to store, ferry and erect means he is very much the 'producer'. 'Garages are always smaller, bigger, longer,' he sighs, describing the variation he has to contend with from track to track. 'Lusail is new and massive. We have to take extra material for that circuit. I could not do my job without the mechanics, and there are some great lads here with a lot of years in the paddock. By Wednesday lunchtimes at a grand prix, the garage is functional with the computers, connections and internet. The lighting is done. It means that after lunch, the bikes can start to be stripped. It's best to keep everything as clean and ordered as possible. If the bosses don't say anything then that means they're happy. They won't tell you it looks good … but I always make a point of asking! Things get chipped, tools and boxes have wear and tear, so I take care to rotate and replace when necessary.'

A grand prix is not a three-day affair for KTM and the other ten teams. It's a full week. Chief Mechanic Mark Lloyd is responsible for Binder's collective. He's the first link from the crew chief to the squad of guys that is constantly maintaining or changing the KTM RC16. Another person with an extensive Honda entry on the CV, Lloyd, or 'Pup', has been around the world with MotoGP since 2004, and with KTM since the end of 2016. Even when he's concentrating and busy, the Briton is one of those who is never too occupied to offer a smile or say hello. He is also enthusiastic and articulate about his profession when I manage to acquire some of his time at Valencia 2023.

'OK, so we always arrive for a grand prix on Tuesday night,' he explains. 'On Wednesday, we'll unload the truck or at flyaway races we'll unpack the crates. We'll be done by lunch, have a mechanics' meeting and then make a plan about any new parts or what engines we'll use, and if there were any problems at the last race then how do we address them. Countermeasures, stuff like that. I'll check the computer for the mileage on the parts – we might need to change a rear calliper or, say, the swingarm mileage is complete. When we strip the bike, we normally try to get everything washed and cleaned on the Wednesday so that when we get to the circuit on Thursday we can start assembling or, as they say, "building the speed"! It is a relaxed vibe because there is no pressure and you have all day to put the bike together. We have music in the box, people are chatting. Friday morning is a bit more tense, but we're already at the "business end". For a piece of equipment that was in a hundred pieces, you have to make sure it's ready to go. After Brad has made his first run, we'll be extra mindful of any issues, especially if there is a new part.'

Lloyd is one of the nine technicians from at least five different countries on Brad Binder's side of the pitbox. Eyre is one of the band, along with Lloyd, and is also the man charged with hoisting the pitboard over the wall and relaying info to Binder on the track. When the bike and the rider are in the pitbox, Eyre jogs back into position and the stream of work and movement begins for what is obviously a tight and well-drilled clutch of mechanics, and a common MO up and down the pitlane.

'Once you get with a good group of people, a good group of lads, then it just gels,' Eyre reveals over a coffee at the Red Bull Energy Station, the three-floored luxury expanse of food and drink and probably the most frequented structure outside of the pitbox for the team. 'In the box, you are aware of where you are, and you are not bumping into each other. We're assembling fuel tanks, wheels, brakes, bleeding brakes, but it happens without really thinking about it. We'll have the tools already in place. It is intense and close, but it all seems to flow without hassle.'

'We've been six, seven years together here at KTM, so it is instinctive now,' Lloyd insists. 'Everybody has a role in the garage. If the rider has a crash then everyone has their area and can focus, and not impede anyone else. The gearbox guy will be able to work on his part, for example, and we give each other room. It's second nature but the togetherness of the group helps. If one person left then it would take quite a long time for a new one to fit in. It would be difficult; it doesn't matter if they are a good person or a bad person, it's just about the system. It's one that people are happy with and we're efficient.'

The KTM team travel, work, relax and go through the mill of sporting emotions together. To apply focus, withstand strain and react to critical situations like bike changes or rebuilds against the clock tests characters and personalities. These guys are not only masters of what they do but also weirdly patient and comprehensible: it's a cloister of high stress populated by individuals who can manage it best.

'Everyone's a professional,' Mark asserts. 'You do get a bit more stressed sometimes but you have to be calm. There is no point shouting and getting excited because it doesn't help anybody. Also, the crew chief plays a part. If he's standing over you then you get to a point where you want to say, "'Mate, you're not helping." But Andres is super-cool and trusts us.'

Andres Madrid is Lloyd's direct link to the rider. He is an immensely qualified technician from Valencia who filtered into MotoGP through university, part-time work in the Spanish Championship, then an apprenticeship as a data engineer and finally a crew chief with Binder in Moto2. Physically, Andres doesn't seem to fit the mould as a leader. He is slight and youthful; only the thatch of greying hair gives away the yardage at the peak of grand prix racing. He projects an air of discernible composure and confidence. 'My job is to look at the timing screen and make sure my rider is P1. If he's not, then I'm not happy,' he tells me from the sun-kissed deck of the 'smaller' Red Bull Energy Station unit at the 2023 Gran Premi de Catalunya. His statement is an oversimplification. A crew chief is an atypical breed: individuals who must apply a hefty dose of psychology to their role.

'When I arrived here, I realized the guys were already a few steps in front of me,' Andres admits of his graduation to the team for the 2021 season. 'I would ask them if they'd sorted something: "done". Then if they had checked something else: "done". It was incredible. The experience was almost overwhelming, and I knew working like that and being surrounded by a crew like this made my life super-easy. It means the job in MotoGP is, weirdly, even easier [than Moto2] because the level of the guys is so high that you can instantly trust everybody.'

MotoGP's seismic transition to Saturday 'Sprints' in 2023 doubled the entertainment potential of the series but it also wound the screw down harder on the teams. Every single lap of every session had to be planned and measured, and time was even more valuable because the first goal of a grand prix is to achieve a satisfactory qualification slot. The bikes are too close, the riders are too good, the lap-times are too marginal and slithers of a second divide the push for a trophy and the second half of the grid. It is a pressure cooker that grills the racer but also applies heat to every crevice of MotoGP labour. The equation of the right tyres for the track state to be deduced, and the complicity of any upgrades for the bike as well as the usual tasks of dialling in the motorcycle depending on the rider's feeling for the best possible attack on the chrono. It's a world in which a deficit of three tenths of a second per lap can feel like motivation to go home.

Readiness is a requisite and the team must be vigilant to deal with contingencies. In other words: changes and crashes. In the case of the RC16, then the space-age carbon chassis means another zone of repair and scrutiny. During any session, the team will be restless, watching the monitors or prepping for the next phase for the forty-five-minute outing.

If the GPS data or the live TV signal shows the number 'thirty-three' unmoving then the whole posse pauses for an update to see if Binder is OK and then bursts into motion. The second bike becomes the object of their attention until the battered first version returns to the box via a trailer from the circuit's marshals. Usually, a trashed bike is returned covered by a tarp, strewn across in some way, but is also discoloured, distorted, broken and spewing small stones and other debris. There is something dramatic about seeing a racebike in this state. It's also remarkable how the resurrection process begins.

'Brad crashed at Valencia on Saturday [2023] and there was a proper mess. A real wreck,' Eyre remembers. 'In all my time in grands prix, I've never seen anything like it. There were only a couple of repairable things; the rest was either bent, broken or completely shattered. In the end, we were shattered as well because we had to build a whole new bike! That day went from the morning all the way to 12.30 at night before we finished and went back to the hotel.'

Like sous chefs, the mechanics have cuts of the RC16 in drawers, primed to plug in and play. 'In the second test of the year, I might take the whole handlebar assembly off, all the brakes, and then build another one from new,' says Lloyd. 'It means I can keep the other one aside because I know it has been run and it's good; all the positions and cables are set and it can be installed right away with a couple of tweaks. The rear brake line will also be built up, bled and good to go. You build as much as you can. You want to look at something and know – without thinking – that it fits and it works. Never put in anything new before a race. It must be checked.'

The KTM RC16 morphs every year in the pursuit of speed and superiority – and, most crucially of all, strong symbiosis with the tyres. The bike also changes in its architecture: how it can be worked on and put together. 'We came from Honda, who have been in racing forever,' says Lloyd. 'Fifty or sixty years. So, setting up at KTM was all about being efficient. You'll have an 8mm T-bar [spanner] – which is the mechanic's "friend" – and you want as many components bolted together with this as possible so you don't have to keep switching tools. Here, at first, we needed a lot of tools for the bike and we didn't have that efficiency, and when you are against the clock you need all the help you can get. The engineers listened and now the bike is at a very high level for working and repairing.'

The mechanics are not alone in the pitbox, however. It will be busy with other staff, TV cameras, management and lingering pass holders. 'For us we don't really notice the pitbox space too much because we are focused on the bike, but it is more annoying for the guys working with the wheels to have to constantly barge past people. Some are not aware of the situation,' says Lloyd.

'Sometimes you might have one of the bosses in the way of a toolbox, but it's because they don't know that you are constantly moving and need access,' explains Eyre. 'You have to be easy-going. At some races, there will be guests and people who have never been inside the box. They don't know where to go, where to stand or even how to act. You just have to make apologies and excuses. When it is a very busy race then you have to realize there is another dynamic to the space. You also have to be aware that for these people it is a once-in-a-lifetime for them to come in the garage, so they don't need a mechanic shouting at them to get out of the way. You have to be placid and realistic.'

In the swirl of noise and hubbub the mechanics have to be diligent. A lack of concentration or absentmindedness can be catastrophic for the rider. The little fist bumps and taps on the legs from the mechanics when he accelerates away from the pitbox are ritual signals that mean 'All is OK.'

'You can never know 100 per cent,' Lloyd says on that fraction of a second when the bike is handed over to the athlete and the responsibility shifts. 'But you do know that the checks have been made. We know, say, the wire harness has been assembled correctly. However, there is still that element of doubt that something could break. We check, check and check, and watch the parts mileage ...

but you still don't know if you will have a "mechanical". We had one in Barcelona 2023. It was nobody's fault. KTM knew what it was and rectified the issue and we learned from that. It's a learning process as well as the chase of the ultimate prize.'

A championship of twenty grands prix, forty races including the Sprints, means there is anticipation inside the pitboxes punctuated by moments of elation. It's the classic sporting drug that fans of crap football teams will know well: the fleeting moments of euphoria. Not everybody can win. From a field of twenty-two riders, there will only be a small handful who give their crews reason for joy each weekend. When the schedule gets hectic with back-to-back meetings or the notorious grouping of flyaways at the end of the season – when MotoGP jets to five or six eastern and Asian countries in succession – then the mutual trust, belief and a good atmosphere around the garage becomes even more valuable.

Jack Miller is pally with his crew, some of whom came with him from the factory Ducati team at the end of 2022. The Australian has been drinking from a shallow pool of results since moving to the Austrian camp (the Aussie 'bootie' celebration, where he'll guzzle Prosecco from the recesses of a sweaty race boot while on the podium, has been a bit dry) but the mood doesn't seem to have suffered.

'You are in tune to it, and you feed off it,' he tells me about the vibe, while sipping from a bottle of water in the shade as the Texan sun cooks the paddock at the Circuit of the Americas. 'I want the team happy around me. I want them all in a good workspace where they enjoy coming to work. I want them to be enthusiastic about the job. There are some slight subtleties because people have bad days or they cannot be f**ked sometimes. As a rider, you pick-up up on it. You can feel it and it might just be a comment.

We're quite sensitive souls sometimes. Some words might make you think that one or some of the guys don't believe in you. I try to keep a good environment because I was in some situations in my early years where I didn't have the maturity or the experience to deal with it. You just want them to be keen and to give you their best day in and day out.'

For all the bonhomie, I've heard both Binder and Miller stride into the pitbox and not hold back with their frustration or their expletives. The crew chief is normally the main recipient of the ire but then he is also the one who is trained to deflate the edginess. Anger is usually temporary. It can be understandable if it is linked to a lack of competitiveness. However, despondency is another issue altogether. Binder's squad sampled this firsthand with Johann Zarco's ill-fated half-season stint in KTM in 2019. The Frenchman was disillusioned with a first factory contract that prioritized development ahead of the chase for silverware. The RC16 simply wasn't ready, and neither was Johann. I remember being close to the pitbox in Mugello and watching his forlorn trudge back to his chair. The body language spoke louder than any words in French or English possibly could. 'Those were dark times,' remembers Lloyd. 'In Assen [Netherlands], he just pulled in. "What's wrong?" we asked. "Nothing," he said. Then people are looking at you … But if that episode hadn't happened, then maybe we wouldn't have ended up with Brad Binder and one of the best riders we've worked with: talented, hard-working, committed. The Zarco thing was unfortunate but it definitely made the team stronger and we appreciate things more. We have a rider now who is the polar opposite.'

I ask Miller if opening the pitbox door ever feels 'heavy'. What if the rider hates the bike, the results are not coming or the atmosphere is off? 'Nah,' he responds, shaking his head, and it's clear that thirteen years in grand prix helps train the shoulders for the weight of pressure. Due to the TV cameras, a rider's entry to the pitbox is a little like coming under stage lights – whether that's before a session or in the aftermath of a crash when the leathers are scuffed and there is anxiety to return to full speed on the second motorcycle. Maybe this is one of the truly outstanding facets of a motorcycle racer's mental resolve: the pig-headed drive to delve straight back into the world of risk and injury after a previous close call.

'To a degree, yes, but it becomes a normality,' Miller remarks, when I ask about the feeling of heading into the 'arena' once he's through the pitbox door. 'It's like I'm stepping into home or into my space. Maybe like a boxer getting into the ring. They know what they are about to do when they get in there. It's the same. I know what I am there to do and what my objectives are.'

'Pressure is there – it always is – but it's also something I've tried to work on,' he admits. 'I've done every f**king thing under the sun, whether it's pumping yourself up or getting in the zone, or the other way when you are just trying to relax completely. I always ride my best when I'm having fun. That's the way.

'Normally you are thinking about everything that is about to unfold,' he adds, reflecting on those lonely moments sat in the chair, poised in leather gear and before the helmet and gloves get fastened. "Thinking about what can happen … but then I can also sit there with the boys and have a chat. It should be fun. It is obviously stressful and there are millions of dollars invested, but perhaps it [the joking and chatting] is a coping mechanism more than anything.'

Long hours. Days and weeks from home. A routine of hotel–circuit–hotel–circuit. A difficult rider or patchy spell of form. An isolated existence. The difficulties of working in one of eleven

MotoGP teams seem obvious but there is clearly some sort of addictive ingredient to it, apart from the clear fascination with sporting achievement and cutting-edge rapid motorcycle technology.

'This isn't a job, it's a way of life,' Jez says, staring at me again. 'I don't think you can class it as a job. When I get home, I still need to be on the computer and be on call. I had two relationships go out of the room because of it. My marriage went as well, eleven years ago. I'm fortunate that I can see my daughter and I've started to see my boy now, which is good, but it all broke down because of the job.'

I don't quite know what to say. But Jeremy doesn't give me a moment to react, thankfully. 'You're away all the time and I think your partner really needs to understand you, if you want to do this. The schedule doesn't help the private lives of people that work here full-time. I believe it's a great experience for a man from thirty to forty-five, and if you're single. You go to these countries but you don't see too much. You can stop out a bit if you want to, but many guys have families. Some don't last too long here. Also, the travelling breaks a lot of people.'

He leans forward. 'All of us in the job are very lucky. Never take it for granted. If I was killed tomorrow by a car then I know that I did what I wanted to do with my life: raced bikes, won a few, did the TT and I got something out of it.' He perks up. 'I think a lot of people just disappear and that's a shame. There have been a lot of nice people who have come into the sport but then they have just left it, and it's gone. I don't think I look bad for my age! I'm fifty-seven. I see other blokes at home close to my age and I think, "Look at the state of him ...." I'm buzzing all the time.'

For all the detectable levels of tiredness, Lloyd is also quick to swipe aside the difficulties of earning money as a MotoGP mechanic. 'I think it is quite unique,' he ponders. 'I think some people do find it hard to understand that you get paid to work in a race team. It is a routine. You don't see too much of the places we go. Thankfully, when we go home then we're "off". We don't have to go to an office. I think I would find a normal job and a commute difficult. I remember Nicky Hayden [the USA's last MotoGP world champion in 2006] saying: "It's better than digging ditches!"'

———————

MotoGP teams are afforded the space and the resources to fit their billing as part of the elite series. The Moto2 outfits all run the same Triumph 765cc triple motorcycles, one per rider, and have to share tighter pitlane boxes. The main Moto3 teams (a division also run to tight technical guidelines and the entry 'rung' to grand prix for racing talent, with an 18–28-year age window in the class) might get lucky with the same arrangement but usually there isn't room for all, and a selection of Moto3 crews will have to occupy temporary white marquee structures in the remoter regions of the paddock. A railing system blocks the crowds so the riders can get to the track through an access point. During a session, these teams will haul tools and materials to a spot in pitlane. It feels like Grand Prix 'by numbers'. There is something earthy and admirable about how teams make Moto3 life work, but it exists at the other end of the glamour scale to the universe of MotoGP.

'I suppose we are!' Paul Williamson half smiles when I ask the MLav Racing's team manager, the coordinator of the sole British outfit in the MotoGP paddock, whether they are like the runts of the paddock. 'But I also don't think of it like that,' he quickly adds. 'Quite rightly, MotoGP is the pinnacle and those teams are massive, so they have more space for the equipment and the machinery. It's only right. We wouldn't want to compare with those teams in terms of budget. Different league.'

We're talking inside MLav's sole truck at Le Mans. It's the same size, with the same interior and amenities (fancy trimmings, air conditioned, soundproof) as any of the other MotoGP versions, placed alongside in rank and file. The French Grand Prix is one of the few events where Michael Laverty's team have their own pitbox 'broom cupboard', where they split a garage with another crew thanks to their barriers and panels. Otherwise, they create their own presentable set-up of boards in the marquee, with tarpaulin 'doors' scraped back and a perfunctory platform raising the flooring a few inches. At non-European grands prix, they pack six boxes to the brim to move everything.

'We work out of a tent a lot but they are the same size and often bigger than what you would get in a little section of a garage,' offers Paul, now into his second year at the helm of the squad that was formed in 2022, and with twenty years on his CV in the likes of BSB and the Supersport World Championship. 'It's not bad, even though the distance from the pitlane can be awkward for logistics – moving tools and parts. You are not on the frontline and it's hard to watch everyone else, especially with the whole Moto3 thing of getting out behind someone. We have the garage working well in terms of set-up and it is pretty much the same everywhere. The length is the same, we change the width a bit, the layout is constant, and we place the desks in the same spot. We have a little tent out the back for the tyres. We have some continuity and the pack away is fast. It is a friendly-enough paddock and the fact that IRTA are British make it a bit more homely,' he adds. 'We just crack on and get on with it. We're not the only team working in those tents.'

Moto3 teams are smaller – thanks to the one-bike policy to reduce costs – and more juvenile but no less assorted than their

MotoGP equivalents. 'There are three people per bike, so we're quite small. Mainly Spanish. One Italian. The crew chiefs are both in our forties. The rest of the lads are young, mid- to late twenties, but the atmosphere is good. There are a couple of new lads here and they have fit in well. It can be difficult to keep morale up sometimes with the results we are getting. It is a struggle but we seem to be doing alright. We are capable, and the bike is always well presented.'

Younger riders, younger staff, less experience, more emotion. Harder job? There are parallels to what MotoGP teams are going through, even though the MLav squad's parameters for success are different, considering they are still pursuing their first podium result in the category. 'I think there was more of a struggle when the team started in 2022. Young British lads with experience in JuniorGP or the Spanish Championship maybe didn't get, or appreciate, where we'd come from or what we'd done to get here,' Williamson says. 'We had to reassure them and build up trust, which is something you have to do anyway with a team and a rider. The rider needs the confidence within the team to push and go faster. It is a mind game and about getting him into that mindset.'

Moto3 can feel like the Wild West of grand prix – hordes of riders roaming track limits to poach slipstreams and rough up opponents. The races are infused with youthful energy and exuberance, where testosterone flows through sometimes outrageous moves on the asphalt. The competitiveness takes place off track as well with 'shithousery' in pitlane via blocking and retribution. 'I'm surprised by the teams that are willing to cheat,' says Williamson. 'They are not trying new stuff. It's a strange mentality, that whole "follow my leader" thing.

'One rider got caught for using the wrong oil and a number of teams were caught last year for doing the same thing,' he expands on the rule bending. 'They got punished. A memo came out but it still goes on! Tests happen. I don't know how they think they can get away with it.'

Curiously, though, Williamson says there is also a unity between some teams. Perhaps a common acknowledgment that most are trying to muck-through and exist on a yearly basis above the bottom line. 'There are not many Honda teams here and we all try to help each other where we can. If someone needs a part then they can come to us and vice versa. There is a camaraderie and it was surprising to discover how good that is.'

Passes to MotoGP paddock are not readily available for the public. To soak up some of the unique vibe – while avoiding silent electric scooters and people constantly on the move – is already a stratum of grand prix. Simply hearing the familiar 'beep-bop' of the handheld scanner held by security staff at the makeshift gates means favoured access into a world where riders, team staff, professionals and guests inhabit a collapsible, colourful, expensive and mobile community, temporarily propped on wheels and ready to wind up and roll off.

The principal avenue of a MotoGP paddock runs alongside the row of race trucks. Most MotoGP teams have a pair, sometimes conveniently stickered for each rider, with compartments that can slide out and upwards, and are joined by stairs, platforms, roofing and other intricate items to form a semi-private operating area of business. The trucks are accompanied by tall 'totem' stands that pronounce the name and number of the 'stars'.

The throughfare is perhaps the busiest place in the paddock from Thursday to Sunday afternoon. It is pounded by foot traffic and plays host to social interaction from morning until night. TV crews and presenters occupy certain areas, while promotional girls click up and down in heels wielding umbrellas. People are seen and want to be seen. From Friday, lucky fans and guests with digital passes wait patiently by the ropes stretched across the narrow passages by the trucks – another MotoGP 'layer' – for their favourite rider to emerge from the pitbox or their own personal hangout room in the vehicle where they will stretch, listen to music, watch other classes on the TV, sometimes conduct interviews and then change into race gear and brief with team personnel.

At some tracks, like the relatively new Algarve International Circuit, the trucks are faced by hospitalities: shiny, exclusive edifices where another type of pass is required. Inside them, LED screens, drinks, food and seating provide a reprieve. At one end of the 'street' will be the Dorna 'carpa': the temporary white, tinted-window offices of the promoters and the second of the three 'nerve centres' at a grand prix, outside of IRTA's grey truck presence, and then the wall of monitors that is Race Direction, normally installed inside a permanent circuit building and firmly off limits.

In this paddock row will also be Michelin or Pirelli tyre 'plants': ceaseless caverns of activity as race rubber is stored and mounted on wheels, and racks with that distinct smell and the endless hiss of pressure hoses and snapping of black to rim.

MotoGP is awash with corporate shades. From the red of Ducati, the blue of Yamaha, the orange of KTM, the black of Aprilia, the white and blue of Honda, the blue of Michelin and yellow of Pirelli. There are logos and design elements everywhere. Team schemes, sponsors, fonts and logotypes. A psychedelic collage of interests and presentation. The paddock is a launchpad, and a home for the business aspect of MotoGP as well as the specialists that help make the sport turn. It's like a concourse between the corporate entertainment, the engineering, and then the real sport and entertainment beyond the trucks and the pitlane.

Layers and access.

As a kid going to race meetings at Brands Hatch, entering the paddock was like getting into a promised land. At British club races, it was a crowded mini-city of tents and caravans; real estate was precious. The higher profile the event, the bigger and more restricted the paddock became. Mostly we'd pay; sometimes we'd try to sneak in.

It was my dad, Liam, who took me to Brands and gave me a love of bike racing. While I didn't own a bike until my late twenties, Dad rode motorcycles from his teens and – knowing his slightly rebellious and cheeky spirit – probably in a sketchy way. My parents had moved to Kent from west London in the search of affordable housing, but the daily commute from Rainham to a British Telecom exchange in St John's Wood, in the centre of the capital, was arduous and undoubtedly justified part of the reason for Dad's two wheels, despite my mum's dislike of the vehicles. There are photos of me as a young boy on a brown Honda, a blue 125cc Suzuki and a Yamaha 350 LC – his last model that was sold before I'd reached my teens. I have memories of waking and watching him dress into a two-piece leather suit, get wrapped up against the dark morning cold and then rattle doors in the cloister of garages as he set off with that rasping two-stroke.

Brands Hatch circuit was less than twenty-five miles away. Dad had a season ticket for the venue and we'd go quite often, picnic box loaded, welly boots on, ear mufflers to hand, to watch fixtures varying from local club races to Powerbike and Transatlantics (the poplar UK vs American series that ran for over ten years through the 1970s and '80s) to early Superbike. Sometimes, we'd drive right into Brands and park on the grassy slope by Graham Hill bend. Other times, we'd have to leave the red Vauxhall Chevette in a distant field. I have one distinct memory of being made to climb into the car boot as we approached the track: admission must have been charged per person on the gate.

I was fascinated by everything that hits most first-time spectators at a motorcycle race: the speed, the noise, the mysterious hidden identity of the riders, their exposure, the proximity of the action, the leaning, the crashes, the response from the crowd to names or sights, and the sensation of danger. Occasionally, I'd get bored and wander off to explore the woods behind Druids Hairpin, dreaming of finding some secret souvenir of a long-crashed race wreck.

Dad said I was 'weaned on bikes'. When we moved to Rickmansworth, outside northwest London, in 1984, the trips to Brands became less regular. But, by then, my dad had taken me on ultra-cheap coach trips to both Spa-Francorchamps in Belgium and Assen in the Netherlands for grands prix, in the last throes of Barry Sheene mania. He would most likely have loved a weekend free of family and kids (my younger sister and brother had come along by that point, and my sister would sometimes get pulled along to those weekends at Brands, purely to give my mum a breather), but instead took along a small, skinny boy who had become fervently immersed in a sport, partly – looking back – as a means to share time and interests with a man that I'd idolize until his sudden passing in 2018 from a heart attack at the ridiculously early age of sixty-six.

Dad took me to Silverstone for the British Grand Prix in 1979. I was only three years old. But I always thought it was quite cool to have been sat, probably asleep, at the fence while Sheene and Kenny Roberts went at it. We went back to Silverstone for the Grand Prix repeatedly in the years that followed, usually spending hours queuing in torrential rain. Silverstone weather – as the deluge, flooding and cancellation in 2018 can testify – could be decidedly evil, although getting soaked through at the British GP and using a programme for a hat seemed like an adventure at the time. I have memories from 1985 of Dad worrying we'd get stuck in the mud trying to get out and me wrapping myself in some plastic we'd rescued from the back of a merchandise stand and sitting at the top of a grandstand as the wind and water battered the hardy fans who had stayed until the checkered flag.

I have photos taken in proximity to Sheene, Ron Haslam and British Superbike heroes such as John Reynolds and Jamie Whitham, and names like Steve Spray and Trevor Nation – when those heroic and potent jet-black JPS Nortons were inspiring a generation of British Superbike fans. From even further back I have a photograph with 1980 sidecar world champion Jock Taylor; the smiling, permed Scot was a big draw at Brands that weekend. I also remember Dad making his best attempt to explain 'internal bleeding' as the reason for Taylor's untimely death at the barely plausible circuit of Imatra in Finland in 1982 at twenty-eight years of age. 'It's when your veins, those blue things in your arm, open up and all the blood runs away.' Heavy work for a six-year-old to figure out, then rationalize the 'here today, gone tomorrow' of an activity that appeared thrilling and fun.

Sidecars looked mental to me and still do. They also used to scare me silly because the thin tunnel that separates the paddock from the pitlane at Brands was like a corridor of fear. It was very dark, with barely any room for pedestrians and race vehicles, and the noise made the situation even more alarming. Sidecars passing through at the same time made me want to squeeze against the wall and hold my breath. The tunnel was surprisingly open to members of public who wanted to cross into the infield section and grassy incline on the inside of Paddock Hill Bend and the outside of Graham Hill: it was a good vantage point, particularly for the shorter 'Indy' circuit layout, but the tunnel was traumatic.

I was smitten by Brands and its green, shallow valley setting. It felt historic and forbidden. Something about the strip of asphalt was inviting but also exclusive. A worthy scaffold indeed. It would become an idyllic location; where the waft of burger stands, bacon butties, freshly fried doughnuts, flat beer and cigarette smoke went along with the sound of a PA (the inimitable voice of Fred Clarke usually), the whoosh of bikes braking and accelerating, and small generators powering the grimy food stands. At one point, the circuit renovated the rusting main grandstand that followed the strange wavy contour of the principal straight and gave the venue a modernized kick up the arse. They created a commercial area behind the stand, and a small model and toy shop become as much of an attraction as the bikes less than 100 metres away. When Dad happened to have a few more pounds in his pocket then my desire for a miniature replica bike would be satisfied and everything felt more special.

I reached an age at which university beckoned. I moved away and wanted to go to more races that either Dad couldn't make or didn't fancy. Occasionally, on weekends when I wasn't playing football then I would get the train across London from Twickenham, disembark at Swanley and then walk three miles from Eynsford station to the track, wishing that I had a crash helmet so I could blag a ride from the bikes that zoomed past on the A20. I'd pay relatively little and watch a loaded club race agenda before setting off back to the station.

In 1995, I sat on the approach to Paddock Hill Bend by myself, marvelling at the 'Carl Fogarty effect' in WorldSBK. Thanks to the success and personality of the Lancastrian, and the interest generated via Sky Sports' coverage, motorcycle racing received some long overdue mainstream exposure and boomed. Friends confused by my ardour for bike racing understood a little more what it was all about. I had less explaining to do.

In a family of five with one working parent and a loving and protective mother, the nearest I came to riding or trying the track myself was through the fantasy of doing sums while studying and working part-time jobs in the summer and at theme parks to buy an MZ and somehow get fast at a budget. Clearly no Fogarty-esque stardom lay in store.

The British Grand Prix faded in importance for us in the mid-1990s. Dad hated Donington Park for the viewing and the traffic. The 500cc class was in a mire with poor grid numbers and Mick Doohan on the verge of turning the championship into a borefest, beating opposition that neither challenged him nor inspired us. Though watching races became simple once British TV had moved into the satellite era and the domain of digital sport flickered into life. Looking back now it was a fascinating time and where media would transition so radically over a twenty-year period at the beginning of the 1990s, the change felt on print mostly (newspapers, magazines, fanzines, books) but also TV (video, four-channel television broadcasters, DVDs to SKY and multiple channels) and internet (email, newsletters, forums, websites, apps, on-demand).

If Dad was a filter for bikes and for another unhealthy fascination, a multi-generational family tie to Queens Park Rangers football club, then Mum encouraged the creativity and airiness of her sensitive and sport-mad son. She always backed and spurred my imagination at school and helped mark my journey, I suppose. I wasn't good enough, or manic enough, to be a pro sportsman but I figured I could tell stories about it. I took confidence from writing, her support, and also from being able to express some thoughts or opinions through a keyboard. It was a craft I wanted to explore and it stimulated me. The goal of being immersed in sport journalism was hardened after two days of work experience on the *Daily Express*'s sports desk, where I got to submit a small slice of copy from a match at Lords Cricket ground and then visit the Wimbledon Tennis tournament. Watching the women's semi-finals from the press box made up my mind.

As a young graduate with a BA degree in English and sport from St Mary's University in Twickenham, I started to write a few pieces for local newspapers. In 1998, I got lucky. From hundreds of applicants, I was offered a job working as a production assistant for an independent TV company called Capricorn Programmes, based on the fringe of Soho in central London, earning the princely sum of £9,000 a year. The TV show I was assigned to work on was a compendium of footage and reviews of video games; the only one of its kind in the UK and an offshoot of what had been a Saturday morning ITV staple called *Movies, Game and Videos*. *Cybernet* taught me a lot; I worked with some intriguing and creative people and learned how you can present content and how you collaborate with different personalities for the best results.

After two years I moved up to the position of assistant producer and rose to the riches of a £16,000 salary.

The video game market was on the point of major bloom, with the online community factor about to kick off, and titles benefited from huge launches and marketing. Free bars, parties and promo opportunities filled the professional and social calendar. My friends used to joke that when the weekend came along, I'd be the only one staying in.

Working in the media and chasing bikes carved a path to Barcelona early in 2001. A weekly scan of the *Media Guardian* classifieds page had revealed that Dorna Sports were looking for a 'multimedia journalist'. I applied and received a job offer to cover the newly acquired FIM Motocross World Championship for Dorna as well as grand prix racing. It was an opportunity too good to pass up, even if moving to Catalunya without knowing a word of Spanish (or Catalan) seemed daunting. The decision significantly changed the course of my future. I met my future wife within a month of being in the country. My former employer, Capricorn, closed and disappeared two years later.

My first MotoGP trip and job for Dorna was the 2001 Japanese Grand Prix at Suzuka. The famous Rossi–Biaggi clash. Honda won their five-hundredth GP that day and I trembled outside the back of the HRC pit waiting to interview Mick Doohan, mostly because of the chilly wind that was whipping around the paddock but also because of the sudden request with a monstrous name of the sport. It was the furthest I'd ever travelled and I was now inside the championship. It was mind-scrambling and the jetlag was horrendous.

It soon became apparent that working two series was not feasible or desirable. Dorna was much, much smaller then and motogp.com was in its infancy. It was a news site rather than the portal for endless video content that it is now. That's when Dorna hired Gavin Emmett to come into the picture to join Matthew Roberts and I while I focused more on motocross, having already made some solid contacts in the paddock for what was the first year of three in Dorna's ill-fated off-road taste, and where applying the same model as road racing was a doomed policy for a more grassroots discipline. Later, as Nuria and I considered a family, the two-day format of MXGP – fewer races, fewer days away – was preferrable as MotoGP ballooned. I did a book with (still) Britain's last motocross World Champion, Jamie Dobb, and also a 2004 yearbook with Tempus Publishing; aping the tomes of the 'Motocourse' annual that my Dad collected religiously. He would get frustrated with me when I'd stuff my face with cereal before school, the splashes of milk ruining the pages, or the dust jackets would tear with use.

Motorcycle racing, or reporting on it rather, became a job. Being able to roam inside the sport offered enough fodder and excitement to stretch on. After two years in Dorna, I had enough contacts to go freelance and worked intermittently in MotoGP when not at MXGP; namely the Catalan, British and Valencian grands prix, when the motocross calendar had ended. I continued to write the MotoGP programmes for a few years as Gav scaled the order at Dorna and then broke free to become a renowned commentator and presenter in his own right. It's a pleasure to see him at every grand prix to this day. Matthew headed the BBC's brief live coverage of MotoGP before starting a family with wife Jayne and leaped into WorldSBK and British Superbike with Eurosport, writing books with riders and other curious avenues like professional coaching.

By the end of 2015, I'd had enough of the full-time grind of motocross and the mountain of copywriting, although the life friendships made there were invaluable, and the work ethic and humour of photographers like Ray Archer, Pascal Haudiquert and Juan Pablo Acevedo left a lasting impression. Sometimes, when dealing with difficult or egocentric riders, I'd think of one of Ray's many little Geordie drops of wisdom: 'Listen, all they do is ride a motorcycle faster than me or you ...'

It was in 2012 when I was fed-up waiting for a year-long outstanding payment from the former publishing group that owned American magazine *Cycle News* that I figured 'why not do this myself? Then there is only one person to blame if I don't get paid ...' It was during a boom time for digital magazines, so I set-up *On-Track Off-Road*, a free, bi-weekly publication backed by advertising. I did it largely by myself and with a small band of valued journos and photographers, before the fad for reading an online PDF faded and the magazine converted to a monthly in 2017. The developments in HTML and the digital reading experience meant it then changed again into something more advanced and fluid by 2020. Advertising remained strong as print clients and outlets evaporated into nothing and brands still wanted platforms for their marketing. By the turn of the 2020s, endemic sport media was altering radically – podcasts were the new trend and quantity replaced quality as the norm for news stories. Long-form, deep-dive articles were next in line for extinction.

It was during the early *OTOR* years that I befriended Roland Brown, a veteran motorcycle tester with a passion for football (and Tottenham Hotspur Football Club in particular) that even outstretched mine. Roland wrote frequently and brilliantly for the magazine and generously shared his contact on the motoring (later 'Cars') desk at the *Daily Telegraph*. Paul Hudson, the editor there at the time, was very open-minded and after pitching a story about the now-defunct one-million-dollar prize pot of the Monster Energy

Cup Supercross race in Las Vegas, I was able to semi-regularly tempt him into more stories and pieces until Paul moved on and 'Cars' drifted into bland content about electric vehicles. Eventually, I managed to breach the sports desk with some MotoGP articles, around the time when UK national media were facing their own revenue and modernization crisis, and budgets and jobs were being slashed continually on an annual basis. The struggle for mainstream exposure for MotoGP continues to this day.

I'd dipped into the MotoGP paddock when I could: writing for Team Suzuki in their comeback wildcard at Valencia in 2014, the same for KTM at the end of 2016, editorial for Monster Energy, for *OTOR* and whatever else. By 2016, I departed full-time MXGP, trimmed a few clients and picked up a couple more for MotoGP. Two years later, and after some guest slots on the Paddock Pass Podcast, I was lucky enough to join David Emmett, Neil Morrison and Steve English, who'd all become firm friends. Sometimes the grind of travelling, routine and minor frustrations of working in a sport (such as broken appointments) can sap the energy levels, and a healthy amount of banter and the chance to share a beer or late-night pizza with them away from the circuit is beyond revitalizing.

On the subject of broken appointments, I can remember a horrifying experience in the mid-2010s at the Grand Prix of Valencia where I dropped the ball massively. I'd arranged interviews with the top two American riders on the grid at that time, Nicky Hayden and Colin Edwards. The two 10–15-minute slots were scheduled back-to-back with Colin, racing for the Yamaha Tech3 team first, and Nicky, who was a factory Ducati rider, second. Both were usually great value for their words and opinions. I sat in Tech3 waiting for Edwards, nervously watching the clock tick down. He was tardy. I didn't have the

Ducati press officer Federica Di Zotti's mobile number on me. It reached a point where I'd have five minutes with Edwards before I'd need to scarper to Ducati and it barely seemed worth it. Stick for Edwards or go for Hayden? The decision was made for me as the Texan bounded through the doors, apologizing. It was a decent chat but I knew my no-show with Nicky wouldn't go down well.

I walked into the media centre a little later, with a half-baked plan to apologize in person or meekly send an email of explanation, when I happened to bump straight into Federica. With a face like thunder she admonished me, allowing barely two lines of justification, and turned her back shaking her head. I felt terrible. And I didn't rush to ask for any more Ducati slots for a while.

Nicky certainly bore no grudges. We'd met a few times at motocross grands prix as he was a zealous off-road fan (like a few MotoGP riders); we also did a photoshoot and feature at his house in Orange County, thanks to the help of the affable Chris Jonnum, and he seemed to be sharp when it came to remembering names and faces. A few years later in Valencia, I was walking through the paddock with an *OTOR* jacket and I felt a tap on the shoulder – Hayden zoomed past on his scooter, throwing that unmissable giant grin over his shoulder. Nicky's death due to a cycling accident just outside the Misano circuit in 2017 at the age of thirty-five felt despairingly wasteful. Aside from seeming like a genuinely good human being, he no doubt had much more to offer the sport beyond his racing years.

Hayden was one of Ducati's star names in a grand prix era that reignited for the Italians in 2003. It would take the better part of fifteen years for the factory to convert the fastest motorcycle in the paddock into a consistent championship winner, but when the tide came it washed the whole series crimson.

TWO

The Red

I t is a warm spring day in west Emilia-Romagna and morning sunshine flashes off the Ducati logo – the red and white shield that has been the company's emblem since 2009. Ducati's factory complex is close to the centre of Bologna. It is stuck in an area resembling an industrial park, but its proximity to both the airport and the time-warped city itself, some five miles from the *Archiginnasio* (a segment of the famous university and allegedly the oldest active institution in the world at almost a thousand years old), only increases the feeling of breathable history.

In contrast to the attention-grabbing looks of the motorcycles, the facility at Borgo Panigale makes an underwhelming first impression. It feels quintessentially Italian: in other words, with contradictions. The building is archaic, with a dated exterior, and seems small for a manufacturer that builds and packages almost 60,000 motorcycles a year, mostly from this location, but also from plants in Thailand and Brazil. Yet, behind the walls that were rebuilt from the detritus of the Second World War, there are objects of beauty, engineered and created with pride, passion and the unrelenting quest for perfection.

Inside Ducati's Borgo Panigale HQ are some of the finest motorcycling technical and design minds in Europe, if not the world. It's a place that can attract fresh generations of talent and ideas from college campuses across the country and the continent. It was a petri dish for the thoughts and creativity of names like Taglioni, Terblanche, Tamburini and Dall'Igna, and therefore some of the most memorable motorcycles on both the roads and the track: the Ducati 888, the 916, the Desmosedici. In MotoGP alone, Ducati's expertise has not only helped to dominate two-thirds of the grid since the start of the decade, but their proficiency has oozed into other manufacturers like KTM and Yamaha: head-hunting in grand prix is not reserved for the racers only.

The faded paint on the bricks in Italy obscures genuine innovation, especially when it comes to the track, with the desmodromic engine, aerodynamics, ride height devices, 'scoops', weight diffusers and other inventions to loop in and around the few gaps of the MotoGP rulebook.

Ducati's desmodromic system is partially a branding tool but also a deep hook to history, and an unmissable tie to Ducati's four-wheel spiritual 'cousins' located just 25 miles west in Maranello. Italy's association with the colour red extends back to the beginning of the last century when racing cars were visually identified by nationality. As the British were painted green, the French blue and the Germans white or silver, so the Italians were scarlet. Ducati followed suit, even though their corporate shade also involves yellow and white.

For all the company's roots and heritage, Ducati has weathered periods of instability. They have changed ownership at least four times and been controlled by Italian, American and German parties. The composition of Lamborghini/Audi and therefore the Volkswagen Group hold the current chequebook and have done so since 2012, but the day-to-day tiller is manned by Italian influence, thanks to CEO Claudio Domenicali; his management structure has helped usher in a period of boom. The biggest milestone yet was reached in 2022 when the company topped a one-billion-euro mark of revenue for the first time by delivering 61,562 bikes, alongside other income avenues like merchandising. This was also the first time that Ducati won both MotoGP and WorldSBK championships in the same year; they repeated the double in 2023. It is fair to say the brand has never been more omnipotent in terms of their racing endeavours.

———————————

I'm not allowed to peek inside the off-limits Ducati Corse race department, but friend and fellow podcaster David Emmett and I are in Borgo Panigale for a different reason. We're ushered into the administration corridors adjacent to the museum. Iconic race bikes from the past are parked on stands in narrow walkways, like deprioritized patients in an overflowing hospital ward. There are yellowing posters covering the old-fashioned interiors, mixed with trophies and insignia from recognizable motorsport heroes.

We're taken to the marketing and management offices. Waiting for Claudio Domenicali has several of the Ducati staff on edge. We are told no less than three times that Claudio will soon be on his way. Our questions, made for the Paddock Pass Podcast, and for a story that would eventually appear on the *Daily Telegraph* website, are vetted again. We make small talk in an office annex, the furniture 1980s governmental style. The glass-walled rooms behind us are closed and darkened; thanks to the heavy rains and flooding in the region, they have sprung a few leaks.

We are shepherded into a small conference room that reminds us of the cultural reach of Ducati: the walls are full of images of fashion models and celebrities draped over the motorcycles. The bikes have appeared in movies like *The Matrix* and *Tron: Legacy* and more.

Domenicali eventually bounds quickly into the room. He smiles and speaks exceptional English in a low-pitched voice. The handshake is firm, and he has the poise of a man who meets, greets and brokers agreements with many different people throughout a working week.

It's an immediate surprise that he refers to Ducati as a 'dimension'. 'A one-billion-euro turnover means it is becoming a big company in this world and without losing the core values: style, sophistication, performance, passion for racing,' he insists.

We talk on a slew of subjects. From the logistical difficulty of the pandemic and post-pandemic and the haphazard delivery of parts ('We eventually stored more than 9,000 motorcycles, which is a huge amount, but that gave us the possibility to quickly put them into the market when the components arrived'), to sustainable fuels ('Everyone is focused on the decarbonization of mobility but that's just one of the big topics'). Domenicali touches on Ducati's place in the Audi Group. ('Where we continue to do good is in product development, racing and all the marketing: it is all completely independent. Of course, we align very clearly on the vision of the company and Ducati is a very minor contributor to the financial part of the group, so it is important for them that we make the brand shine, and to shine even more in the future.') Of Ducati's costly lunge into MotoE as the sole machine supplier from 2023, Domenicali says, 'We do MotoE because we basically want to understand the option, the potential and what are the limits of a full electrical motorcycle, with the current technology; the one in five years and then in ten. We still consider it as a kind of learning "laboratory", a development of understanding and skill.'

I remember when I first became aware of Domenicali, now in his late fifties and with a thirty-year career at Ducati, a company he joined as a mechanical engineer from Bologna University. It was during a press conference at Jerez for the 2001 Gran Premio de España. He sat with Dorna CEO Carmelo Ezpeleta and then-FIM President Francesco Zerbi to announce that Ducati was entering MotoGP. They had accumulated eight titles in the last ten years in WorldSBK but were aiming to confirm the spec of their prototype Desmo engine by early 2002. Domenicali said that it would be a full factory team and that the cost of the whole project was likely to deprive the firm of around 30 million dollars with an estimated running cost of 10 million dollars per year. It was bullish, ambitious and entirely expected.

At the time, WorldSBK was not under Dorna's control (that acquisition would come in 2013), so it felt that MotoGP had peeled a significant scalp. The impending four-stroke era (the last premier class race to be won by a 500cc two-stroke was in Brazil, 2001 when Valentino Rossi beat Carlos Checa by a tenth of a second) meant the grid was ripe for some Desmo.

Domenicali cited three main factors for the MotoGP transition that day. Firstly, that Ducati means 'racing' – the firm's fervour for sport dictates that it *has* to compete, and it wants to win. Secondly, a buoyant financial state afforded attacks both on MotoGP and World Superbike fronts. And thirdly, motorcycling to them is 'fun', and to design, build and race a new machine would be the most fun they would have had in a long time.

Ducati aced the BMW Qualifier at the Catalunya pre-season test in 2003 with a top speed of almost 204mph and then scored a podium on their debut in Japan. Their first grand prix win came five races later but a maiden title didn't materialize until Casey Stoner's talents broke the mould in 2007. Ducati felt confident enough to court Rossi for an ill-fated two-year stint in 2011–2012 (the start of the current Audi-era where neither the motorcycle nor the process inside Ducati Corse were ready for such profile), but the real deviation in the journey came when they persuaded Dall'Igna to defect from Aprilia in 2013 and built up to the point where they had eight motorcycles of the twenty-two on the grid in the 2021 season. A shrewd and reactive strategy meant Ducati signed two other stable teams aside from the factory effort and Paolo Campionoti's Pramac squad that was the official 'satellite' unit. Therefore, an octagon of bikes not only gave them beef in numbers and effectively guaranteed Constructors honours, but also bestowed on Dall'Igna the power to cover the shoal with a vast net of data-gathering potential that only increased the team's responsive capabilities and competitiveness further.

Other manufacturer's race management would begrudgingly credit Ducati's business acumen (on the lease of race bikes, both current factory spec and year-old tech) in press conferences and interviews over the years. The clamour to halt what had become Ducati's onslaught reached a point where countrymen Aprilia were desperate to confirm a second team; their gain with the then-RNF squad in 2023 was Yamaha's loss. The fortunes of the Iwata music firm tumbled with only two Yamaha M1s on track compared to four, while the Italians from Noale gained pace and started to post their first podiums and victories, less than two seasons after their flaky engines had made them the whipping boys of MotoGP.

Fast-forward more than two decades from that announcement in Jerez and Domenicali is able to be more concise about Ducati's ongoing investment in MotoGP. 'There is a lot that we can learn and carry over. The Panigale [sportsbike] is a perfect example. The engine is a very close interpretation of the core engine principal we did in MotoGP in 2015, that was the first bike that Gigi Dall'Igna thought of as a global product. The counter rotating crankshaft, to name one, is part of that whole layout with the cylinder and the general frame. We learned a lot from MotoGP to make a bike behave in an easy way, which sounds a bit strange because MotoGP is very complicated and difficult, but the more you are into racing the more you learn that putting a rider at ease is very relevant. When a rider can play with the bike at the front of the field then this is like the perfect state; where rider confidence is so high and the effort needed is not dramatic. He can change direction pretty quickly and turn where he wants, the engine is not aggressive, and he does not put the whole chassis into problems. A lot of this concept transfers to the production motorcycle and the current Panigale is far easier to ride on the racetrack than a bike of six/seven/eight years ago. Take the electronics, the TC [traction control] – all of this on the Panigale derives from the software we had in MotoGP when it was the "open", which now we cannot do any more and that's a limitation. It is always a fine balance between leaving the championship open to develop the technology or trying to control the cost. All the electronics we give to the Panigale now is like a "black box": it is all our own code that we make and when it's compiled it just needs input and output.'

Domenicali can be spotted at various grands prix. As a former engineer, he has a knowledgeable shortcut to some of the R&D ramifications for the business but, as CEO, he is also acutely aware of Ducati's stance and appeal as a luxury or exclusive brand. This is where the singular success of MotoGP and all the marketing worth adds up. 'This is Ducati,' he underlines, opening his arms. 'It is a very nice-looking motorcycle, very polished, very refined, very long thought-out in terms of balance of volume because it is not just a motorcycle but a piece of art.'

Our thirty-minute slot concludes, and we are chaperoned

into the Ducati canteen, where tyre fitters are sat alongside sales directors. Darkened cargo pants mix with clip-on ties, everyone having passed through the self-service counters. The food on display looks ordinary enough but the taste, unsurprisingly, induces saliva. Again, the interior gives the impression that a lick of paint would go a long way, but the high cornice is layered with a collage of racing action and riders of the past. It reminds me of a teenager's bedroom. A lot of it is Superbike photography, perhaps indicating the date of the last decoration. Next door, the bar for coffee is like a crowded pub. The post-lunch espresso is taken standing up, over a quick conversation, and downed like a medicinal remedy for the afternoon shift. Jostling to the bar to apologize for wanting a milky coffee involves some careful weaving in and out of elbows and loud chat. Caffeine applied, the world of Ducati starts to close as we walk away and hear the grind of machinery and graft on the factory floor below.

The curling road into the night becomes taut as the turns get more torturous and acute. The darkness through the back window of the bright green, 60,000-euro Audi gets more mysterious as the route twists upwards. Somewhere to the left and right, the Italian mountains are creating a large, imposing blackness. The car is new; Albi, our driver, is friendly enough, and the long journey from Milan to the depths of the Dolomites is arduous, taking almost four hours to pass the lakes, carve through remote towns and hamlets geared entirely for the winter ski activities, and into the climb to Madonna di Campiglio. There is something about the trek that strikes a chord with Ducati's own surge in MotoGP.

In pre-season 2023, Ducati revived their winter team launch

event from the original 'Vroom' edition, where Philip Morris International's tobacco cash would underwrite a star-studded and fanciful press junket on the slopes of the upmarket ski town, and where après ski was mixed with small talk, racing chatter and a fully comped experience for media and guests. Instead of cigarette cash, Ducati now had Audi horsepower. They camped in Madonna to celebrate their first MotoGP and WorldSBK double and present their line-up for the coming term. The snow tumbled in abundance during the first day of presentations and press conferences. Now, in 2024, it was milder and with less white coating on the *pistas*, and Ducati would bolster the occasion by unveiling their first motocross project.

Madonna di Campiglio is a sanctuary of hotels, 'wood cabined' shops and restaurants, with a few amenities geared to all-out tourism in ski season. Audi have adopted the location as a symbolic 'testing reserve', that gives their move towards sustainability and more eco-friendly vehicles an apt setting for promotion. For the three-day Ducati gathering, gleaming cars and people transporters glide and slide around the narrow, gritted roads and white inclines. Dinner takes place in a sizeable reserve high above Madonna di Campiglio. In 2023, we were loaded into a ski lift capsule for a jolting fifteen-minute journey in a pitch black, steamed-window claustrophobia. In 2024, the commute is achieved by piling guests into a fleet of snow tractors that powered up the mountain. I was sat next to former WorldSBK race winner, grand prix rider and World Supersport champion Chaz Davies – a man seemingly far too intelligent to have been a professional motorcyclist.

The food and treatment were first-class, as was the effort to remove the usual barriers between media and race team personnel. Rarely would Ducati management fraternize so freely with a ream of inquisitive journalists, their guard only partially raised between canapes, wine and coffee.

One of the main targets for the press is a tall and bushy Italian: the wiry and gravel-voiced Luigi Dall'Igna, Ducati Corse's General Manager – an innovator and a technician so revered that Honda tried a cheeky swoop for his services midway through 2023. The Japanese wanted him to end his tenth grand prix season in red with the challenge of subverting HRC's rudderless dysfunction. On the track, Ducati would not be where Ducati is without Dall'Igna.

'I always said to Domenicali that we needed to make Ducati a huge brand and Claudio, first as an engineer in Ducati Corse and then as CEO of Ducati Motor, really improved this idea in the proper way,' Team Manager Davide Tardozzi tells me. 'We have to remember that Claudio is the guy who decided to hire Gigi Dall'Igna and it was one of his best decisions for the racing.'

From Thiene, between Verona and Venice, as a child Dall'Igna was fascinated by how things move. Motorsport is a glamorous and mainstream sport in his homeland, but this aspect was not the main pull. 'I was passionate about the "technical". I wanted to study physics, but it's hard to reach good results and a good position in that field. Only a few people can achieve it. I didn't feel I was clever enough!' A big smile and raspy laugh distorts the voluminous goatee.

I first interviewed Dall'Igna in 2022. I walked through the paddock in Jerez, Spain, and he popped out of the aisle between the Ducati trailers as we headed to the office at the same time. On the way, he was stopped and asked for a selfie by a young female fan, and I could sense his bemusement, shyness but also friendliness. Inside, Gigi eased into his chair across a dark grey table and clasped his hands. The interview process is undoubtedly not his favourite aspect of his work, but I had the impression that he was approaching the questions in his second language in a studious manner.

My colleagues and I have tended to file interactions with Dall'Igna as initially plentiful and engaging, but, upon transcription and 'rustling through the swag' of the interview itself, realize that he's very frugal with details. Quizzing him on his personal background, his philosophy and preferences yields a little more fruit than, say, the rationale behind the angle rate of a particular piece of aero.

'I have always been passionate about motorcycles but, honestly speaking, I am not a racer,' he told me during another grilling in 2024. 'I prefer to make a trip with a bike with a tent and live for the freedom of it. This is my vision of motorcycles. I am really passionate about the technology. I am curious about the innovation, the technical aspect of the world – aerospace, boats, bikes and so on. When I was young, I watched all the Formula One races and most of the motorcycle races, but it was not my passion. I was not passionate about one brand.'

Dall'Igna identified 'automotion' as a realm in which he could satisfy his inquisitiveness for forces. A year spent in the car industry and with Michelotto, a sub-brand of the Ferrari group, proved difficult after the racing division folded and the relatively sedate pace of car production was not attractive. The proximity of Aprilia, just an hour away, was a temptation. 'You have to think that when I started, [technical] drawing was not done on the computer, it was on the paper! 1992 was my first year in the motorcycle industry. I was too young to understand the differences in the cars and had only spent a short time with four wheels. For sure the motorcycle had many more interesting possibilities but then the budget was far lower. You had to be clever if you wanted to do things.'

Competition offered Dall'Igna a vocational palette but also an apt mixing bowl for his ideas, his ingenuity ('I like fantasy. I like to do things in a different way') and his lack of patience. 'You learn a lot when you start to work for racing. When you have an idea you can put it on the table, design the piece and test it on the track – soon!'

Dall'Igna eventually headed the sport department at Aprilia in an eleven-year association that included utter dominance in two-stroke 125cc and 250cc grand prix, and mastering the RSV4 V4, WorldSBK spoils and championships, and even MXGP and Rally contests with the ill-fated twin-cylinder concept.

'It was a very small department and we moved through the two-strokes and into the four-strokes, so it wasn't easy to manage all the time, but it was a very good education,' he said. 'I don't mean just for the technical side, but also for the politics and from a management point of view. It came with more freedom but also more difficulties and more work to do.'

For Superbike, Dall'Igna was a spoon of sugar in Ducati's tank. 'Aprilia is the main enemy of Ducati,' he said, mouth curling at the memory. 'I remember very well when I first saw the 916 at Mugello because we shared the track between the companies for testing to spend less money. The 916 was a bike that made an impact on me because it was beautiful … and it was fast.'

Admiration for his rival apart, his toils for Aprilia disrupted Ducati's push for WorldSBK titles in 2010 and 2012. And when the MotoGP dream combination with Valentino Rossi proved so disappointing in 2011 and 2012, Domenicali and co decided they had to clear decks and make the call. 'I became managing director ten years ago and when I was head of the company racing was in a very poor situation,' Domenicali had told us in Bologna. 'It was just at the end of the Rossi period. He left the company and the team was very down. Also, the technical part was at the end of a period where they tried many different things and they lost the idea.'

Dall'Igna, however, saw potential, and perhaps more resources for racing outside of Aprilia's Piaggio Group remit. There was also the challenge of reversing a special brand's fortunes. 'When I was in Aprilia, the Desmosedici was, in my opinion, the fastest bike on the track but it didn't have a good balance,' he said. 'It was focused on the engine point of view, on the power, and it was not a "package". That was my opinion from the outside. Filippo [Preziosi, Ducati Corse General Manager 1994–2012] made a step out two years before and Bernhard Gobmeier was the project leader and the general manager of Ducati at that time. He changed the bike a lot and he reduced the power, so it became the opposite! I had to come in and bring it back! The power and the speed of the bike is always important because it is easier to overtake another rider in the straight … so it's an important part of the strategy to win the race.

'Having one clear leader was the first and most important [fix],' remembered Domenicali. 'I looked around and there were not many available. We met a couple of times with Gigi but we did not need many meetings … we found an agreement and he started with us at the end of 2013. Then it took a while because he had to start from scratch. But he was very clever because he understood immediately that there were a lot of good people here but without a clear direction.

'You have to think that for my first day in Ducati, I was the main enemy for most of the people.' Dall'Igna was smirking again. 'It was not easy. It took time to know them, to learn the people and to change the organization. Before making any technical decisions, I wanted to organize the people in a different way. The first six months in Ducati I spent knowing the staff, forgetting about the technical problems. I had to understand what I needed to move and what I needed to change to improve the system. The people and the group is the main thing if you want to progress. It is the engine of the system.'

Dall'Igna took only one other member of staff from Aprilia to Borgo Panigale. The Desmosedici needed some time to take shape, and the Italian had to correct what he felt was Ducati Corse's biggest vulnerability. 'The delivery time of the new ideas was the worst point of Ducati because they wanted to be sure that their ideas come to the racetrack in a perfect way and sometimes this doesn't work,' he told me. 'You have to make a balance between time and the durability and whether it works for the system, but if you can manage some small problems then you gain a lot in terms of knowledge through the new idea and you gain in performance.' The ideas soon started to spring forth from what he believed was one of Ducati's strongest aspects: 'The people inside Ducati Corse, the technical and the human side, are really clever, and also the spirit was really, really strong. So, I was very happy about that. I changed the mentality in the sense that I wanted to speed up delivery of the new ideas on the racetrack.'

By 2016, Andrea Dovizioso's GP16 had sprouted winglets and the race for supremacy in aerodynamics, vehicle dynamics and behaviour – Dall'Igna's beloved physics – had begun in earnest. At this time, the triumvirate of Dall'Inga, Sporting Director Paolo Ciabatti and Tardozzi was an alliance that spread Ducati's red shadow wider and wider across the sport, sparked imitation and resentment, and seeped into the industry itself. Dall'Igna had prioritized, nurtured and boosted the latency of an underperforming group and back-to-back world titles were complemented by records such as Ducati having a bike on every single grand prix podium for more than two seasons and thirty-two trophies with seven different riders in 2022 alone. By the end of that year, there had been a Desmosedici on the front row of every grid for the last forty events.

'Gigi has his own ideas but he is also very good in letting the younger engineers come up with things,' Ciabatti said to me in 2022. 'Everybody has their responsibility in a certain area and they have to think in an unconventional way – but within the regulations – and to come up with some ideas and technical solutions that will then be evaluated with Gigi. If they see some potential, then we go ahead. One of Gigi's strong features is to let the talent of the engineers be expressed. If there is potential then he will fully support and develop it, like we have seen since we brought aerodynamics back, the ride height device, the holeshot device, swingarm deflector and so on. He is a demanding leader but people work hard under his guidance.'

What about the other side of the man? 'He is a very clear leader. The [weakness] – like we all have because you cannot have the positive without the negative – is that he can be difficult to work with because he is very opinionated!' laughed Domenicali. 'If you have a different opinion then it will be a bit more complicated … but we work quite well and we were able to take together the most important decisions and guide the team in the proper direction.'

In contrast to Tardozzi's wonderfully rabid celebrations, the Dall'Igna slow smile and nod of approval is about as animated as it gets for post-race merriment. And there has been a lot of congratulations, with Ducati winning eighty-seven grands prix from 2003 to 2023, and enjoying at least one victory every season since 2016. By the mid-point of 2024, Ducati had set a record for seven consecutive podium lockouts ('This is what happens when you have the best riders on the best bikes,' said Pecco Bagnaia after the British Grand Prix). For all the acclaim and the highest form of flattery up and down the pitlane, Dall'Igna still has the air of a man who could close his tablet, saunter out of the paddock and leave MotoGP to the memory banks. 'Sometimes with my son, daughter or my wife, we will talk racing but I think it's important to not carry it with you and don't always think about your problems. It will become an obsession and sometimes you cannot find a way to fix a problem,' he warned me in 2022. 'Time in the garden, time with the dog, the bicycle and the skis. I love music, so I love to put on records and open a good wine. I have a lot of hobbies,' he added.

Dall'Igna held the biggest and most significant knife in sculpting the Desmosedici to become the finest forward-thinking expression of performance. A chiselled and jolting exemplification of design, it exploited the gaps between the rulebook lines as well as vanguarding the first spec software. It is a motorcycle that would empower at least eleven different riders to achieve grand prix success during his tenure and spawned a small clutch of racers that blended with the demands of the technology: most evidently in the form of Bagnaia, who entered MotoGP with a GP18 and was able to extract the full possibilities from the machine.

Aside from a large scrawl through the record books, one of Dall'Igna's more fecund legacies will be the infiltration of Ducati scholars into MotoGP. Already, some of his most trusted lieutenants have been prized away from Italy by other manufacturers. Ducati have defaulted to their prosperous tactic of cherry-picking the brightest and youngest minds from institutions around them. This is the generational 'cream' of new specialists for whom Ducati is the top name and the most striking brand in a sport that warrants high billing on the national news.

'The theory is important and the simulation is important,'

Dall'Igna explained of the recruitment policy and the proliferation of new techniques and advancements. 'It's important to have a mathematical or physics model of the bike to understand what could happen when you put the new idea on the racetrack. Our philosophy is to bring engineers from the university, work with them and grow with them to become really technical. We are probably the only ones that build our talent inside. The rest? They bring people in from Ducati, or from Ducati or from Ducati …,' he smiled again, clearly as irked as he is proud of the poaching.

'Or from Aprilia …' I reminded him.

'Hahaha, yes, sometimes.'

March 2024. I've lost count of the yawns. It's an early and chilly start from Barcelona on yet another full Vueling flight. Thankfully, the Airbus has the heating pumping through the cabin. I try to resist dwelling on the mileage and the hours required to fly to Venice and drive over 250km to arrive at Valentino Rossi's impressively dayglow yellow VR46 building in Tavullia. It's a hike and so I'm hoping the 2022 and 2023 MotoGP world champion, Pecco Bagnaia, is in a chatty mood and charitable with his time.

Tavullia is much smaller than I imagined, and a lot closer to the Misano World Circuit than I realized – a mere ten-minute jaunt past the flat, open-plan race facility. Faded yellow '46' flags hang from the lampposts. The brightly coloured VR46 *bottega* shop stands out like a homing beacon and is, perhaps, the sole attraction for anybody on this hillside hamlet populated by 8,000 people. I drive past the 'Yellow Garden' – a mini kids' play area created by Rossi and featuring the seven dwarfs of his 2005 championship celebration. The equally fluorescent VR46 office is a few kilometres outside of the town and presides over an industrial park. Though surrounded by a dark, tall, green hedge, the distinctive logo and corporate colours of the two-floor building are still unmissable. The location is not only home to the VR46 merchandising and business operation but is also the nerve centre of the VR46 grand prix team and the VR46 Riders Academy.

I've arrived slightly early and I have time to swoop past the black gate, park, check some messages and have a glance at some of the other cars around me. Nothing too flashy. Then, on cue, the deep growl of a Porsche trundles by. The dark GT3 RS with a red race trim and an imposing spoiler quickly fills a space and Bagnaia emerges, dressed down in a grey sweatshirt and sweatpants, carrying a holdall and a helmet bag. I also jump out of the car. He greets me warmly and we walk into the reception to get out of the rain. The receptionist looks at me and melts into a large smile when Bagnaia quips, 'He's with me.' We walk past several of Rossi's old race bikes on display and straight up the stairs. Bagnaia is eager to find his sister and PA, Carola – the facilitator of our appointment and a shy, reluctant conversationalist.

We walk through the wide office space with floor-to-ceiling glass. There must be twenty people at work. They all turn and greet or wave at the rider, but then return to their screens. It's clearly not unusual to have motorsport heroes, stars and legends strolling around. The merch and trinkets, posters, pictures, helmets, gear and trophies are almost overwhelming. As is the endless presence of yellow. We find Carola outside in the smoking section with Uccio Salucci, Valentino Rossi's childhood friend and confidante, and one of the founders and overseers of the VR46 Riders Academy, who provides a friendly welcome in his thickly accented English. I gesture to the grey, watery sky and he rolls his eyes. 'Too long, this shit,' he laments.

Pecco drifts to the two large Nespresso machines and makes us both an espresso. Not a drop of milk in sight. After a bit of small talk, we walk back through the corridor to Rossi's vast office at the helm of the floor.

The large executive desk near the window has a Mac screen, a keyboard and several unopened packages. On one side of the room there is a big TV with a low-set, wavy, brown sofa as well as two armchairs. Opposite is a long boardroom table with at least eight yellow chairs. Pecco briefly vanishes behind a pillar and raids a fridge for a bottle of water which he places neutrally on the table between us. Before we start to talk, he takes his helmet out of the bag and starts to scribble a message across the dark visor with a silver pen. Clearly not a new model. He smiles. 'It's for my manager, I said I'd give him one.'

I mention, looking around, that I'd never been to Tavullia or the VR46 'hub'. Pecco is momentarily surprised and kindly says he'll conduct a tour after the interview, but then we both look at our watches. The clock is ticking. In exactly one week we'll both be in Qatar for the first grand prix of the season, and will most likely be sitting in the same press conference room for the first official act of the 2024 championship. Bagnaia is rolling through the last duties and acts that precede an all-encompassing MotoGP tilt, and those involve sponsor and team obligations and special requests from media. He's squeezed in this appointment between training sessions. 'Cardio was this morning, now I need to drive to Pesaro for stretching,' he says. There is no feeling of urgency but when we've finished our interview, a few minutes short of an hour, he's left with little time to get back to his trainer. The tour will have to happen another day.

I first spoke to Bagnaia back in 2017. It was the first in a series of in-depth interviews I was writing for Monster Energy: one of

Valentino Rossi's long-term sponsors. Therefore the deal covered all his VR46 proteges. The Italian was thirty years old then.

Bagnaia is undoubtedly the Academy's finest export and Ducati's greatest lab rat. From his entry in MotoGP in 2019, when, like many rookies, he struggled to gauge the braking demands of the machinery but eventually became one of the strongest at 'casting the anchors', the Italian moulded his style to the idiosyncrasies of the Desmosedici and was able to harness all of its qualities to marry them with his focus and ability to tunnel-vision. In 2022, Bagnaia overturned a ninety-one-point deficit in the championship in eight races with seven podiums. Bagnaia was and is a rider for pressure.

There are traits of Pecco, sat upright in Rossi's office in front of me now, that were in evidence six years ago. He is still softly spoken, easy to smile, slightly monotone and makes a lot of eye contact. His English is much better (he also knows how to take a compliment) and seems like he has barely aged: the same short curly crop and prominent facial hair surrounding a youthful and attractive face and complexion.

His frequent tendency to chuckle at comments or himself is endearing. He can also be sarcastic, and that makes him even more likeable. Speaking for an hour in a second language (or third, as he is also fluent in Spanish) cannot be his idea of fun, but it doesn't seem like a chore either. Fifty-five minutes of thoughts and inquisition pass by swiftly.

He doesn't verbalize much with his hands but it's not the first time I notice how well manicured he is. It's a notable feature, usually because motorcycle racer's fingers are notoriously crooked or misshapen thanks to endless fast-paced contact with the ground. Pecco looks like he could be a pianist, in stark contrast to the curl and callouses of say Marc Márquez or even the sizeable grip of his mentor. 'Rossi's [hands] are huge,' former Yamaha teammate Jorge Lorenzo once told me, and having shaken his claw once or twice, I can attest to the claim. MotoGP fans will remember well Rossi's four-finger front braking style, something that's not altogether comfortable with stubby digits. Bagnaia is tall, slight, fit and even through his casualwear it's easy to see muscular definition. He's neat.

'Pecco' was labelled by his sister, Carola, three years his senior (he's a middle child), when he was small and the name stuck. His father, Pietro, and uncle rode motorcycles and would head to circuits. That was Bagnaia junior's way in. After a trip to Paul Ricard, a journey of some 250 miles from the family's home near Turin, Bagnaia's fascination took hold. He claims he was five or six years old, and the arrival of a Beta 50cc minibike for Christmas started a routine of laps around his grandparents' garden. 'It was my thing to ride a bike,' he insisted to me in 2017. 'I wasn't pushed. I saw my dad riding and just really wanted to try. I had a go at basketball and football, but I wasn't good enough to play these games. The first time I rode a minibike was in 2005 – or 2006, maybe – and it was incredible that I was able to touch the ground with my knee straight away. I was thrilled and that was the start of it. It was all about the speed for me.'

Bagnaia was hooked but not, it seems, totally obsessed. He would ride the motorcycle a few times a week, sometimes once or twice a month. In a 2018 interview, that would run on the *Telegraph*'s website, he told me constant laps were 'boring and repetitive'. School was also 'boring'.

Bagnaia's 'less is more' take is even evident today: he will not always be the rider with the most laps in a session but he is pin-sharp with his objectives and has the concentration to achieve them as quickly and efficiently as possible. His mental compartmentalization to the task for a chrono, a day, a meeting or a season is a forte. 'One of my strongest points is this one,' he affirms, 'and [keeping] my confidence. When I realize I can do something well, then I know perfectly what I am capable of. For example, if I ride motocross or flat track then I know there is a risk for me to go fast and on the limit, so my mentality is already set lower. When I go with the Ducati Panigale to ride at Misano I know I can put it the limit right away.

'This [realization] is automatic for me but I still try to improve it,' he says. 'I know at a grand prix some others might be faster at the start of the weekend but our way to work will bring us to the top and we can be quicker.

'When you do something too much … then it [life] becomes just about that,' he opines on saddle time. 'You start thinking too much. When you ride [then] you have to do it to the maximum. You can be more focused on giving that maximum and taking full benefit. If you ride every day, then you start to make habits and maybe not reach that maximum. I don't know if my mentality is the correct one but it is helping or directing me to improve our work, I think.'

Minibike potential, results and his family's support meant his rate of development was quick and he caught the eye. By 2010, he was travelling to races further afield and his involvement with former 125cc world champion and Marc Márquez's manager Emilio Alzamora and his Spanish pre-GP talent team with 125 Metakit bikes was serious progress. He started to learn Spanish and spend more and more time in the country, competing in the CEV national series (arguably the strongest in Europe and the best 'shop window' for the world championship). For three seasons, he won races and took top three finishes in the series.

At the end of 2013, Bagnaia's life changed. 'So has this building,' he says, looking around. 'This office was still here, though. I remember walking in, it was December 2013, and it was the first time I signed a contract for the academy. I felt like I was amazed the whole day.'

Bagnaia was one of the first clutch of kids to be acquired, trained, schooled and managed by Rossi's scheme. The opportunity to befriend and receive the backing of an Italian motorcycling icon was a major accelerator for his career, but the deal came with a catch: he'd have to relocate to the east coast while midway through his teens. 'I never had any doubts to be a part of it. When I signed the contract, I accepted the possibility that I would have to live here. It was more of a sacrifice for my family than me. I was living my dream but it was not easy at the start because I was in a hotel for one or two months, I don't remember how long, and I was seventeen. It was a difficult period because I was alone, without a car. There were other riders from the academy around but they were living their lives with their friends.'

Teenagers on the verge of professional sport usually have to sacrifice their childhood and other conventional hallmarks of adolescence. They grow up quickly. If they don't become serious and learn to say 'no' to distractions that can affect their competitiveness, then they don't make it. Bagnaia was trying to work this out in a strange environment, while under extra pressure to unearth results in what was a second term in Moto3 and the first as part of Rossi's freshly established VR46 race team. It must have been a confusing time. His smile is knowing. 'Also, I was really, really shy. I have never been an arrogant guy. Never. And I will never be. I was enjoying everything I could, and it was useful to be close to tracks and to ride motorcycles when I wanted, because at home it was only possible one or two times a month to go to a motocross track … and I hate motocross. I like watching it but doing it scares me. When I moved here, it felt like there was a kart track or a mini-bike track fifteen minutes in every direction. The mentality of the people was totally different.'

'The first time I saw the name "Bagnaia" it was in the newspaper,' Uccio Salucci recollects. He is grinning already. We're in the VR46 MotoGP team office space in the Portimao paddock a month after my trip to Tavullia. The stairs between the two trucks lead into an impressive mezzanine of small, contained areas separated by an aisle. One has a massage table, another two seem like hangout spaces or more offices. At the end, Pol Bertran, the ever-friendly Catalan press officer, opens another door. Straight ahead is a yellow exercise bike. Uccio sits next to it at a desk made for two. Undoubtedly this is also Rossi's cubbyhole when he's making fleeting appearances at MotoGP. I wonder who uses the bike.

Uccio is on the phone but gestures for us to come in and waves a remote at the huge TV suspended on the wall opposite to lower the volume. I mention that he can finish the call and we can wait, but he says, 'No problem, it is just Valentino, sending me audios.' I briefly ponder if Rossi is a texter or a talker – probably a talker.

Apparently, the academy surfaced from Rossi's acute business sense … but also the desire to gain some peace and quiet. 'It was four of us: me, Vale, Carlo [Casabianca], Albi [Tebaldi],' Uccio recounts, clearly a decent raconteur despite insecurities with his English. 'Vale was training in the gym in Pesaro. Young riders would come in: Simoncelli, Morbidelli, Antonelli, Marini. They would come to Vale and say: "Please, Vale, help me with a helmet [deal]." I remember well Morbidelli asking for help with the leathers! Vale called me and said: "Help these guys for gear." Then, he started to think.

'So, he calls us for a meeting on the boat and he told us about the academy idea.' Uccio is warming up now. 'We thought, "F**k, OK … we're doing it." He said, looking at me first, "You know people in the paddock and the teams. You, Carlo, are good for the training, and you, Albi, are good for management and the contracts. We will do it … but because you are getting paid for these jobs already there will be no extra money." OK! *Grazie* Vale! Good idea! As always, he was right because it was a good system to help these riders. We started to organize. The first year we were five, second year eight, then ten.

'In 2013, I was full-time in charge of the academy,' he tells me of his part in the Bagnaia conscription. 'My mission was to try to find good, young, Italian riders. At the end of that year, I was looking around a lot. I think my attention was caught more by Bagnaia because of the face, the eyes. When I first saw him, it was at Dainese, because I was taking care of something for Valentino. Bagnaia was there. He didn't smile. I introduced myself and asked if all was OK. He complained about his bike, saying it didn't turn, and also had pain in his wrist, which he had broken. I reminded him that he has to try to smile a bit more because he was in the world championship. He was too young to be that way. I think he looked at me like I was a crazy man! A few years later, he told me that when we first met I gave him some support and he was happy for that. Anyway, when we decided during 2013 to make our own team for 2014, I knew I already wanted Bagnaia, and [Romano] Fenati also. They both had something a bit special. I'd seen a lot of videos but Bagnaia was already very fast with braking and I liked that. I went to Vale and said: "Please take Pecco for the academy and also the team."'

Considering his words, I wonder whether talent or character was a more discernible initial quality. 'Both,' he says immediately. 'They have to go together. Fenati is maybe one of the best talents I have seen in my life. He was unbelievable. I think it was 2014, or maybe 2015, at Mugello, he passed [Alex] Rins on the outside into Arrabbiata 1 and was so fast that he then passed Álex Márquez on the inside of Arrabbiata 2. This one was a *phenomeno*! Rins and Márquez: not slow riders. But the character of Fenati was not easy. If the character is not good then it is more difficult. If the character is good but not so much talent then the work is easier but then it's harder to arrive to the top.'

Bagnaia was timid and maybe disillusioned in 2013 at sixteen years of age. In his first grand prix season, riding a Honda was pointless, almost in both aspects, as progress was slow and he barely entered the championship rankings. He didn't finish in the top fifteen once from seventeen races. 'That was the hardest moment of my career, for sure,' he had told me. 'I was not getting any results and I was slow. My feeling with the team was zero. It was a total disaster. I was not thinking about giving up at that point but I knew there was also a possibility that I was going home.'

He paused: 'I was scared but I also recognized that my results were not good enough. I was doing the maximum ... but it was difficult. One big thing that I learned was that if I didn't have a good feeling with the people I was working with then I was not able to do good results.'

Uccio, VR46 and Tavullia provided sanctuary and possibility. There was also training sessions, riding sessions at Rossi's nearby exclusive 'Ranch' dirt track, English classes and tuition. It was a haven for ambitious sports kids where camaraderie sat alongside competition. It also involved disorientation for Bagnaia.

'He was too serious!' laughs Uccio. 'But it was not an easy

situation for him. He came from northern Italy and 500km away, to the south at sixteen years old. He lived alone. Sometimes when I went to bed at night I would say to my wife: "I wonder what Bagnaia is doing now? I hope he is OK …" She told me to invite him over for food sometimes because he was stuck there without a car or a scooter and Pesaro is not a big city. You won't have a taxi at 11pm at night. He came over for dinner, we spent some time together and when he was more comfortable in our world then he started to relax. Life became easier. He was still very young.'

Bagnaia chuckled at the memory of a kid from the north trying to blend in with the 'beach life' attitude of the eastern coast. 'At the start, they used to say it was impossible to make a joke with me because I was more serious than them, but it did not take me long to understand how they enjoyed themselves and what it meant to have fun. Where I am from it is more about football, only football. Here is it only motorbikes and then football! This is something I really liked.'

Pecco had an alternative personality to his academy mates but I was compelled to ask him if he felt different to everyone else, period. Breathing at 150mph while sixteen or seventeen years of age and retaining the levels of drive to constantly test oneself personally and professionally are not the normal hallmarks of a teenager, even those overly flush with youthful urges.

When I had put that to him, the lightly bearded smile appeared again. 'I have to say that, for me, until I reached the world championship, this [racing] was like my favourite game. Inside the world championship then this changed a lot. I never thought I was different compared to my friends, and they also never said anything to me that made me feel like I was different. It was just normal that I was being taken three hours from my home just to have a ride while they were just crossing the street to play football.

That's how it was. I never used motorbikes as something to put me on another level. I think that is still the same. As you grow, then your group starts to work, some are still studying, others move away – I'm four hours from home – but we still have normal dinners together and it doesn't feel that much has changed.'

Another small lifestyle milestone was passed in 2014 when VR46 paired Bagnaia with another racer, Lorenzo Baldassarri. 'They arrived at the academy at the same moment,' Uccio says. 'Balda from the south, Pecco from the north. Vale had a house in Pesaro and we wanted to rent it out so we put them both together. It was just the circumstances.'

'I moved to live with Baldassarri and it only got better from that moment,' Bagnaia remembered.

Baldassarri had been one of Bagnaia's contemporaries going back to his pocketbike days and also a teammate when he was competing in Spain. They raced together in 2013 for that first trying year in Moto3 and then became housemates. 'We started living together at the end of 2014 and until 2019,' 'Balda' tells me from his car via video call. The tall World Supersport racer is another I'd interviewed several times at the end of the previous decade when he was winning grands prix in Moto2, prior to several hard crashes that diverted his career away from MotoGP.

'I moved from Marche, further south, because it was 1.5 hours from Tavullia. Pecco had come from Turin, which was four hours away. We decided to share a house for training because the gym was there, the Ranch, Misano … it was in Pesaro's port, surrounded by all the boats. We had a lot of great times together but, because my home was closer, I was often going back at weekends to see my girlfriend or my parents. It was harder for him. We never had any problems but it obviously got a bit "tight" when we started to have girlfriends and there would be four of us. We'd watch films, play

Gran Turismo, train. Our relationship towards the end was not as close as it was at the beginning because we both had partners and we were both fighting for the Moto2 world championship. Not as easy as before … but always friends outside of the track.

'We'd made some real disasters in the kitchen,' Balda explained, in his high-pitched but raspy voice. 'Some weird experiments. I cannot say more because it is better that people do not try it at home! Pecco is a funny person. He's a friendly guy and was always talking, whether it was bikes or whatever. He did not keep to himself, and me neither, even though I'd say we were both shy guys. It was a good group in total. We'd go out together in the evenings as well.

'He learned from Valentino because at the races he was very good at being focused but also having some fun times and speaking with people,' he added. 'Sharing time at a GP with many others can take a lot of energy that maybe you want to save for the sessions or with your technicians, but Vale was really good at that. He actually took energy from it.'

Bagnaia swiftly deduced that having the right professional support network around him at the circuit and in the pitbox was just as crucial as the environment at home. 'The year 2014 started quite well but again, the team was not right for me. There were three or four people inside it that were not friendly to me, I have to say. I remember perfectly after Vale's win in Misano we were in his home and Uccio said to me, "We have a small chance of riding for the Aspar team and the Mahindra, just focus on doing your best for the rest of the season." We signed the Aspar contract on Monday after Valencia and the last race. I was quite scared up until that point but it turned out to be one of the best choices of my life. As soon as I got to Aspar, my feeling with the team was incredible. In my first race, as soon as I started, I was fighting for the podium, only Fabio Quartararo pushed me out of the track on the last lap! The confidence from that and the whole two years with Aspar really helped me to grow and also forget about the previous two years.'

The first grand prix win arrived for the Spanish team with the Indian brand at the TT Circuit Assen in 2016. As the Aspar team were also contesting the MotoGP class with Desmosedicis, Bagnaia was given a nine-lap mini 'test' run at Valencia at the end of the season as a prize for his Moto3 achievement. It was his first contact with Ducati power and where his braking ability received a reality check. 'It is scary because it feels like the whole world is stopping around you,' he told MotoGP.com at the time.

'Honestly, I don't remember too much,' he said of the outing to me at the 2024 Dutch TT after he had topped every practice session and obliterated another lap record on Saturday afternoon. I asked him to look back and bring some context. 'But I do remember that moving from the Mahindra to the Ducati in a day was the biggest step I ever tried! It was very powerful, was very difficult to brake with the carbon [discs]. The corner speed was fantastic, so the bike was more stable, but, compared to today, it was another story.'

The housemates would become Moto2 competitors in 2017 and 2018 as Bagnaia briefly drifted back into the VR46 race team operation after his Aspar stint. Baldassarri was fast but inconsistent, while Bagnaia really found his stride, clocking up finishes, podiums and wins. Their careers were already heading in different directions by 2018. It initially looked like Balda would be the one to graduate to MotoGP first but Bagnaia took the championship with eight wins and twelve podiums. Lorenzo broke free of the Academy. 'Pecco believed in it 100 per cent,' he said. 'I was not the same. There were many riders and I felt their interests came before me. I wasn't into the project 100 per cent. So, I decided to stop and go by myself. Uccio had a lot of work with Valentino. When I asked for more support, it was not possible but we finished with a good relationship. Pecco was very quiet and went along with it all. I gave my best and sometimes more than Pecco, but he was cleverer than me in that moment and went completely all-in with the people involved. I was more worried and didn't have such a free mind on track.'

'The difference was the character,' stated Uccio. 'The Academy is like an institution. You need to believe in it all the way, and Pecco did that. He said, "Guys, I'm in your hands." It wasn't just him but also his family. I have a very, very good relationship with them – Pietro and Stefania. Baldassarri's talent was similar to Pecco's and he demonstrated that. In 2019, he won the first two or three races in Moto2. He fought for the championship. But Baldassari did not trust the academy 100 per cent. Not just Balda, but some other riders. The ones that made it, trusted the system; not only the fact that they would have a good bike, good tyres, mechanics, a good programme, support – it was about mentality. Trusting our advice. People want to come to the academy because it is the academy of Valentino Rossi … but that should not be the main reason that they want to *stay* in the Academy. It should be because they believe in the work. The riders that stayed and they had faith in it were the ones that arrived to MotoGP.'

'One thing I'm lucky with is the people around me: Carlo, Gianluca, all the guys in the academy, Vale, my family, girlfriend,' Bagnaia said. 'They help me to remain free in my mind and just focus on the objective, which is winning and improving. I'm lucky that my girlfriend is super-good at managing me! She is more mature than me. I try to follow the way she is growing [in life]. That makes it easier.'

Domizia and Bagnaia were engaged when I interviewed him in Tavullia. The pair married in July 2024. 'She is magnificent in everything and that makes it easier. She is a buyer, for a boutique in Pesaro. She has to travel to Paris, Milan, Roma and there are periods where she is often away, sometimes more than me! And at the start it was quite difficult to combine.

'In MotoGP, we are more like athletes now, not just riders. It is quite different and not everyone, the public, understands that. Right now, the preparation, the mentality and the race weekend is managed by *athletes*, and the level has increased a lot.'

Friend and 'academy-mate' Franco Morbidelli was the first from the VR46 collective to win a world championship when he ruled Moto2 in 2017. He was also the first to enter the MotoGP class in 2018, even though a broken wrist and the disintegration of the Marc VDS Honda team meant it was a frustrating term for the laidback Italian/Brazilian. Bagnaia was quick to follow in the slipstream and his Pramac Ducati deal had been confirmed by late February 2018. It was a clever gesture and allowed the rider to concentrate fully on bringing the VR46 race team their first world championship that year.

'The first request for Pecco to go to MotoGP was a really good moment,' recalls Uccio. 'I told him, "We don't need to sign now, Pecco." But he said, "If we sign now, then my mind will be more free. I will win seven races and become world champion." I said, "No way! F**k off!" But we did the deal with Pramac, he won eight and made it happen! Funny story, no?!'

Bagnaia's 'Go Free' mantra was doing the rounds frequently at this point. For all his ability on the motorcycle, and the force and courage to brake harder and later than most, it was his mindset and disposition in the face of sporting adversity that was arguably his main strength. As Miguel Oliveira – his principal rival for the 2018 title – would tell us in 2024, 'feeling is everything', and Bagnaia would roam, search and probe for the best sensation with the Ducati and in an intensely systematic way. Some of the emotions and irritations spotted in the garage during his Moto2 phase and the first year in MotoGP would fade to be replaced with a blank wall of resistance, but then acknowledgment that improvement had to be inevitable.

'In the past I would get the results, but I would get even more stressed or angry if they sometimes would not come,' he explained during our interview. 'Right now, that is not the case. I know if I am fifteenth fastest in the first session that we will work through, I will work on myself and we can arrive [to the front]. That experience and knowledge helps so much. I think it started in 2018. A few times, I would be [only] in the top ten during warm-up and I'd be so angry and frustrated, but then I'd finish on the podium or win the race. Keeping calm and working things out is always the best way.'

I remember being one of only a few journalists standing outside the back of the old Lusail pitboxes in Qatar to speak to Bagnaia on his MotoGP debut. He was not overly happy and still trying to get his head around the Michelins and the limits of stopping the Ducati. In truth, his first campaign was not the definition of 'stellar'. One top ten result in the first ten races, with five DNFs, hinted at a troubled conversion. Fourth position in Phillip Island was the highlight but fifteenth in the championship was concerning.

Thankfully, the 2020 season, late starting because of the pandemic, thrust Bagnaia further up the order. He would have had a podium at the second grand prix in Spain but the Desmosedici went bang in the oppressive Andalucian heat and he then broke his leg in the Czech Republic for round three. On his racing return at the fifth GP, he was runner-up at Misano and that result and his betterment led to the Ducati factory team. A first win came in Aragon in 2021 and ignited a sequence of four victories in the final six events of that year. He was second in the championship behind Fabio Quartararo and the ball was rolling.

'He took that lesson – that we learned from Vale – to never stop improving and changing, and he continued working on himself and his weaknesses. A lot,' says Balda. 'I see the same guy on the inside, but on the outside he put all the puzzle together. The difference between me and him is that I wanted to win every time … but you cannot do that. And I learned from him how to [judge races] better. He was sometimes too quiet, but I think he improved that also. His training and his physical strength. He put everything together to win in Moto2 but still had a lot more to do. To be at the very top of MotoGP he did not stop building.

'Sometimes you can get to the position when you are winning and you sit back and think, "I'm the best,"' he added. 'So, you do the same things, the same routine for the next year but then everyone else has improved! You cannot stop your own journey.'

Jack Miller was Pecco's teammate for four seasons, two in Pramac and two with the factory team. The Australian and the Italian bonded, and Miller, two years older than Bagnaia, saw the trajectory. 'He is one of those guys who can ride off feel and doesn't have to force things,' Jack told me. 'The Ducati is a bike that gives you a lot of feedback but then there is a point when it doesn't, as well. He has a great finesse with it and understanding of what he feels: it's like a Spidey Sense. It means he can use the maximum of each corner and in each braking zone.'

'I'm very precise in understanding every situation and the potential of every rider,' Pecco revealed. 'For example, before setting the lap record at the 2024 Qatar test, I did a 52.1 with twenty-four laps on the tyre and I said to myself: "If I can do that with twenty-four laps on the rubber then now we go for 51.0 or 50.9," because I knew about the tyre drop. I understood well and could judge my situation, and I think I've always been like that.

'Sometimes I am slowed down a bit by wanting to be perfect on the bike,' he pondered. 'It takes energy – too much – because you never have perfection, it is easier instead to find a balance that works in many places. In 2022, we didn't touch anything on the bike in the first races, just the forks and springs, but in 2023 we changed many things because my feeling was not the best. After a few GPs, I was struggling with engine braking, so we started to move things around and, instead, we worked perfectly because after the sessions we were ready to make the qualifying or a race in the best way.'

'Technically, he was really good but sometimes – away from the track and in training – he'd give up,' Baldassarri remembered of his friend and rival's weakness. 'From what I see now, he never does that. When you are top of the championship, then you need to know when to take second place or just take the points. I can see in his eyes that he is going 100 per cent all the time. Sometimes, in the past, he wouldn't be that strong. But in MotoGP he is really precise from the middle to the end, [Jorge] Lorenzo style. The hammer!'

Bagnaia's 2022 season was defined by his face-off with Quartararo and that fightback from a ninety-one-point shortfall at the halfway mark to be the first Italian to win on an Italian bike in the premier class since Giacomo Agostini with an MV Agusta exactly half a century earlier. It was Ducati's second championship and the first for Italy since Rossi twelve years before. After an impeccable triumph by just 0.2 of a second at Jerez for round four, Bagnaia bounced through prangs in France, Catalunya and

Germany, initiating a sequence where he'd own fourteen of the next thirty-four events in his two title years. After Jerez and apart from the season finales in Valencia (ninth in 2022 and fifth in 2023), when Bagnaia finished a grand prix then he was always on the podium, stretching through to the end of 2023. In 2024 his peak arrived with the devastating expressions of perfection at Mugello and then the Dutch TT.

There were, however, a few episodes that punctuated this rise. In the summer of 2022, he celebrated his Assen Grand Prix win by using the short summer break in the calendar between Dutch and British dates to travel to Ibiza. When his car careered off the road past a roundabout in the early hours, he was breathalysed and found to be three times over the Spanish legal limit. A contrite Instagram post followed, as both the rider and Ducati hoped the attention generated by the incident would subside. At Silverstone for the next round, and after his second win in a row, a journalist from the *Sun* asked in the post-race press conference if he planned on celebrating with a few soft drinks. 'For sure, this night I will take a taxi,' he batted back. 'But I think everyone can make a mistake. I did a mistake. I *said* I did a mistake. Everyone can make mistakes. I'm sorry about it.'

Two grands prix later in Misano and his home fixture, Pecco unveiled a custom helmet in tribute to former NBA player, Dennis Rodman. Bagnaia's fondness for basketball had been fed by his trainer Carlo's interest in the sport. In the eyes of some, honouring the livery of a person convicted for domestic violence in 2004 and with a history of drunken misdemeanours was not the wisest choice, notwithstanding Pecco's claims during the pre-event press conference that the paintjob was to acknowledge Rodman's sporting prowess as one of the best rebounders and defensive players in league history.

It was a tumultuous two-month period in his career. My personal view was that Pecco had been naïve, and obviously so absorbed by the MotoGP 'bubble' as to not realize the full extent to which his actions and gestures would provoke reaction and debate. He was not a MotoGP world champion at this point, but he was the hottest star on the scene as Quartararo struggled with Yamaha's fading competitiveness in the wave of the Ducati tide and Marc Márquez was mired in injury doubt. What he said and did was bigger than who he was. There was vilification from some quarters (when isn't there in this judgmental and relentlessly outraged era of society?) but I felt the indiscretion and choices also made him seem more human and more fallible in a time when MotoGP requires almost robotic, clockwork commitment.

The year 2022 was Bagnaia's last metres on the ascent to a peak of fame, where endorsement deals with the likes of fashion brand Bulgari and voice cameos for Pixar movies became normality. I asked him about the concept of celebrity, especially in his country where MotoGP is much more part of the mainstream sporting culture.

'For some people [athletes], it is impossible for them to go to a bar and take a coffee,' he reasoned. 'For me, I might have to do one or two pictures but it's a pleasure to do this. Vale has always transmitted to us that it's important to have your feet on the ground and be happy and smile always for someone that wants to meet you. They have to enjoy the moment, while you also have to have the feeling that you can have a normal life. I love to walk my dog and go shopping. People in my town are used to seeing me buying the groceries and asking me things about bikes. It's normal, and I love it. It's a pleasure and a privilege to have these kinds of things when you get invited to events. It is important to try to understand it [the attention] and to enjoy it. It means I am doing quite a good job.'

It's a rational and rehearsed response. There must be occasions when being Pecco Bagnaia can get on his tits; when he tackles comments that his titles were won in Márquez's absence and that Dall'Igna's engineering is the only reason for his success. Bagnaia has defeated Fabio Quartararo and Jorge Martin (another Ducati rider) and has pierced through Japan's grip on MotoGP. His mental resolve extends to external perception, it seems. 'In my case, I am quite clear and transparent: what I think, I say,' he stated in Tavullia, as the interview became quite direct. 'Most of the time, comments seem to be against me but I don't really care what people [critics] at home or online are saying about me because I know I am doing my job to the maximum. If I know something is wrong, then I will say it.

'All this bullshit of the "angry rider" and the characters is not really [relevant] anymore,' he added on the subject of rivalries, and the accusation that MotoGP is too 'nice' among the pack and there should be more needle. 'There will always be a rivalry on track but we are all working hard and there is a respect among of all us. I think it is the best way to deal with a championship like this, and to work together to improve it. I don't care to lie to the media. I will just try to talk as clear and as clever as possible. For sure, when you are in a factory team you need to be more polite … but I am also in a team where Davide Tardozzi is the first one to be direct to a camera!' The smile was back.

There were also herculean feats in this two-championship spell (he is only the third rider to take back-to-back titles since Mick Doohan in 1998) that showed just how special Bagnaia is.

In a steamy Malaysia for the penultimate race of 2022, the pressure around the Ducati pitbox was dense. The air was laden, the expectation as smothering as the humidity at the Sepang International Circuit. Quite often, TV pictures would cut to Pecco sat in the pitbox in his helmet, sweating. He looked like he had the weight of a career, a lifetime goal, a team, a brand, a country wedged somewhere inside that lid. He was only fourteen points ahead of Quartararo but had fallen in Japan and had taken two third positions afterwards in Thailand and Australia. His French rival was making a decent fist of resistance and Bagnaia looked to be struggling after a crashy Friday and needing to go through Q1 to sit ninth on the grid. Finally, in the sweltering race he was flawless, finishing 0.2 of a second ahead of Bastianini for his first win in five rounds.

At that grand prix, I stood at Turn 1 as the riders hurtled along one of the longest and fastest straights on the calendar. I couldn't help but marvel at the control and the rigidity of the number 63 Ducati as it hopped and slid into position, deaccelerating from 200mph to 45 in around six seconds of whoosh, by putting almost 6kg of pressure into the front lever. Sepang (alongside Lusail) tops the scale for braking difficulty and drain on the equipment. Brembo actually made a 355m carbon disc for the race in 2022 to cope with the temperatures. Pecco was braking but also breaking the others.

'Friday was not good. Saturday morning also,' he said, shaking his head when I asked him about the episode. 'But when you put so much pressure on me or there is some *absolute* task that I must do, then it somehow becomes easier for me. In 2022, the only way to win the title was to win races. It can be quite difficult to understand, even for me, but there was a point after Sachsenring when we decided that we had to be more precise. I won four races in a row and then took second in Aragon simply because I knew I was getting very close to Fabio and I knew he was out of that

GP. If you just need to win, then you enter a dimension where it somehow gets easier – it's hard to get your head around it! In Malaysia, I simply had to win to have a good gap for Valencia, but it was not easy because Enea was pushing a lot and it was not true we had "team orders". It was really important.

'After that win I was finished,' he continued. 'I told my team that I used all the energy I had that weekend, mentally more than physically.'

The Valencia finale was two weeks later and he only needed to finish fourteenth if Quartararo won. The pressure was back but less severe than in Malaysia and one metaphorical hand was already on the MotoGP champions 'tower' trophy. The Ducati team, the VR46 unit and the voices of experience helped cloak Bagnaia, who looked tired in Spain. A ninth place allowed him to add his name and metallic tag to the climbing cylinder of twenty-eight champions. 'In Valencia, we had to manage everything. I was not living the situation well. I was nervous. I was not eating well. They [his crew] were always speaking to me and reassuring me, reminding me of the advantage, what I needed to do and the importance to stay calm, to relax. When they said, "You only need fourteenth" and "Not everyone has the chance to win a championship, enjoy!", I appreciated it. There are always suggestions and advice, but I never feel that I had to tell people to shut up and just let me focus.

'On Sunday, I think I was the only one not having a party afterwards!' he laughed. 'At 11.30, I went back to the paddock and the GP room to sleep because I was destroyed.'

Thinking of Bagnaia's slender defeat of Bastianini in Malaysia only a fortnight earlier, it seemed that he'd weathered close attention for most of the year. I looked it up and the biggest margin of all seven wins had been 0.6 of a second. I asked him in the Valencia championship press conference whether he'd carved a reputation as a pressure-handler. 'This year, I was always with a lot of pressure,' he replied, red championship t-shirt covering his leathers and the dedicatory pitboard in the background. 'I knew that a second position was not allowed, and we did it. It's the worst situation possible when you have someone behind you on the last lap and you can't commit any mistakes. It's the situation where you can easily lose your concentration. I think we worked well.'

In Tavullia in 2024, he was a bit more blasé about this capacity to carry a 'shadow'. 'I don't care if I win a race by seven seconds or one tenth of a second,' he said. 'The result is the same, the points are the same. One thing that I really love is controlling the gap. I can control seven or eight tenths of a second for twenty laps. I did it in Moto2 and many times in MotoGP.'

He relived the Valencia 'decider' predicament again in 2023, this time against Martin, but had a 'déjà vu' card up his sleeve. Bagnaia had been partially annoyed at his title defence and the first year wearing the coveted number 1. Mistakes in a wet Argentina (round two), in the USA (round three), and a collision and crash with Maverick Viñales in France (round five) meant an alarmingly poor return from the beginning of the championship. He recouped points thanks to two 'Saturday' victories in the new Sprint format. The Sprints had served to ramp up anxiety and narrow the margins for misjudgement in MotoGP but Bagnaia cleared his head for Mugello (the second win of what would be a hat-trick on home turf) and then ripped off three wins and two runner-up results in the next five GPs.

Then came Catalunya, round 11. A dramatic highside in front of the chasing pack on the first lap saw the stricken champion's legs smashed by a pursing Brad Binder. The images were horrific. 'I was very lucky. Absolutely. For years in Barcelona we have been asking them to resurface because the grip is so low. My rear tyre was not working and the crash was quite huge! It's something that can happen, unfortunately.' I asked him if he'd watched the accident back. 'I watched it because Dorna TV put it everywhere! I saw it many times.' Bagnaia denied it was a rider error. But Ducati and Michelin were also not too forthcoming on the cause.

Remarkably Bagnaia was relatively OK and not only managed to compete the following weekend in Misano but also take a pair of third positions on Saturday and Sunday by using crutches to mount his Ducati. It kept the championship chase alive. 'In Misano I felt quite destroyed physically, but mentally I was set on the front. I was conscious of what could happen by not being 100 per cent to make the lap-time or win the race but I did not let it affect me.' That mental resolve kicked in again. It was the closest he'd been to injury since the 2020 leg break. We talk about the danger of his job and the way in which he was so shaken by the 2021 tragedy at Mugello when Moto3 youngster Jason Dupasquier lost his life. Rushing around a circuit at 350kmph can have consequences. 'I never think about it,' he states. I struggle to believe him at first and then realize that it's a reconciliation – a denial – that racers need at this level. 'For sure it's a dangerous sport but we accept the risk, and we know what can happen,' he follows up. I'm a little disappointed at the normalcy of the response but then it's a subject that is probably tucked in the corner of a racer's recess as long as possible.

'The fact is … we are getting used to the speed,' he then says matter-of-factly. 'After a two-month winter break we will go to the first test at Sepang and on the third lap of the first day we'll already be near the race times from the previous GP. Your muscles have a memory, and it is difficult to forget. Then to go that extra bit faster and hit qualifying times is a bit more complicated. Things are always improving: us, the bikes … right now I think the bikes are safer than seven or eight years ago when they were wheelying more on the exit of the corners and it was harder to control the lines or the highsides. Now the grip on the exit is incredible and the rear ride height device helps with the same line. Also, the run-off areas are increasing everywhere, more or less. So, I think our sport is improving.'

At round thirteen of 2023 and MotoGP's first visit to India, Pecco's 'demon' reappeared and another crash and DNF saw him trudge back to the pitbox, helmet on, visor down in the searing heat, almost to hide some embarrassment. I wondered if that was the case. He flips the question. 'I'm lucky that my team is 100 per cent with me and they try to remove pressure. I love that: we always say that we win together and we lose together. If someone makes a mistake, then we say "sorry" and we move on … like I did in India. I made a mistake then. Like I did in Japan in 2022 or in Austin 2023. It's better to not invent excuses and just be smart about the situation.' It was his last gaff in 2023. He was a podium fixture for the last seven races and then battered the field at Valencia for the crown. Fourteenth? How about P1 instead.

At Mugello in 2024 he also silenced some of those who intimated in varying degrees of subtlety that he was not fit to buckle Marc Márquez's boots when he went toe-to-toe with the Spaniard and took the win. Márquez was riding a GP23 during 2024 and was in an acclimatization phase after ten seasons wrestling a Honda but was operating at lap record pace with the champion and came out second-best that day. Absurdly, I heard comments around the circuit and in the media centre that Bagnaia had gained some credit, as if he hadn't earned enough as it is.

Being the best of eight riders on Ducati machinery was enough to bash Bagnaia it seems. 'Props' will always come from within the manufacturer and, as he previously said, there is a common level of respect among MotoGP riders where they will recognize the talent or work of their like. Further vindication of Pecco's status easily flows, and from sources that see his efforts up close or know the sum of the man. 'Like every good champion, they make the difference somehow at the end of the day. I don't think it's only the bike,' opines Miller, dismissive of the perceived heady role of Ducati superiority. 'There are a lot of good guys riding that bike at the moment … but he is clearly doing something better.

'Everybody in this paddock has an ego … but the way Pecco presents himself and goes about his job and the things he's achieved is quite remarkable,' he continues. 'It's probably different to some of those past champions where it is all about them and they are "legends". He gives a lot of credit to the team, the bike and the people he has around him.'

Baldassarri: 'In this sport, talent is not enough. Just working hard is not enough: you have to be mentally good and strong. You have to have good people around you that help a lot and support. Valentino, Márquez? Yeah, a lot of talent but they had great mentality and great condition. Márquez is a talent but works a lot. Pedro Acosta the same. Maybe there was a phase where just talent was enough and you didn't have to work that hard to be world champion. Now, you must work a lot. Valentino was forty years old but continued to work, to change and to never give up. He was good with the people. [Casey] Stoner was another great talent but maybe missed some of the "people" side. In racing, you cannot just think about the racing and the bike, full gas and finish. You have many things to manage. Stoner was a great talent but, in the end, did not win like Pecco because he didn't work on the other parts. You need more than just speed.'

'For me, the best moment in a race weekend is during

qualifying: it is only time when you can demonstrate to yourself and to others true performance,' Pecco said, looking at me intently. 'It's when you can feel the maximum strength and power of the bike – and of yourself. I love to do time attacks. You feel you are doing something incredible. And you are so focused that it feels easy. It is amazing. It's the best reason to keep going for it. There is nothing that comes close in my life to reaching for perfection in riding. If I had to tell you something for comparison then maybe going for the best lap in a shifter kart; it is a brutal experience but still only 30–40 per cent of what is a MotoGP bike.'

I suggested to Pecco that he could try to emulate his mentor Rossi and race for another fifteen years. 'I think motorbikes are changing and, right now, the style of weekend we have is really demanding mentally,' he replied. 'It is more difficult to reach thirty-seven or thirty-eight years old like this. Last year, when I finished the championship, it was tough and when it was time to start again, I was not recharged. But … maybe we will adapt. It's a matter of enjoyment.'

Recorder switched off, Pecco offered a firm handshake. We started to walk out of Rossi's office and I mentioned the long return drive to Venice airport. 'Maybe we could have done this at a test?' he said. I smiled. The chances of securing an hour of the world champion's time at any MotoGP event would be slim to none. But it's testament to Bagnaia's personality that he's the same whatever the setting. Under duress and in demand for his sport, or dressed for the gym and driving around in the rain, he is even keeled. Maybe that is its own kind of 'special'. These are rare sportsmen.

THREE

The Gift

'm loitering outside the main gate close to the large, red-helmeted ornament at the Mugello International Circuit, north of Florence, deep in Valentino Rossi country. I'm looking for people I think might have a decent grasp of English. It's 2017, round six, and Rossi, the Peter Pan-ish, flamboyantly brilliant racer, has taken three podiums from the first five grands prix of the season. In a matter of weeks, he will claim the top step of the rostrum at Assen for the Dutch TT for his 115th (and final) grand prix victory. I'm surrounded by Rossi's yellow 46s as well as copious Yamaha apparel.

Rossi has battered grand prix statistics sheets, captured hearts from Argentina to Australia, and entertained, competed and defined a sport for the better part of two decades. 'Transcended' is probably an overused term but it sums up Rossi's profile and synonymity with MotoGP nicely.

At thirty-eight years old, Rossi is working hard to shift his style and attitude to the changing technical face of grand prix, as well as match the energy and expression of the latest generation of adversaries, thanks to his boots-deep involvement with the VR46 Riders Academy. Rossi guides and advises his proteges through his presence at training and riding sessions, but he also feeds off their vibrancy. He gleans fresh interpretations of style in the search for more speed to cope with changes to spec electronics and the Michelin era.

Rossi, son of charismatic 250cc GP winner Graziano, seldom has an issue in conveying how much he relishes his sport. The seemingly permanent happy-go-lucky disposition under the semi-rigid uniform of the cap, Oakley sunglasses, team shirt and shorts and Nike Air Max 95s is a well-practiced veneer of presentation, an image projected to fans, media and television. Early in his career, he sharply deduced how he could make the waves of attention work in his favour commercially, psychologically and for the sheer power of influence. The jovial side of his character is genuine, but it's also a tool in his large box of promotional tricks – from the increasingly inventive post-race celebrations (the Mugello speeding ticket is still 'all-time') to the well-crafted personal imagery (sun, moon, animals), and the custom-painted helmets to the A-list sport and entertainment contacts. Rossi takes his on-track panache from riders like Norick Abe, Kevin Schwantz and, naturally, Barry Sheene, but away from the asphalt there is hardly any precedent for what he does and how he works his audience. At Italian rounds of MotoGP – at most rounds – the dominant colour of the championship is that blinding yellow. No wonder he needs the sunglasses.

However, I am hovering by the gate at Mugello because Rossi's sporting prowess has begun to be eclipsed. His reputation in the eyes of some (still the minority) was tarnished by the ill-tempered but utterly gripping spats with Márquez in 2015 that introduced an ugliness to MotoGP. It is unusual to hear riders booed on the podium at grands prix unless there has been a radical race-altering incident, but the clashes between the pair (in Argentina, Netherlands and Malaysia) meant that Márquez bore the brunt of the *Rossitisti* and even needed a security detail at Italian fixtures in 2016.

If Rossi is in the final laps of his career then why is he still so damn popular? I want to try to find out. My first targets are two younger fans, two girls. A mistake, as they keep giggling at me and my attempts to talk to them. 'He's a wonderful person, with lots of emotion … and he's funny,' is all I manage to glean.

A number 46-bedecked guy in his early twenties stops to talk and I get a more impassioned reaction. 'He's been my idol since I was four,' he says. 'From my brother and my father; I just love motorcycles. We have grown up with him and he races for all of us.'

A gentleman with a yellow t-shirt, a fold-up chair and an icebox: 'I'm from Tavullia. So I'm in the fan club,' he smiles. Not much insight there then.

My next approach is to two guys standing together. They turn out to be South African. 'He's just a character,' one tells me. 'When I was thirteen or fourteen, my dad said, "Watch this one; he's special." And from the moment he jumped off a RS250 and went to the toilet he was the one,' he adds, in reference to Rossi's 1999 250cc Spanish Grand Prix victory at Jerez, where he stopped on the cool-down lap and briefly disappeared into a Portaloo.

My final interviewee is a father accompanying three kids, each decked out in VR46 garb. They are from France. I walk with them through the gate and towards the Arrabbiata 1. 'He is very good at marketing,' the guy opines. 'For the kids, he is fun, and with "The Doctor" and the colours he is like a cartoon and has become such a part of MotoGP it is hard to imagine it without him. The other riders are more neutral. We know Márquez is a god but the kids like Rossi for the fun.'

Rossi expresses an era. He symbolizes a sport. At this time, he is still both a commercial boom and a crutch for Dorna. The wins, the podiums, the championships, the impact is immense. But is he the greatest motorcycle racer? Or, what makes a great motorcycle racer?

It is easy to forget just how much excitement Rossi's emergence generated. Magnetism apart, he took a season to learn a class and then won it in his second term, every time. Before the greatness were the germs of a phenomenal motorcycle racer. 'Vale is the son of Graziano,' Uccio Salucci says to me in Germany 2024, when I quiz him on the skill factor of his lifetime friend and employer. 'When I was younger, I didn't really get it. Now I am older, I understand that Graziano gave Vale all of his experience. Vale drove a kart before the bike but every time he was driving or riding he did it with a smile, he was not pushing him, and this young guy when he was sixteen years old was driving a 100cc kart so very fast, too fast, for a child. It was like he was twenty. He already had the "system" to drive. A big talent. He was very impressive. But Graziano did not have the money to pass to the bigger kart and the minimoto was the next choice. In a very short time, he was riding as fast as the other riders who had a lot more experience.'

Graziano was a charismatic and naturally talented Grand Prix racer. His career was curtailed by injury but he evidently funnelled his stronger attributes into his son. He was a slightly eccentric figure. I'd sometimes see him at grands prix. One of the oddest episodes involved pulling into the car park at Donington Park one morning for the British round and seeing Rossi senior rolling around in sheets in the back of a BMW estate. He didn't like sleeping in hotels apparently.

ABOVE: Valentino Rossi's media debriefs were always big draws. This was the packed session inside the Yamaha hospitality at Valencia 2015, where the Italian had finished fourth after starting from last on the grid but lost the title by five points to teammate Jorge Lorenzo.

BELOW: Technical magician Gigi Dall'Igna talks to the media from the confines of the Philip Morris hospitality rig, flanked by Paolo Ciabatti. Ducati were still circling MotoGP greatness at this point and dominance was not far away.

ABOVE, LEFT: Cal Crutchlow was popular with the press, and his daily debriefs for the last six years of his career were lengthy but often unmissable. Cal was/is an expert in using the media, but sometimes his more outlandish comments would froth the MotoGP soup.

ABOVE, RIGHT: The lane of MotoGP hospitality units flanked by the shallow hills of Tuscany; it can only be Mugello. This was taken from the top floor of the immense Red Bull Holzhaus, inside the Autodromo paddock.

BELOW: Dry but with a menacing sky: welcome to Assen. The TT Circuit is one of the oldest venues in MotoGP and lays on a section of a century-old road network in Drenthe. Few love their racing as much as the Dutch. [Photo by Rob Gray/Polarity Photo]

ABOVE: It'll buff out. Jorge Martin's scratched Ducati after sliding out of the long Turn 16 at the Circuit of the Americas in 2022.

RIGHT: Ready for coronation. Pecco Bagnaia, smirking in contentedness with his championship T-shirt in place, waits in the wings for the official press conference to finish at Valencia 2022 and before his own star turn.

OVERLEAF: MotoGP is never more hectic and hair-raising than through the first corners of the race. Jorge Martin (left) is distracted by the sliding antics of teammate Johann Zarco in 2023, as disaster looms behind the Frenchman.

[Photo by Rob Gray/Polarity Photo]

ABOVE: A car window snapshot during the commute from central New Delhi to the Buddh International Circuit in 2023 – MotoGP's first ever visit to the country. Bikes everywhere but also desolation.

BELOW: In complete contrast are the picturesque climes of Phillip Island. When the weather behaves there are fewer more spectacular settings for motorcycle racing than the Australian mecca for speed.

ABOVE & BELOW: Pitbox confines. From inside and outside of the Red Bull KTM structure. Lights, monitors, cameras, concentration and tension. John Eyre (below, standing), Daniel Petak (right) and Mark Lloyd service Brad Binder's RC16 at the 2023 German Grand Prix.

ABOVE: Red Bull KTM's Motorsport HQ in Munderfing. The facility is a three-storey, 18,000m^2 hub for racing, bursting at the seams. MotoGP begins here for the brand with the build-up of new motorcycles for the season.

BELOW: An expensive wreck. Enea Bastianini turns his €2 million factory RC16 into a 'low rider' at the first 2025 test in Barcelona towards the end of 2024.

'Vale never got "bigger"', Uccio continues on Rossi junior's trajectory. 'He has always been like this [holds up his finger]. He doesn't need to take the bike all the time and be "Grrrr!" [mimes aggression]. If you see his data then he was braking and accelerating very smoothly. A lot of people say to me, "I stay behind Vale and I am like huf-huf, pushing hard, and, f**k, he is ahead doing nothing! I see him for two laps and then no more." This is talent.'

The fact that Rossi claimed the 2003 world championship at the 'rider's circuit' of Phillip Island in Australia by accelerating above and beyond a ten-second mid-race penalty for passing under yellow flags shows just how much he could stretch the limits, even taking into consideration that the Honda RCV was the dominant motorcycle at the time.

I ask Uccio if Valentino ever won by edging out of his comfort zone. 'For sure, with Honda in 2001, 2002 and 2003, maybe yes, he was [only] at 70 per cent. But in 2004 and 2005, with Yamaha he rode at 100. In 2004, because the bike was not very good but he won the championship. In 2008, also we passed to Bridgestone tyres and the first few races were not very good but then Jeremy [Burgess, former crew chief] had one idea to make the swing arm longer and Vale said, "This is my bike." He had a good race with Stoner in China and also Laguna Seca. He rode at 100 per cent for sure. I would say three or four years he had to do that ... for the others 75 per cent was enough. But ... he's Valentino Rossi.'

That's as may be, but what kept Rossi plugging away at MotoGP in the later years of his career when he had absolutely zero to prove?

'You know, Vale always dedicates himself 100 per cent,' he tells me. 'When he said he was tired and too old for the bike and he was switching to the cars he had three options: a lower level like the Italian Championship, a medium level like the GT Open, or at the highest. He went straight for the highest and in just one year he was at the top. In six months he did it because that is his personality. Sometimes I say to him, "Vale, dinner tonight?" And he says, "Ah, no, I am in the gym." I say, "F**k, you stop with MotoGP and now you are in the gym again?!" In the last three years of MotoGP he could be there eight hours a day. Now he is driving he has gone from four to six and is nearly eight again! In a day! He is like this. His mentality is 100 per cent. He is like [Francesco] Totti, [Michael] Jordan, these guys. It's only one way. I have never seen another rider like this. Maybe Pecco … but he is very focused. Vale just talks about bikes, performance, bikes, performance, every minute! And now he is just like he was before [with MotoGP] because he is very fast in the car. This is Valentino Rossi.'

The first time I interviewed Rossi was at the 2001 Spanish Grand Prix at Jerez. It was for the fledgling MotoGP.com website and the-then twenty-two-year-old had a mini-train of media commitments; evidently, media work promoting Honda was still a requisite. Rossi, clearly fed up at another dose of questioning but looking fit, trim and tanned with very close-cropped hair and sideburns, offered up his stock reaction to my small talk about his recent London address. 'It's cold,' he uttered, perhaps for the thousandth time.

He already had a way of transmitting his personality. 'I think it's very important to have a lively character; for me this is a normal thing,' he said, leaning across the table. 'I'm just a boy who is twenty-two, so I have fun just like a twenty-two-year-old! I think the riders who are very reserved are just older and maybe have a more mature view of the whole thing. I think it's good for the people and fans to see someone who is having fun in what they do. The sport is hard and serious but riding for me is always enjoyable. To go fast, for me, is the most fun.'

In an instant, he then switched to show some of the dedication that Salucci would eulogize twenty-three years later. 'My preparation for this season has been different. I have been more quiet, and have had serious ideas about my racing,' he said, after having won the opening three rounds and on the way to his first championship and the final 500cc crown before the rebranding to 'MotoGP' in 2002. 'I think I understand the 500 better.'

Rossi quickly became MotoGP's supreme Claudius – a man who could so easily smile and smile and yet also be a villain to his rivals that he would systematically dismantle with superiority and mind games. Márquez was his most robust opponent. A man who bettered his speed and was (publicly at least) immune to the comments and the yellow army. Rossi had other classy challengers, like Dani Pedrosa, Lorenzo and Stoner, but Márquez had this sheen of invincibility, abandon, and he changed the game, like Rossi's effortless style and fluidity had done more than a decade before the Spaniard entered the premier class.

The very first premier class FIM World Champion was Les Graham, a former RAF bomber pilot who Mike Hailwood (one of Britain's first outstanding and wholly dedicated grand prix stars) described as 'a daring and talented rider'. Bestriding a temperamental AJS Porcupine in 1949, in the last throes of British engineering dominance, Graham won just two of the six grands prix to become the inaugural world champion. He was then one of the first of the British elite to defect to the faster Italian Gilera machines at a time when nationalism and patriotism obliged motorcyclists to remain loyal to partisan brands. Graham had won his title by just one point after his bike had been punted out of the Nations Grand Prix at Monza by Carlo Bandirola's tumbling Gilera while fighting for the lead. The template for MotoGP action and sensation was established from the outset.

In the first years of the world championship, riders competed in thick two-piece suits with cork, wore pudding bowl helmets and still racked up average speeds of 90mph. Graham strived to enlarge his win total with Gilera and then MV Agusta, but his fate highlighted the peril and the plight of grand prix racers when he crashed at 130mph on lap two of the 1954 British GP on the Isle of Man at Bray Hill and lost his life.

Since Graham prevailed in 1949, almost thirty other riders have risen to the status of premier class number one in seventy-five years. Meanwhile, grand prix has claimed over one hundred lives in the pursuit of similar glory. The juggling act with mortality is part of the package with top level motorcycle sport.

There must be a separation between the average person, the average motorcyclist, and those who have the physical coordination, the mental fortitude and sense of denial, the coordination, the balls and the outright confidence to throttle a bike in order to prove they are faster and better than the rest? And then there is the next level: the gifted.

Jean-Michel Bayle is the only person to have won FIM Motocross World Championships, AMA Motocross and Supercross titles and then retire on the dirt to enter grand prix road racing, scoring a best finish of fourth and taking two premier class pole positions. For a generation, 'JMB' is still the most talented racer there ever was. 'In road racing, there is a lot of technique, but if you want to go faster then you have to push yourself more every time and have a lot of motivation to take risks,' he told me of the transfer between one elite contest to another, while we were in Bercy, Paris, in late 2012. Our meeting came before the start of the yearly Supercross spectacle in the French capital, where Bayle is a celebrated figure.

'The speed [of grand prix] – you feel like your eyes are three or four times bigger than normal,' he continued. 'There was too much information to take in. I had to learn how to relax and see exactly what was going on, but that was very difficult, and I had to get used to it. With the start of every new session, you have to build yourself up from the bottom again. You can rely a lot on your technique in motocross. If, for example, you say, "I don't feel good today" you can still hit the top three. In road racing, you always have to push otherwise you are in tenth place.'

There is a lot to be said for a grasp of motorcycling that people such as Bayle, Joey Dunlop, Toni Bou (record breaking trial rider) and the likes of Stephane Peterhansel (a six-time Dakar conqueror), Scott Parker (flat track legend) or Tony Rickardsson (one of the kings of speedway) displayed, but motocross combines heightened technique, speed, improvisation and physicality. It depends on throttle control and sensitivity, the perception of grip and balance. It's little wonder that so many in MotoGP train frequently on the dirt and risk injury to sample all the crossover benefits it can bring. Some staunchly dismiss the hazards of 'MX' – Pecco Bagnaia being one of those – while others – Marc Márquez, Fabio Quartararo, Maverick Viñales, Jack Miller – draw nothing but energy from it and live in constant admiration of the grand prix and AMA stars that are doing it much faster and better than them.

'If MotoGP guys can feel so much with the tarmac, imagine us when we're riding a motocross bike! We have a lot of feeling with the dirt. We ride so much that we can feel every single stone on the track and then it is up to you to take the risk,' 2023 MXGP World Champion Jorge Prado tells me over a coffee at the Red Bull Energy Station at the 2024 Italian Grand Prix at Maggiora.

Prado is one of those generational 'freaks' – a junior competitor who was lauded for his natural management of a motorcycle at the age of twelve, and whose family thus transplanted from Galicia to the Benelux. Following in the prodigal teenage footsteps of other world champions, like Ken Roczen and Jeffrey Herlings, Prado, who finished on the podium in his first full grand prix as a sixteen-year-old, would dominate the MX2 class in 2018 and 2019, earning a reputation as one of the best starters the sport has ever seen, with a glut of holeshot awards confirming his superior timing out of the gate. Prado, who speaks four languages fluently and rides a 450cc dirtbike with such grace that he barely seems to be breaking sweat, is another rider in the Rossi/Márquez mould, where the smile betrays the fun that he mixes with the day job, but the serious scowl that appears occasionally shows a ruthlessness that he can unveil to others who want to sharpen their elbows with him.

I first interviewed Jorge as he was moving through the European Championship in the middle of the 2010s. He was barely in the series before he was deemed too fast and grand prix beckoned. Prado has become a reference for MXGP in more ways than one. The pin-up looks come with an awareness and also an admirable humility for a twenty-three-year-old who has won everything there is on the table in MXGP. He is the best Spanish racer in the history of the sport and has long been hailed as the saviour of Spanish motocross – a discipline in which the country badly lacked serial winners and competitiveness in comparison to their authority in virtually every other two-wheel FIM series.

'I have *that* feeling through the handlebar,' he articulates of a sport that has a higher injury rate than road racing. 'When you see me riding then I look slower than I am. That helps me to improve my speed because doing everything with a certain level of comfort helps you to step it up a bit more every year. I almost never go over that 100 per cent. I'm below. I'm always secure, and this is important.'

MXGP travels at a rate incomparable to MotoGP. Top knots might 'only' hit 60–70kmph through rough terrain but that pace across a sea of bumps tests basic physics and the sanity of human endeavour, especially over the large jumps. It is awe-inspiring to watch the judgment of athletes as they maintain race-winning momentum lap after lap and on a circuit that constantly metamorphoses.

Prado's approach of constraint seems at odds with the violence of motocross but the precision and capacity to pay unceasing attention to detail link these dirtmasters to their kin on the asphalt. 'I will always detect if I am approaching a moment where I will be out of control and avoid it,' he claims, moving his hands in illustration. 'I always try to ride in a percentage where I feel I have everything under control. It's my choice to "send it".'

I ask if his process of judgment is something that happens every lap of a thirty-minute and two-lap 'moto'. 'These are decisions that you need to take every *corner*,' he stresses. 'Every turn you ask yourself, "Shall I give it a little bit more or not?" You take the risk but you need the feeling. It's not easy!'

Then a world champion racer needs a higher level of instinct and analysis. 'Exactly. And all in 0.001 seconds,' he nods. 'You are already thinking about the next corner and the next obstacle all the time. We know our limits before getting to the next section of the track. That's why we ride so much. We are in MXGP because we can search for those new limits quicker than other riders. It's all about how you feel and how much trust you have in yourself.'

I drain the rest of my cappuccino as motocross bikes gurgle past the Energy Station windows. I ask Prado if he thinks he is a phenomenon. He shakes his head firmly. 'No, I'm normal! I just do some stuff better than others.' I have trouble buying it and tell him as much. 'I need to recognize that I'm good at motocross,' he concedes.

I would have perhaps picked a better adjective, although with his next comment we get a little more substance: 'I ride my bike because it's fun, and that's why I'm racing.' Three months later, Prado would be world champion again.

***

Precision and commitment, then, and also a sense of understanding boundaries. These are key components of a motorcycle champion. But I wanted more. I needed further rationale about the motor skills and mental aptitude that sets these people apart. Like millions of others, I had a basic reference. I finally passed my motorcycle test in the UK in my late twenties (on the second attempt, having failed the first exam for apparently riding too slowly in a 30mph zone. I thought it was better to keep just under thirty than go over it … obviously not). So I knew how to ride a bike, but the idea of exploring any limits on two wheels was still hard to grasp.

A search for answers led me to Simon Crafar, the owner of a single, superior premier-class win at Donington Park in the 1998 British Grand Prix and a visitor to the podium twice more before plaudits also in WorldSBK. I first interviewed Simon in 2001 when he was drifting from racing to a brief spell as a technician for Swedish suspension specialists Öhlins. He then transitioned into a racetrack tutor, producing the well-rated *Motovudu* book and DVD before being hired by Dorna in 2018 to join their pitlane and commentary crew for the live international feed. The New Zealander adjusted to the demands of TV broadcasting in the first year and, by trying to bring balanced and editorial reactions to news, events and technical developments in the pitboxes, he quickly became a tremendous asset to Dorna's visual and informative output. He has an uncommon knack for dissecting matters of motorcycles or on-track incidents that satisfies the curiosity of both new fans and the well indoctrinated. When he talks, you want to listen. And you always learn. 'It's like I am the link between the ideas and the actual experience,' he told me of his work with Öhlins in 2001 and the same principal rings true now. He's done it, he's taught it, he's explained it.

Simon seems eternally friendly but also has a narrow threshold for bullshit. Considering how busy he is on a grand prix weekend I'm grateful for his time over more caffeine and again in the Red Bull hospitality unit, and at the 2024 Dutch TT. I know there is a hefty quota of psychology involved in MotoGP but I also want some clues to this magical 'feeling' riders have that all the speed and confidence stems from.

'These guys feel where the tyre has grip, it is almost like a subconscious,' he says, sometimes breaking eye contact to focus on his words and strive for maximum clarity. 'You ride around willing to push yourself beyond what is necessary but you are also getting "warnings" all the time. You don't physically feel the tyre move but you get that warning that it's on the edge. When it's old then it feels like a puncture; it's easy. But trying to find the edge or the limit in, say, qualifying, with a new one, is not as easy. You need acute feeling. The fast riders could always figure out how much grip there was. And edge grip – some would just use it for lean but others knew there was more to it for acceleration. They could feel that. But there are so many pieces of that puzzle because you need to figure out where to use that grip; if it's in the wrong place then you will only go slower.'

What about these supposed hard brakers? Surely all twenty-two riders in MotoGP are scratching the maximum edge for a corner. How do they make a difference there?

'There is a difference between doing it when you are relatively upright and when you are turning in, and then being able to transition from being hard on the brakes to off-brakes,' Simon says, gesturing with his right hand. 'When you haven't got confidence then you stay on the brake because you want to be able to feel where that front end is. The people with confidence can get off that brake really fast and are able to trust the tyre. It's a "feel thing" to understand what the tyre is doing. When they say of a rider "He can brake really well" I would say that's the result. A better way to say it would be "He's got awesome feel for the front tyre, to be able to know how to use it and get the most out of it." That's where I think someone like Pecco has his confidence.' If there was a rider renowned for his extraordinary feel then it was Australian Casey Stoner, one of only four individuals – up until mid-2024 – to have won premier class crowns with different manufacturers, after Giacomo Agostini, Eddie Lawson and Rossi. Casey's brilliance (he claimed GPs in every class) came from an intense dirt track background, and his quest for excellence was accompanied by an acquired purism that eventually butted against the technological march of MotoGP in an increased electronic and aerodynamic age. He retired aged twenty-seven and with 38 wins and 69 podiums from 115 MotoGP starts.

Admiration for his dexterity only increases with time. His

high-speed drift and delicacy around Phillip Island's Turn 3 was one of the most magnificent examples of grand prix expertise in modern times. It was artful. 'In the beginning, everyone said I was over-aggressive, hard on the bike, hard on the tyres,' Casey explained in a call from Australia for a special chat made for *On Track Off Road*'s hundredth edition. 'It was only because I allowed the bike to move. A lot of other riders don't want it to move. The way the bike was moving for me, people maybe thought "dirt track is not so bad …", and being silky smooth doesn't always mean lightning fast. I adapted to what I had.'

What about physicality? What do the greatest riders have in common in terms of fitness and physical traits? One way in which Casey Stoner was similar to his peers was his size and stature. MotoGP does not have a combined minimum weight limit and larger riders like Crafar, Danilo Petrucci, Scott Redding and Luca Marini compromised against racers such as Márquez, Andrea Dovizioso, Maverick Viñales and Jorge Martin through the way they had to manage tyres or manipulate ergonomics. The case of Dani Pedrosa, tipping the scales at fifty-odd kilos, was one of contrast, where the small Catalan's finesse of feeling a motorcycle's behaviour was sometimes countered by the fact that he could not heat and work the rubber as much as others on the grid.

'I think we need the weight limit because it's quite clear that we won't have any more big guys and that's not fair,' Crafar had explained. 'Imagine a kid who has everything but might be a bit tall. That's really sad, and the engineers have told me that they have to be in the 60s [kilograms]. It is better for the sport to have a wide range of people.'

Looking at Cal Crutchlow's sinewy 'Popeye'-style forearms was a reminder of how much g-force and stress racers' bodies experience when they brake and accelerate. Viñales' 190bpm heartrate readings during a race emphasize how much general fitness is necessary. Fabio Quartararo looks as though he could carve a half-decent career as a distance runner, judging by how much he pounds the pavement. I recall Colin Edwards telling me that the first day of pre-season testing after the winter break, typically at Sepang, made his wrists ache, his arse ache, his legs ache. It sounds gruelling, until both the body and the mind come up to speed.

Racers get to VO2 max during a grand prix, and from 2023 that cardiovascular limit began to occur twice in a weekend thanks to the introduction of Sprints. It's something that cannot always be replicated in training. That's when chemicals come into play. 'I cannot get to 190bpm if I am cycling like crazy on a hill,' Scott Redding, a grand prix winner in 125cc and Moto2, told me for a story for the *Daily Telegraph*. '185 is my max in a VO2 test … so the rest must come from adrenaline. You don't feel that you are at 180 when you're on the bike. You should be struggling for breath and you're not.'

'My highest heart rates have come on the MotoGP bike and I haven't been able to replicate it in cycling or running, so that does show the level we are riding at,' Bradley Smith, a MotoGP podium finisher and rider between 2013 and 2020, remarked. 'I think adrenaline plays a role, as does heat dissipation with the leathers we are wearing.'

'Another thing is confidence: flow and mental state,' he added. 'There are some days when you are not in a battle and you can be at 93 per cent heart rate and you feel like you are dying, and there are others when you're in the flow and you're hitting 103 and you feel like you have another step you can make. You can never quantify the mental side, and things like focus, where you can be just a little bit off and things become ten times harder.'

Surprisingly, breathing requires its own kind of focus, just through the combination of forces. 'On these GP bikes, we hold our breath for such a long time entering the corners,' said Crutchlow. 'If a zone is, say, on average four seconds on a hard-braking corner then you'll be holding your breath for that time and you might have five of those in a lap.'

'Not everybody is the same, but if you try and breathe in the braking zone then it is actually hard to stop the bike because you are concentrating on breathing rather than the deceleration process!' he adds. 'You go tense when you brake, you tense your whole body. When you lift a weight in the gym – and the bike is a heavy weight with all the g-force – you are doing the same. Imagine doing it for something similar to twenty laps and around a track like COTA with all those bends. We try to get time to breathe and suck-it-in on the straight but a lot of the straights are not exactly "straight" and you are still fighting the bike.'

MotoGP riders are taking a powerful mechanical foil to the limits and, apart from the difficulty of doing that, they also have a set of handlebars and a dash with a host of different 'Smartie' coloured buttons, winches and levers to change engine mapping, engage ride 'height' devices on straights, lock a suspension compression 'start' device, activate pitlane speed limits, and other functions like trimming traction control. Teams try to make life on a MotoGP machine as simple as possible but there is still a lot a rider must comprehend, and with only a pitboard once a lap or a short message that can be flashed up on the dashboard display as a means of communication.

A hectic life while safeguarding life. There is a suppressed uniformity to MotoGP currently because of the aerodynamics and devices that are emphasizing downforce, and the (general) effectiveness of the Michelin tyres means fearsome grip and new lap records and race times every year. When I spoke with Wayne Rainey at the 2024 Grand Prix of the Americas in Texas, we were sat in one of the vacant commentary boxes adjacent to the media centre, next to the final turn at COTA. He told me to watch how all the bikes and all the riders displayed the same smooth progression onto the start straight and how the settings of the machinery stopped them getting out of shape. It was a fascinating few minutes of style critique from one of the very best and an opinion held by many, particularly Stoner, that the overt presence of electronics and devices diminishes a rider's input. Still, it looked bloody hard to gas and hold onto those banshees and I don't think Wayne was undervaluing a MotoGP rider's work.

Alongside the electronics, the rider's faith in the bike's hardware is as important as the hardware itself. 'In 1996–1997, I got to a point where I knew I was riding really well and I kept that for 1998, but it went pear-shaped afterwards because we changed tyre brand and I lost my confidence,' said Crafar. 'I never got it back. The feeling of confidence is unbelievable. You can give such clear feedback, especially for one flying lap. Back then there was a tyre war and, no kidding, we'd use five different fronts and three different rears in one session trying to sift through and find the best one. I had the confidence to go into one fast lap but then bail out of it because I knew the tyre wasn't the right one. It was really clear: as soon as you are a bit off – up to one second – then your feedback drops and you don't quite trust yourself.'

But regardless of technique, ability, physical fitness and the compliance of their bikes, there is no getting around the sheer amount of graft involved for any rider who gets to the top of the sport.

'There is natural ability and then there is work ethic, which comes after. It seems so obvious but is so important,' Crafar said. 'I don't think my natural ability level was anything exceptional but I worked f**king hard to try to improve and improve.'

———————

In the MotoGP paddock in 2024 there was another clear 'marker' for indisputable motorcycling mastery. Freddie Spencer is a MotoGP legend, a three-times world champion and distinctive for being the only rider to have won two crowns in two different categories in the same year in 1985 (250cc and 500cc, the equivalent of ruling both Moto2 and MotoGP now). From 2019 to the end of 2024, the American was the chairman of the Race Stewards Panel, and therefore a big target for riders' and teams' indignation for penalties. He was usually ensconced in a room full of monitors within the permanent circuit buildings. We had a chat at Valencia 2023, when the MotoGP Championship decider between Bagnaia and Martin vaguely echoed the 1983 showdown between Spencer and Kenny Roberts exactly forty years earlier. The countrymen had a terse rivalry. They won six rounds each of the twelve that year, famously clashed in Sweden, and Spencer triumphed by just two points for the first of his titles.

Spencer was a trailblazer for achievement when he entered the world championship. His first attempt came at Spa-Francorchamps in Belgium in 1980, where he raced a 500 at eighteen years of age. He flew over from the States again in 1981 for a crack at the British round and was Honda's main man for 1982, winning his first race as a twenty-year-old in what was his second attempt at Spa. That record for age stood until 2013, when another HRC-mounted youngster from Catalunya broke it by just 129 days. Spencer had just one full year before going face-to-face with a hardened veteran like Roberts, who had created the American wave in grand prix with a revolutionary approach of applying flat-track style to the tarmac. Roberts made his own legend through riding, winning, team management and engineering innovation, as well as outspokenness and individuality. For some, his grand national CV on the dirt was just as definitive as international efforts in grand prix that dominated his life from the late 1970s until effective retirement in the late 2000s.

Spencer is arguably the only rider to have confronted and beaten a fully fit Roberts. Although his career was punctuated by bouts of injury and episodes of insecurity and unreliability, Freddie is widely acknowledged for the natural knack that led to twenty-seven wins and thirty-nine podiums from seventy-three GP starts and, of course, that milestone in 1985.

I speak again to Spencer at the 2024 German Grand Prix. We sit down to talk in an office next door to his Race Direction hub. Spencer is polite and gracious, with that Louisiana lilt to his accent. His memory is pinpoint sharp and he is another ex-elite-level performer who can articulate quite well the contrivances needed to make it in his former vocation.

'From riding a minibike in my yard up to the point where you are battling for a world championship, the first thing you need is some ability, and that ability is not only muscle-quickness and eye-hand coordination, but what you see, and how you react and implement it with timing,' he says. 'It is also the anticipation. The ability to see things before they happen. It's innate and intuitive. It is an incredible open-minded willingness to trust, which is what motorcycling gave me – this shy kid – to take whatever those skills were and to blossom and develop them.

'You know, it could have rained outside in the yard but I didn't care. I learned to look at the leaves and if they were darker then they were wetter, and I knew how the ground would be. To be able to see this at speed, your brain has to be able to absorb that image. So, it is ability and other tools, and I consider those [mental] abilities also, those are gifts that separate riders from others.

'Most things in life are about "seeing things" but also about perfecting your intuitive side. The rhythm of riding. People always said, "You make it look so effortless," but that's because it is hard to make it look effortless. It is not easy! That all comes from anticipating the timing and seeing the opportunities. I kind of transfer all of that to pretty much everything: my relationship with my kids, my understanding, my patience, my discipline. Then, desire. I was relentless in my desire to hone those skills.'

Where did that come from? 'Probably the exposure I had. My dad, and my brother, who was twelve years older than me, was already racing by the time I was old enough to go along and know what I was looking at. From a very early age it was not about beating other kids – I almost felt bad about that. I've said it many times: that was the hardest part for me. I was very self-driven to get better. I can remember from a very early age I worked on drifting and rotating the bike and I would play with lean angle. I can still close my eyes now and feel a course around a particular set of trees that I would weave between, and then go around the outside of others. I'd slide the bike in and control how much that would be and how much I could drive into the corner. A lot of these things just felt right instinctively. How to get between trees as quick as possible utilizing the bike, without thinking, "Cool, I can slide the bike."'

What age are we talking here? 'Eight or nine.'

It's curious that Spencer did not have a will to crush opposition that many youngsters believe is some sort of requisite to get anywhere in sport. He was competing and winning from a stunningly early age and his mentality was honed on the objectiveness of self. Total focus. 'It is a quickening of the maturity process,' he believes. 'I am not saying every [successful] rider is mature but there is a thing among the exceptional ones, let's say. There is a difference. It might not be in their personality as such … but it is in their thinking. I understood what I was doing and I suppose I knew where it was taking me because getting better inspired me to keep doing it and allowed me to keep graduating. I was riding and racing a TZ750 Yamaha when I was fifteen.'

I can't end the interview without asking about 1985. He won seven from the first nine 250cc grands prix and finished on the podium from ten of eleven 500cc races, claiming seven checkered flags. 'Everything I'd done in my life was to get ready for that,' he says, with the faintest hint of a smile. 'Riding is, truly, about discipline. Picking the right time to perform. But nothing is perfect. We didn't even have a 250 for 1985, we had to build it, and the 500 was the '84 bike so there was not a conventional one until we got the '85 spec model. So, there were all these problems that could have derailed us. It took all of the skills and mental capabilities to pull it all together and be always ready to go.'

Freddie needs to get back to Race Direction. There is a host of Moto3 penalties to issue. The youth of today still cannot gauge that touring around the track during a session will result in a grid position sanction or a long lap castigation. 'It always seems to be the same culprits,' he sighs. For a moment, the flash of that wonderfully cranked blue and white number 4 Rothmans Honda with the rider in perfect symmetry flashes to mind. I thank the sixty-two-year-old for his time and he sees me out of the office with a warm 'Good luck with your book'.

It wasn't quite the right timing, mainly for a lack of time, but Freddie's rough years post-1985 are undoubtedly a fertile ground for the subject of mental strain of top-level sport. Spencer never finished on a grand prix podium again after his epic double – his best result was fifth while riding the factory Marlboro Yamaha in 1989. By the second third of the 1989 season, his GP career was over. He had sustained several injuries, notably to his wrists. The motivation and the energy subsided. The mentality had softened.

'Our sport is more mental than it is physical,' Simon Crafar had said at Assen. 'I think the first thing that I learned both as a racer and then as a teacher is that the rider has to have – and this sounds crazy – a lack of self-preservation. Everybody has an in-built level of it, but these guys have one that is so low that they can do whatever it takes. For whatever reason, their brain allows them to do this. I realized this in 1993. I was riding a Lucky Strike 250 [Suzuki] and I didn't have much experience on a 250 but, at the time, the results to me were more important than my body. I said that to myself. It was my first year in the world championship and I got hurt. There is nothing you can do to ignore that in-built preservation ... but some guys do: Kevin Schwantz would race with a cast on his left hand and still be fighting for the podium. There is something "missing" with those exceptional dudes. I know there are more ingredients to it though, because not all of the top boys have such a lack of self-regard. It's one piece of the puzzle.'

For a more extreme example of the motorcycling racing mentality, swap the MotoGP circuits for the roadside hazards of the streets. In 2024, Michael Dunlop, nephew of Joey, son of Robert, brother of William, made history on the Isle of Man by winning his twenty-ninth TT. For many, the 'IoM' is its own form of insanity. Motocross doesn't look so starkly into the mirror of mortality but the injury rate is shocking. The 'acceptance' of these extremities is hard to unravel.

Work, mental grit, a deftness of touch through the bars, iron-like confidence, delusion, a sense of enjoyment, razor-focus … Add 'game-changing' to the list, and for many Marc Márquez's silhouette is impossible to ignore. Neil Hodgson told me that if you could create the ideal MotoGP 'robot' for performance then Márquez is the mould.

Many riders have set benchmarks, overthrown underdog status, and defied prejudice, antiquated attitudes and stunted technical improvement, but few have had the substance to move the limits of a racetrack to their will. In this aspect, it is hard to dismiss another grinning assassin, and Márquez will top many bench-racing 'best of' conversations.

I saw Marc's brilliance close-up at Valencia in 2014. I was standing on the inside of the Turn 2 left-hand hairpin and he would fire into the corner with such utter conviction in the front end of the Honda RCV (which was not always the best bike and rarely the easiest to ride in his ten-season tenure with HRC) that he seemed to be pitching and turning at an impossible angle. The complete commitment in that one moment alone was astonishing and addictive. I also watched him trackside at Mugello and at Catalunya, where his lean angle was quite astounding; an unhealthy proportion of one entire side of his body seemed to be in contact with the pavement at pace. That inclination became a spectacular part of his racing repertoire as he would often linger near the top of each year's crash statistics sheets: the method involved scratching at the hard line of his and the Honda's limits in practice and therefore having a reference and a barometer for the GP distance. Some of those crashes have been ruinous and have highlighted the high risk of the strategy. The highsides in Indonesia 2022, Thailand 2019 and Germany in 2024 take the breath away and led to vision problems and fractured bones. The 2020 spill in Spain and the broken right humerus that needed four operations and altered both his career and steepened the spiral for HRC almost signified the end.

On the bike and in splendid full flow, certainly in mixed dry/wet conditions, where he is untouchable, Marc's proximity to the ground provided another useful calling card. Márquez's 'saves' have given MotoGP golden material for social media video clips through the previous decade. Perhaps the finest was the 2017 recovery at Turn 1 in Valencia, where he could have lost his fourth world championship. The front wheel tucked and slid at more than 150kmph and laid a black line for more than 50 metres at 64 degrees. He somehow propped the bike with his elbow and knee and went on to finish third.

More recently, he lost traction with the Gresini GP23 Ducati into Turn 15, the intimidating Ramshoek curve, at Assen in the 2024 Dutch TT. The tyre smoked at 120mph and cranked over at 60 degrees. He halted the cascading scene with his left arm, the wheel righted and the bike remained upright. 'Yes, [a] good one!' he told us later, grin appearing. 'I mean, that one was impressive [scary] but everything was under control. In that corner this morning I was super-fast. This afternoon I was struggling more and I said, "OK, I will try …" but I was ready for the reaction. Then when I see that I was losing the front, just I use a bit the elbow, a bit of gas and pick up the bike.' Like popping out for some fresh bread, then.

I have had a few chats with Marc over the years, since he started to slay MotoGP in 2013. I travelled to the Rufea motocross track next to the western Catalan city of Lleida, close to his small hometown of Cervera, to speak with him about his love of the dirt (his crashes while trying to brake into a berm for an action cover photo sent my heartrate higher than necessary) and we also had an interview at Sepang in 2019. I asked him then if the 'Márquez Saves' were becoming a bit too much of a calling card for his liking, especially as that season would be his most ruthlessly effective, with first or second positions in all but one of the nineteen rounds. Only his ten wins in a row to open 2014 rank with equal distinction.

'Two or three years ago, after some saves and comments from people about good things I was doing, it was strange; I did think, "Is that me?" But more in the way of "Can I do that again? Can I make it work next season? Am I just lucky?" I had that question mark. Over the last three years, we [HRC] have always been quite competitive and always with the same riding style and philosophy and the way to win and approach the championship. Now, I don't think any more about it.'

Then there is Márquez the person. People have often asked me what Marc is like and the truth is that the friendly guy you see on TV, stopping for fans and appearing as though MotoGP is a fun lifestyle as well as a job, is also what I see at the circuits. The guy has presence. Sometimes, it does seem like the shoulders are beaten down, which is comprehensible in an environment where everybody wants a slice of his time or attention. His 2023 season – the last with the stubbornly unresponsive RCV (a motorcycle that was also partially a result of his own development cycle, it has to be said) – was deflating as Marc staggered around the ring, often grappling with the ropes of grand prix in frustration, like a featherweight facing a clutch of heavyweights with maligned and ill-fitting gloves.

'I'm like this because, in the end, I cannot act …' he explained of his transparency. 'I think if you tried to play that way then sooner or later you will show your real face. I'd like that the people remember me – or that I give the image – as a guy who gives everything on the racetrack. Whether I lose or I win, every year, I give what I have. The way to ride and the passion I give to bikes.'

We bumped into each other a few years ago at Milan airport. We'd both been attending the EICMA show and sat down eating an ice cream, waiting for the flight to Barcelona. Aboard the plane, Marc was in the window seat behind me. We were taxying onto the apron and near the runway when a loud blare of bike noise thundered from a video on a mobile behind me. I turned around to that recognizable and endearing laugh. 'Motos!' he laughed apologetically.

In 2024, Márquez is harder to reach. The change of management has pushed him further into the limelight with an Amazon TV series and high-profile product endorsements. The whole saga of scrutiny over his future with Ducati means that media work seems to be more of an inconvenience to him than in the past. By all accounts, he detests the interview process, but it speaks well of his character and professionalism that he does it with passable humour.

After asking, waiting, then more asking and more waiting, another one-to-one chat was fumbled by Marc's personal team. Initially, the plan was to speak at his home in Madrid. This was eventually scratched. Extended time for an in-depth interview was also shelved, with Márquez eying his own book project. Or so I was told. Despite having a good relationship with Marc's friend and training partner Jose Luis Martinez (a former Spanish motocross champion), who also tried to pull a few strings for me, I found that the Márquez media team couldn't find the will to assist.

I pushed a bit further for our interview to take place in the motorhome he shares with brother Alex (a double world champion himself), via the eternally hounded Gresini PR rep Cristian, and this was put into limbo. I decided against trying to crawl up the Márquez team's backside further after the clamour for him got even worse in the wake of his 2024 Aragon Grand Prix double, when he was unequalled to win both the Sprint and the Sunday race at a hot and greasy MotorLand. The flash of 2019 form reset the Márquez fan-o-meter. It ended 1,043 days of hurt since his last victory at Misano in 2021. That first day of September also represented something of a zenith with his GP23 and being able to extract every ounce from the year-old motorcycle, while Bagnaia was busy clashing with Marc's brother in a controversial incident vying for third place that sent both into the gravel pit at Turn 12. Jorge Martin meanwhile continued to play a champion's game with a third consecutive grand prix of 2–2 scores.

Marc is too wily to sit on a cloud of puff. In Aragon, he recognized his higher level of speed, credited his team (although this was weirdly offset by hanging out with his former HRC crew at the following race in Misano; it's hard to imagine him doing that if Joan Mir and Luca Marini were even half as competitive as they were) and also played down talk of his 'return' to former form. Reality seemed to have resumed somewhat only seven days later. At Misano, where he had celebrated that last success with HRC and still had the boos of the Rossi-loving locals in his ears on the podium, he ironically crashed in the attackable Turn 14 lefthander in qualifying and snuffed out his chances for a repeat success by having to accept ninth place on the grid.

Misano is always chaotic and outdated, and I still cannot work out whether the basic facilities are part of the charm or are a pain the ass. I guess a bit of both, occasionally at the same time. The 2024 San Marino Grand Prix was a grim experience for the media in the debrief process: too crowded, too tight and very unlike a world championship looking to portend as a global entertainment product. Márquez, as usual, commanded the biggest audience. On Saturday, and after a gutsy ride to fifth in the Sprint, where he provided the best overtaking moves and more than his fair share of fun factor once more, I was positioned right behind him as he sat at a long desk and spoke to press. It was hard to take my gaze away from his limbs. His left hand sported large pink circles and blotches where the skin had worn away, like the painful patches under blisters. The palm was dirty and callused and the fingers wonky; both arms have scars and lines of operations and previous stitches. The famous right upper limb is distorted, thinner than it should be, missing muscle shape. I could barely hear what he was saying but I thought the image of his ravaged body parts spoke so much for the obsessive approach he has towards his racing. I thought, does MotoGP define Marc? Or perhaps Marc defines MotoGP?

On Sunday, he used the brief flurry of rain to his advantage and underlined his almost matchless skill for win number two. The series will get another two years of him. If Rossi is the sport's greatest, then Márquez must be labelled as the best: pure performance, pure expression, pure want.

Perhaps Pedro Acosta is the most obvious successor to the Rossi/Márquez lineage. Not even the Italian and the Spaniard ripped through grand prix like the current MotoGP newcomer. For all of Acosta's overt potential, he hasn't yet displayed the evident insatiable craving for victory that Márquez still retains. MM93 might be celebrating podium finishes in 2024 on the Ducati with particular zeal, and this is understandable considering his injury hardships for the better part of three years, but for this multi-millionaire (still the biggest rider in the sport) to still be reaching and risking for the same prizes and the same gratification after a decade and with similar standards (never mind the six titles and his 33 per cent win rate in the premier class) is unbelievable. One of the most touching moments of the Amazon documentary is when Marc and his brother visit his elderly grandfather before undergoing major surgery again to Marc's right arm. He asked his grandson a question to the effect of 'Why carry on? You've done everything'. Márquez's reply was a 'I'm not done' gesture, with a light shrug of the shoulders. Somehow, it was sweetly innocent. Racing (and winning) is who he is.

The only time I have seen a likeness is with five-times world champion Jeffrey Herlings in MXGP: the Red Bull KTM racer is now surpassing Stefan Everts' supposedly unreachable 101 grand prix win tally and has broken bones in most parts of his body in the unfailing chase to be number one. These people breathe a different air.

'The best fuel I have in my body is the taste of victory,' Márquez told me in 2019. 'I see that all the effort I make during the season has a very good conversion. This is the best thing. People sometimes say, "You win many times" [makes a gesture of boredom] but it really is the opposite. I want more, more and more. When you win, then you can do many events, lots of training and many kilometres on the bicycle and you don't get tired. When you have hard moments, then that's where you feel tired. It is different. The body is somehow happy when you win. Anything you want to do seems like a good idea. It is difficult to understand ...'

The analysis and the opinions and the personal references

from experience can never fully tap into the complexities or the causes and creation of MotoGP merit. Márquez and his kind across the board are difficult to comprehend, but that's what makes them fascinating to us. To see the balletic shapes and exertions taken by these athletes (and they *are* pro athletes) to make MotoGP sing and sizzle and meet their own realms of personal satisfaction is a narrative that never fades as the next boundary is flexed or broken.

FOUR

The Layer

Silverstone, 2023. Pecco Bagnaia has finished runner-up to an elated and typically unreserved Aleix Espargaró. The Italian is shifting around on his seat-stool in the press conference. At one point, he even crosses his legs, and it occurs to me that the full get-up of leathers and boots looks incredibly supple. Almost comfy. The logo-plastered protection is custom made and constructed from a complex weave of materials, including PVC, Kevlar, moisture-wicking fabrics and impact-absorbing 'foam'. Suits cost several thousand pounds each and, despite the high-technical blend and all the R&D that has gone into the product, the bulk of the outfit still comes from the backside of an animal.

Leathers and protection. I think back to the 1975 ITV documentary (*Barry Sheene – Daytona 1975*) which showed Barry Sheene crashing in practice for the Daytona 200 at more than 170mph. With a broken femur, wrist, ribs, several vertebrae and collarbone, his suit was still remarkably in good shape, despite sliding over 100 metres and the MotoGP legend recalling that he felt as if he'd been 'barbecued'. In the aftermath, a graphic photograph was taken of Sheene with the same leather set mounted on the wall of his house like a *Silence of the Lambs* movie prop, having been cut away from his broken body in Florida.

Almost half a century later and MotoGP riders are still relying on the same basic properties of livestock hide. Alpinestars coat the skins of ten racers, nearly half the grid, and is one of five companies providing suits in MotoGP. The Italians offer a choice between bovine leather or kangaroo: the cow being thicker, stiffer and generally more resistant, while the Australian mammal is more flexible, thinner – around 1.1.5mm – and more expensive, but dependent on the fibre quality of a particular cut. Casey Stoner was a bovine fan. Jorge Lorenzo and Valentino Rossi, with Dainese, favoured the kangaroo. Of the current grid, all Alpinestars reps have their suits made from kangaroo and will have between ten and fifteen made during a racing year.

The process of getting leather ready for a suit is precise and highly involved. At Alpinestars, it is tested, tanned, chemically treated and prepped for printing. More sprays are added: antibacterial, resistance agents, and for the wet weather suits, a solution that hikes the waterproofing performance up by 70 per cent compared to dry versions.

Combine the leather with other panels concertinaed for movement and fabrics to deal with friction heat, and then stitch in protective elements like back, elbow, knee and shoulder guards, and the suit starts to take shape. They cater to old injuries, body peculiarities (perhaps most noticeably with crooked fingers in their gloves) and of course personal preferences.

Quite clearly, the suit is designed to feel like a second skin, one that can resist the burning graze of tarmac at 150mph plus, as well as the rough serrations of gravel. They are fabricated and even punctured for ventilation. Inside, some use an undersuit. It's startling just how good and reliable the outer shell can be; the sight of a rider falling during a grand prix session, getting back to the pitbox and then going straight out on a second bike without having to change is now a regular occurrence.

From 2013, and Marc Márquez's barrelling gatecrash, Alpinestars started to add elbow plates to the exterior of the suit to help with the Catalan's exaggerated lean and the extent to which he dragged various anatomy across the pavement. Márquez was by no means the first to scrape his elbow – British racing fans will remember the sight of Frenchman Jean-Philippe Ruggia painting a black line on his leathers through Donington Park's Coppice Corner on his 250cc Gauloises Yamaha in 1988 – but Marc was the first to regularly employ the elbow as a stilt. Jorge Martin's spectacular style meant the manufacturer had to add upper arm guards around the shoulder as the Spaniard shifts his diminutive figure around the peak of the Ducati. Martin's intimate caress of high curbs at the Circuit de Barcelona-Catalunya with his 'hombro' has generated some of the more unforgettable photographs in recent years. Fabio Quartararo is another excessive tilter.

Most exterior knee sliders are made of chunky PVC. The Velcro attachment system is so adhesive that riders often have to prize them off with the assistance of a screwdriver. Signed sliders have become a popular fans' keepsake in the last decade or two.

Every suit now has the aerodynamic 'hump' that is crafted in shape and size to sync with a racer's helmet profile when they are in the full tuck position. Motorcycle manufacturers spend a great deal of money on wind tunnel research and aerodynamics has become the main field of innovation in the last ten years of MotoGP. The rider's bulk and the way he or she squeezes into the lines of the bike are part of the careful technical set-up. In this way, brands and companies collaborate for the sake of performance. There is not much more that can be done to streamline the pilot. He is already moving around the motorcycle and 'ruining' the patterns of data acquisition of the bike's behaviour. The pitch, roll and irregularities of a motorcycle – even in the uniformity of hard aero and ride height devices that almost 'lock' the machines to lines and places on the asphalt – are still the biggest differential to the information gleaned from cars. For me, and for many, a bike's submission to the will and impulses of a rider is still one of the most appealing aesthetics of the sport. Long may it remain as haphazard and mysterious as possible.

Modern materials need to be crafted, cut and stitched to allow them to stretch and breathe, so individuals can remain suited and booted for hours after the checkered flag, through the requirements of media work and content creation.

The addition of the back bump immediately gave more real estate. Naturally, those who like to ride in hotter climes with a hydration pack had room for liquid, but the space has also lent itself to onboard cameras, with the rear-facing 'back cam' making its debut in 2023, as well as personal data logging equipment.

At the start of the century, during the 2001 Spanish Grand Prix, I attended a press call by Dainese for the presentation of their D-Tec Procom under-suit. Max Biaggi, never one to shy away from a camera lens, half stripped and posed to reveal the tech that involved thirty-two humidity sensors, thirty-two temperature sensors and a heart rate sensor, which took readings every five seconds. The info was collected by a unit in the hump. At the time, I wrote that the system could 'see which parts of a rider's clothing is not allowing the body to function in optimum conditions. Implications can lead to the comprehensive testing of new materials and combinations, and of course improvements in safety.' Dainese were investing in this stuff well before personal GPS, the possibility of data transmission and the minimalization of hardware: advancement that has allowed Dorna to become genuine pioneers and world leaders of onboard live camera production.

Nowadays, the suit's deformity houses an airbag. Dainese stole a march with the introduction of their D-Air in 2007 and were initial innovators in the field. Stefan Bradl's 2007 125cc crash and activation of an external airbag made him look like a stunt replacement for *Robocop*, but it marked the arrival of the technology in its most rudimentary form. Dainese's thunder has been silenced in recent times by the prolificacy and quality of Alpinestars' Tech-Air offerings, but the company still banks on their valuable career-long association with Valentino Rossi. Rossi's last kangaroo-leather suits (around 80 per cent) in 2021 weighed just six kilogrammes with the airbag installed.

Airbags have become faster, more reliable and bigger in terms of the coverage they provide. Alpinestars' Tech-Air autonomous unit blew up in MotoGP from 2009, six years after they had first begun to collect data with sensors positioned in the suits of Nicky Hayden, Casey Stoner and others. In 2014, the first commercial systems for the street appeared and, at the time of writing, there are four different airbags for different purposes, ranging from sport to the most casual road rider who is still safety conscious. The Tech-Air Race edition became available in 2016 and is used by other leather suit brands that do not have their own proprietary technology. This was a pertinent situation from 2018, when the FIM had seen enough statistical evidence of the airbag's advantages, and the reliability, to not only embellish their homologation (a rule parameter) standard but make it compulsory in MotoGP. There is no other rider tech in motorcycling that feels both highly advanced and physically effective.

Alpinestars have been increasing the surface area of the airbag in MotoGP. A crash by Alex Rins during the 2019 season gave the skinny Catalan an hourglass figure with his leathers expanding by the ribs and also the hips. Not the most flattering form while trudging through the gravel trap but more encompassing for protection. The company had an unwilling crash test dummy in Márquez, who provided reams of information and even awkward marketing value when the Italo-Americans were able to publish recordings from the former HRC man's suit that showed the sheer violence of his ejections. There have been accidents in the last twenty years of MotoGP that have caused awe and anguish. Some with benign consequences and a drama-free aftermath provoking marvel at modern rider equipment and how it can perform under stress.

Perhaps the accident that, to this day, still most impels me to watch and wince is Marc's 2022 highside at Turn 7 during warm-up at Mandalika for the Indonesian Grand Prix. He does a full midair somersault and the Honda stubs into the concrete, disintegrating with the force of the dismount at 180kmph. Márquez's suit numbers show that the whole horrific episode lasted almost four seconds. The airbag fired its canisters 0.99 of a second before a humongous blow that registered well over 27G. Marc was glancing at the treetops while his suit was puffing in half the time it takes to blink an eye. He had already fallen three times that weekend and had said on Saturday, 'I need to attack, I need to take a risk.' The crash and head impact instigated another episode of double vision, meaning he missed the next race in Argentina. The mire with Honda and the mess with his right arm sunk both the rider and the manufacturer into a slump. Both needed 'surgery'.

MotoGP is a sport where limits are bent and molested in the rush for an edge. Riders accept that scrapes, bone chips, hematomas, brittle collarbones, deformed fingers, crushed toes, concussion and sometimes far worse will be on the agenda. That stoicism and flippancy is another bizarre mark of motorcycle racers.

'I've been having stupidly big crashes since I was seven years old,' Jack Miller told me in Texas. I felt guilty for bringing up the subject when I find out that a film crew had conducted several interviews with Jack only a few weeks previously about crashing. Though it was a topical subject as the rate of falls in MotoGP had been climbing every year since 2019, when 220 premier class prangs were logged. Ignoring the truncated 2020 season, there were 278 in 2021, 335 in 2022 and 358 in 2023, the first year of the Sprint format.

'I feel like I'm riding fast and then it's normally at the point where you think, "Nothing can be wrong, everything is mega." Then it catches you,' the Australian explained of the roots of a crash. 'I don't know whether it's to do with letting your guard down. Sometimes, you know when you are coming in [to a corner] f**king hot and it's the last three minutes of qualifying and that [fast] lap needs to get done. What will I do? Run wide and ruin the lap or throw it onto the side with all my willpower and see what happens? There is a 50–50 chance you will come out the other side. You might not. It's the gamble you have to take quite often.

'You know when it's a big one,' he added. 'The fear aspect never comes into it because you never plan for it to happen. Maybe we're blind or we're in denial, but we think it won't happen again. Maybe it's the way we're wired up or something.

'It is a bit mad when you think about it. But the protection and the safety gear we have is all very good now. We can slide, jump up and sprint back to another bike, if you have enough time and nothing has come to pass. In the past, I think it was considerably different; you'd walk around the paddock and it seemed like every other bloke had a missing pinkie. Step by step, everyone has kept their fingers.'

I've heard countless riders explain the process. How the shock of a crash quickly transforms into a personal health check, an urgency to evaluate the condition of the motorcycle, and then sporting concerns about whether the error or the problem will ruin the session. It's only when the clock has stopped ticking and the session is over that the flow of bodily chemicals slows and the non-physical effects of the fall enter the fray. 'When I think about it then, it's more about "What do I need to do to prevent that? What were the steps that caused that crash?", Miller said. 'For those qualifying ones, you know it's because you are pushing to the absolute limit and she said: "No more." The ones that play on your mind are when you are flying and everything had been going so well. You mull them over quite a bit more.'

In recent times, the biggest amount of mulling occurred in 2017, when riders in all three categories hit the floor over 1,100 times. Marc Márquez has habitually been one of the worst offenders, ensuring his crew have had plenty of work since he fell off fifteen times in his first MotoGP term in 2013. It set a trend with double-figure accidents every campaign; even during his phenomenal 2019 championship, when he won twelve of nineteen races and finished on the podium at another six, he still needed fresh fairings after fourteen thuds.

The aforementioned Alex Rins, a MotoGP racer since 2017, crashed heavily into Arrabbiata 1 during the Sprint at Mugello in June 2023, breaking his lower right tibia and fibula. He said to Spanish TV broadcaster DAZN that the injury was like 'an explosion, there were many little bits everywhere'. He needed an epidural for a four-hour operation that caused him to 'cry with the pain'. After another procedure and a bizarre period towards the end of 2023 when he felt the need to return to MotoGP despite barely being able to walk, he was still limping in the summer of 2024. 'I was never a good runner,' he half-joked at the 2024 Austrian Grand Prix.

Alex was interesting to talk to on the eve of the 2024 Italian Grand Prix a few months earlier where he returned as a Monster Energy Yamaha man as opposed to a LCR Honda rider (his April 2023 success with the RCV in the United States is still the last grand prix win for the mighty HRC brand at the time of writing), his first competitive comeback to the track after his day-to-day life had been significantly altered. MotoGP riders have a habit of being able to submerge themselves back into harm's way only minutes after a fast crash, having been ferried back to the pitbox on a marshal's scooter and to their waiting second machine. But, of course, there is residue when they feel the aches every morning and carry the scars. Rins had made some test laps at Mugello prior to the grand prix but it required help from other experts to open the throttle again fully at one of the swiftest layouts on the entire calendar.

'Luckily, we were able to ride [here] some weeks ago and it was more easy than I thought. We worked a lot with the psychologist to avoid the memories … but for sure, the first lap at the test I was thinking of it. But after five times, the head resets!' he said. 'You forget the moment. The day before the test, I did it [the corner] ten times on the scooter, trying to keep the mind on the way and doing a good line.'

Compressed air is not only parcelled around the hump of the leathers. MotoGP sessions and races have been halted due to damage to the resilient air bulbous fences that shield immovable walls or Armco barriers. Perhaps the most notable was the fiery destruction of the cushion bordering Turn 1 at the Red Bull Ring by Maverick Viñales' Yamaha in 2020, when the Catalan ditched his brakeless M1 at 215kmph.

'Suddenly, in Turn 1, the brakes exploded,' the Spaniard told us via Zoom, the only way to communicate with riders during that Covid-19 ravaged season. 'It's something I have never had in all my MotoGP career. I understood very well that the brake was broken, so I decided to jump.'

Only one week earlier, the carnage of Franco Morbidelli and Johann Zarco's collision into Turn 3 at the same track had caused one of the most remarkable escapes for Valentino Rossi and Viñales, as the twisted wreckage of a Desmosedici catapulted past their helmets with inches to spare. 'We have to pray to somebody. Everybody has to pray to who he decides. But, f**k. I feel bad. I am scared, very much,' Rossi admitted. 'I saw Franco in the medical centre; we hugged each other because we have been scared together,' Zarco said. The incident was so outrageous, and so fortunate, that the Red Bull Ring neutered their layout with the installation of the '2a/2b' chicane and also changed the aperture of Turn 3, the airfence having been totalled by Morbidelli's Yamaha, but the trajectory of Zarco's Ducati meant it became a missile for the riders ahead negotiating the curve.

Circuits like Jerez, Sachsenring, Red Bull Ring, Mugello, Misano, Assen and more rely on the expertise of Austrian company Alpina to install permanent or temporary air safety barriers to different dimensions or even blocks. The 'walls' are more than just a rugged balloon. There are forms that prevent the bikes from sliding underneath and a tougher outer buffer.

At Jerez in 2024, I went for a walk during the one-day test on Monday after the race. After watching an Andalucian hare look at me and dart away into a little hole by the fence on the outskirts of the entry to Turn 2, I continued to the edge of the wall by the corner (recently infamous for the major pile-up in 2023 between Fabio Quartararo and Miguel Oliveira) and prodded the airfence.

It felt as solid as concrete and rough as well. It was difficult to imagine how fast a projectile must travel to penetrate the white puff. Then, two months later, I stood trackside in Germany and was impressed by how quickly the track crew at Sachsenring dismantled, replaced and inflated a new Alpina structure at Turn 1 during the 2024 grand prix. It is one of the crashiest corners in grand prix thanks to the slow, off-camber swoop of the apex and exit. 'Turn 1 is really tricky. It goes up and then down, and if you touch the gas when you go up then for sure you don't have front weight and *whoosh*. It happened for me in FP in the morning. I stopped the bike better but when I touched the gas it was on the crest and *wheep*. Nothing! You have to be so careful,' the endlessly luckless Viñales said of the corner.

Márquez didn't arrive to the air fence when he flipped out of a riveting comeback at Jerez in 2020. Bravely, brazenly and disbelievingly, he tried to ride the following weekend at the second Jerez Grand Prix, but the fracture to the right humerus opened a two-year void of despair with plenty of lows (eighteen crashes in 2022 in just twelve grands prix) that required three more visits to the operating theatre, including an expensive (and final) reparation in the halls of a specialized clinic in Minnesota. Márquez's biggest ailments otherwise have involved the head trauma that has caused at least two debilitative episodes of diplopia – double vision.

His concussion symptoms could have been worse were it not for advancements in helmet engineering. The improvement in EPS architecture to combat rotational acceleration (the movement of the brain in relation to the rest of the cranium, the cause of concussion and the root of most brain injury) has not been as spectacular or evident as the implication of airbags, but the research and development in the last few years have shifted the sands. The ground-breaking investigations by the Swedish scientists and medical experts behind the Mips system, and staunch advocation for better protection by the likes of small Californian firm 6D Helmets, forced far bigger and more established helmet brands in MotoGP to revolutionize.

The requirement for certification and a 'standard' to apply to elite level motorcycle racing eventually obliged the FIM to invest and make their own helmet protocol – from a FRHPhe-01 regulation in 2019 to a second phase (with even more demanding tests) that will be mandatory for all lids in GP competition from 2026.

6D was the hood ornament on a rushing vehicle of change in motorcycle helmets. Soon, brands like Leatt and Fly Racing were offering rotational motion solutions in their off-road wares and eventually major names like Shoei started to follow. Another American firm, Fly Racing, was noteworthy for their off-road 'Formula' lid and the use of Rheon gel 'padding cells' inside the liner, as well as resistant EPS structures like Conehead

At Silverstone in 2024, Nolan took part in the seventy-fifth anniversary celebrations with a spread of their MotoGP helmets from the last twenty years, models from riders like Pedrosa, Stoner, Davies and more, complete with scrapes, scratches and caved-in sections. The products had fulfilled their purpose. If the display was a touch macabre, it did however reveal another slice of how Dorna are preoccupied with safety. The work of IRTA and the late Mike Trimby cannot be overstated for how it gave teams and riders a voice and some leverage to express concerns over circuits or facilities, and Dorna hold a 'safety commission' meeting with the riders on every Friday of a grand prix where they can air their grievances. Although the themes and the comments of the meetings are normally guarded by a mutual code of silence, it is a well in which journalists frequently like to dip a bucket. Sometimes the pail comes up with some drops of gossip, especially if a rider is sharp in terms of using his words to publicly criticize another for their conduct. Not everyone attends. Valentino Rossi snubbed the meetings after the 2015 kerfuffle with Márquez.

Dorna's attitude to all potential safety avenues to protect the riders is openminded and eager. I know their meetings with people from Mips at Valencia in 2022 were positively received. Also, in 2014, Leatt had decent traction in their talks to bring their award-winning off-road neck brace to MotoGP. The South Africans were hoping to have similar influence in road racing and were working with former WorldSBK champion and grand prix rider Colin Edwards in his final MotoGP season when he was wearing NGM Forward Yamaha colours.

Consciously or unconsciously, the Texan might have leaned more to the possibilities of neck protection after his tragic part in the last MotoGP class fatality. On Sunday, 23 October 2011 at the Malaysian Grand Prix, Marco Simoncelli, a twenty-four-year-old Italian, a former 250cc world champion and a consistent top-ten runner in MotoGP with a factory Honda, lost control while running fourth. Simoncelli, a contentious but flamboyant racer who had been on the receiving end of criticism from Jorge Lorenzo and Dani Pedrosa for his aggressive style, tried to save the floundering RCV, but the repercussions of the slide pulled him across the track and straight into the lines of both Edwards and Rossi. The sickening collision ripped Simoncelli's helmet free and caused the tumbling Edwards to dislocate his left shoulder. Simoncelli, clearly unconscious from the outset, suffered upper torso trauma. Before 17.00 local time, he was declared dead and became the first rider to be killed in MotoGP action since Daijiro Kato's high-speed crash into the wall entering Suzuka's Casio

Triangle chicane during the 2003 Japanese Grand Prix. Kato passed away after a two-week coma and from another neck injury.

In contrast to the 2003 Japanese Grand Prix (incidentally, MotoGP has not returned to Suzuka), the race in Malaysia was stopped in the immediate wake of the accident. Images of a distraught Valentino Rossi in the pitbox, then riding for Ducati, one of Simoncelli's close friends, showed the face of a man confused, shocked and lost.

'Eeeeesh,' Uccio Salucci gestured when I asked him about the memory thirteen years later. 'In Sepang, when that happened, Vale said to me later, "Why are we here? For what?" and I said this is our life and our story. He said to me, "I know, but like this, it is too much." But, after one week, we tried to think about our future. When you are a rider in MotoGP for twenty-five years, some moments like this unfortunately happen. You must analyse the situation in the right way … and continue.'

Sepang would be a hoodoo circuit for Rossi. With six wins there it was his joint-eighth most prospective territory, but, four years later, MotoGP would be kicked into hysteria and he didn't win again after his last victory in 2010.

Back to Edwards' neck brace, though. Integration was hard to achieve and although Leatt persisted, the brace was not officially approved and never appeared in MotoGP. At this point, in 2014, airbags were dominant and only three seasons from becoming obligatory.

Dorna upgraded the old 'Clinica Mobile' medical unit in the paddock to the 'MotoGP Health Centre' in conjunction with Spanish medica care company Quiron. The Clinica Mobile, helmed by Italian Dr Claudio Costa, formed part of 1980s and 1990s grand prix racing lore. Costa was as much in front of the cameras as the riders, in a period when the brutal 500cc two-strokes regularly chucked them to the moon. The shiny new two-floored MotoGP health centre parked up in 2023 to service MotoGP in general, not just the collective of sore, wincing and hobbled racers. 'It helps the paddock but it is also a way in which Dorna wanted to help the riders and the teams and to think more in a combined manner,' Dorna SPO Carlos Ezpeleta told me. 'If each team had to have a physio for each rider, then it would be much more expensive. We're really proud of it.'

The smell of cream, of sanitization, greets you entering the 'MHC'. The pristine white truck has two slide-outs and sits in a corner of each paddock like a beacon for aid. The structure looks appropriately clinical from the outside and is a contrast to the logo-splattered appearance of the old Clinica. Inside, the décor bears the signs of a place that has a lot of coming and going.

I'm in Mugello at the 2024 Italian Grand Prix and I'm swiftly greeted by Miguel Suarez, a tall, athletic-looking *Madrileño* who has been heading up the centre for just over a year and couldn't be a better embodiment of rude health himself. The main *sala* of the truck has five treatment tables arranged in a tight formation. Moto3 rider Ricardo Rossi is the only inhabitant, receiving some attention on a shoulder he smashed in a crash at the Catalan Grand Prix. There are scanners and other physio aids propped against the walls. I see containers and boxes carrying gels, straps and more. Everything is bright. Mirrors line the far wall. Opposite the door, the five-man therapy team (with a radiologist and nutritionist also on the roster) have a tablet which the riders use to book a time. The windows have a tantalizing view of Arrabbiata 2 and the final looping Bucine corner – talk about a perspective that is both motivating and maddening for the inhabitants. The main treatment area is a bit claustrophobic; with a full complement of riders, it must be a noisy place. I instantly ponder how a professional football equivalent must be with banter and gossip bouncing back and forth between athletes that find themselves sharing some close personal company.

Miguel shows me the upper section where a makeshift gym allows riders to 'warm up' if they want. Small weights, bands and other utensils lie around, and a panel of 'reaction lights' lines one of the walls for those partial to sharpening their reflexes. MotoGP Medical Director Dr Angel Charte has his office up here and there is another desk where Suarez and I can talk in Spanish. 'For sure, yours is better than my English,' he admits.

Suarez and his crew are from the private Hospital Ruber Internacional in Madrid, where they are accustomed to working with many athletes at various levels. 'Pro, semi-pro, amateur and some of us have experience at elite level.' They attend every grand prix. 'I think this is one of the strong parts of the project because we have continuity with the riders; we know about their crashes, their problems, their tests, their treatment from one week and one race to the next. We can follow their progress closely and with the best attention,' he reasons.

The MHC is very much a first contact and a secondary phase for MotoGP rider conditioning. 'The protocol of each GP means that when a rider has a crash, the first thing that happens is that he goes to the medical centre and they make any relevant or necessary scans and checks,' he explains. 'They pass through this filter and then if there aren't any major problems – trauma, neurological issues – and they can work with us, then we take control with the information passed to us together with direction from Angel Charte and Nacho Gallego [radiologist] and the treatment needed. After the complete medical check, the rider might have, say, a fractured finger and this doesn't stop him competing. The rider then passes to us for evaluation and the phases of recovery and physiotherapy.'

Miguel talks quickly and quietly. He comes across as man who can react to situations in the same manner. The Spaniard sees MotoGP athletes in a way that very few do. Some racers have their own personal physios and specialists at the circuits. Otherwise, the MHC door hinges are well worked, particularly for those in the Moto3 and Moto2 classes. I ask how he sees the debilitation of MotoGP riders, most of whom are in their twenties. 'We see the extra stress, physically and also mentally,' he ponders. 'Since the Sprints and higher speeds coming into the championship, we see the psychological effect but also the extra concentration and the decision-making. You have the normal injuries like contusions and scratches, cuts, but also fatigue and overload and the wear and tear of the sport. We see lumbar and cervical problems – but quite a few people have those normally – also with the extremities like ankles, feet, hands and fingers that get smashed around. Sometimes the elbow and the AC joint.'

The Spaniard and his team witness racers at their most vulnerable. Most work with sports psychologists but asking riders about this area of their preparation is usually met with a muted response. It's a highly personal subject after all. 'I went to see a couple of sports psychologists when I raced because I was aware of the [importance of the] mental side of it,' Neil Hodgson admitted to me. 'And I learned nothing from them. I tried two different ones and they focused on the danger side of it, which was an aspect ... but I wasn't half a second off the pace because I was worried about getting hurt; it was some other reason. Maybe I just didn't believe in myself.'

'It's a stressful sport and it affects them all at some point,' Suarez offers, clearly not wanting to wade into the complexities of psychology. 'It has these peaks of adrenaline and some riders suffer because the results have not been arriving.'

I ponder aloud if the health centre can be as hectic as an emergency ward. 'Haha, sometimes, yes!' he responds. 'And that's where the appointment system helps us. We don't deny or defer anybody but we do prioritize when necessary, maybe between people from the paddock or riders. We've never had a problem in this respect and we always complete our full schedule.'

Knowing that riders can be gossipy (they are only too happy to quiz a journalist for the latest sleaze or can drop their eaves with the best of them), I ask Miguel if he and his team also have to exercise discretion in what they hear and see. How gobby are riders when patiently undergoing attention? 'Behaviour is good,' he smiles. 'We don't know them much outside of the general paddock. It's natural and that makes our job easier. There are rivalries in this sport and sometimes these guys find themselves together in the treatment room. There is normally a good vibe though. They know they are in a space to seek help and we always get decent feedback. They know they can relax and there is a professional team for their needs. They also know there is confidence, and knowledge of their cases, and they can be comfortable.

'They know their bodies very well and usually the higher the level of athlete, the more knowledge they have, mainly due to previous injuries and consequences. In this medical environment, they hear and share stories of injuries and treatments and things that helped and others that didn't, mainly for their own interests. They talk a lot. It's like a changing room sometimes.'

What about the variations of MotoGP injury and prevention compared to other sports? 'One of the main differences is that in other sports, the athletes are not playing with their lives,' Suarez understates. 'Yes, footballers, say, can have cardio problems but here is a real threat of loss of life. Motorcycle racing, in terms of risk, and in our experience, is at one of the highest points. Common injuries are the contusions and concussions, but then there are also a lot in rugby, for example, and the protocols are very advanced there.'

Before Miguel has to adhere to his appointment schedule, I enquire about the biggest constraint on his work and that of the health centre. 'Time: it's a constant challenge,' he almost sighs. 'It's not just about reacting to accidents or incidents that happen on track but also a general question of time. It's not like you can go slowly with a patient. Here, they have to try to follow a recovery schedule but also consider how they can still compete when they are not 100 per cent. On many occasions, there is not the time to do what is necessary. They might not have slept well, have a stiff neck or are unwell, but only have a couple of hours before they have to give the best of themselves. It means that you have even less time to help or make the best decisions to assist. There can be a lot of tension and various problems to attend, sometimes with just one athlete! I think we do a good job and we get good feedback, and it's great to have that knowledge of the riders. And, being a team here, we can interchange and still do our best. Communication is constant and fluid, even when we're home in Madrid.'

Dorna's medical provision is comprehensive, but circuit and event standards have also been raised to a point where they are barely questioned any more. This was not always the case and generations of grand prix riders could have only wished for the facilities and assistance prevalent in MotoGP today. The system was last put to the harshest test at Mugello in 2021. The whole structure at the circuit in Italy went into overdrive on a sunny Saturday in late May when nineteen-year-old Swiss rider Jason Dupasquier crashed out of Arrabbiata 2 during Q2 and was hit by his own bike as well as the Red Bull KTM machine of Ayumu Sasaki. Thoracic and vascular injuries caused the youngster to become the 104th person to lose their life in seventy-two years of grand prix racing.

'I met Jason and his mum in 2019.' I'm sitting with Florian Pruestel, owner and team manager of the squad, with whom Jason was racing at the time. We're in the Pruestel racing team's hospitality two years after the accident. 'We had been watching him in the Red Bull MotoGP Rookies Cup and also JuniorGP and we thought, "We need more riders from northern Europe at GP level." Tom [Luthi] was his coach and I thought, "Let's push into a different market and close to Germany." Jason also spoke a little German. We had some meetings and he made a test. There was a good match. He was a calm guy with an easy character and his father [Phillip, who I'd known for his failed attempt to win the 2002 125cc Motocross World Championship] was a title-winning rider, so there was a good background. So we signed him for 2020.

'We have the eighteen-year-old age rule now in Moto3, but before, they could be as young as sixteen. They could grow in the teams, and they also change quickly with their character. To sit on the bike and to perform is one thing, but to really work and understand what they are doing can be very different and it depends on maturity. This is something particular to Moto3 and they don't really have it in Moto2 and less in MotoGP. Jason had made improvements and he was adapting, because in 2020, as a rookie, he didn't score a point, but I said to him near the end of the season that I would give him a second chance although he had to train really hard in the winter because this is the world championship and as a team, we wanted to improve.

'He trained with Dani Pedrosa. He was pushing hard with his dad and was coming up to the level of the Spanish,' Florian continues. 'Like riders in some other northern European countries, Jason, being Swiss, could not train as much as the Spanish. There just wasn't that culture. At the beginning of 2021, he was quite strong. We had put that pressure on him and the family, but the improvements were there.'

Pruestel betrays no emotion when speaking of 29 May when his rider fell, his team was decimated and his life affected. 'I was with the family in hospital in Florence and saw what it all meant,' he tells me. His eyes and the poise behind the glasses while recounting the episode convey a composure and the mileage of a person who has been through the mill and somehow made his peace. 'He was nineteen years old. The situation changed my life and [made me] think differently about racing. Everyone knows the risk … but they don't *really* know it because if it happens, then it's a different feeling.'

In an ill-advised move, there was a minute's silence for Dupasquier on the grid before the MotoGP race on 30 May, after confirmation that morning that the rider had succumbed to his injuries. It was not the time nor the place. Pecco Bagnaia was visibly struggling. 'I crashed in the race because of that, absolutely,' he told me. 'I was not scared to race but I was not happy to race. It had been a shock. I was eating before the race and I heard the news that Jason had passed away. I was trying to focus but I went to Davide [Tardozzi] and said, "I don't want to race." He said I had to. I was crying on the grid when they had that one minute of silence. I was completely out of my mind. I think another two, three laps into the race and the focus would have come back, but I crashed because I was distracted. I know Mugello perfectly and I knew that if you touched the white line through Arrabbiata 2 then you'd crash, because the gap between the asphalt and the kerb is huge. I lost the front and if I had been concentrating then it would never have happened. I was quite angry with Race Direction, but we told them …'

If anyone was as affected as much as Bagnaia then it was not so obviously apparent. Fabio Quartararo made his own dedication on track with a Swiss flag after winning the race. Bagnaia would go on to triumph for the next three years at Mugello. I asked if the experience had hardened him or if he would be troubled in a similar way again. He paused, but only briefly. 'No, I think I would be the same,' he said. 'I never knew or had met Jason. I had never spoken with him but he was a rider, and we are all riders. We all know perfectly the feelings of a young rider trying to reach his objective and in a moment, everything can be lost, especially for the family. You can feel bad for everything about it … not only because it might have been a friend. Like with Marco Simoncelli. When he died, I was at a test in Valencia and we stopped riding. I was fourteen years old. I'd never met Marco but I was young and of course that means you don't really understand situations well. Still, I stopped the test because I wasn't focused. And it's dangerous.

'It was one of the hardest periods,' Pruestel continues. 'I was still young in this paddock and I was "automatic" about it [accidents] when it happened to others. But in 2021, it came to my team. You cannot really describe the emotions you have but, all of a sudden, you don't want to come to a circuit or a race anymore. As a team, we stopped for three races. But then we had the chance to change bikes with CFMOTO, the colours, and make everything new for

2022, so we went for it. I was thinking about stopping. I stopped my academy for the younger riders. Racing was still in my heart so we continued but it was thanks to the CFMOTO opportunity because we'd been through the worst you can have.'

Returning to Mugello in 2022 was traumatic. 'I walked around that corner … everything came up,' he says. 'When you send out a rider and the rider doesn't come back, you see the helicopter, you see the family, you get all the messages and then finally you have to tell Dorna that a life has finished … yeah … it is a big experience.'

In the aftermath, causes, reasons and explanations are sought. The nature of Moto3 was held largely to blame, thanks to the technical regulations that bunch the bikes together in such tight proximity. Moto3 owns sixteen of the closest grand prix finishes of all time (all points scoring positions, so first to fifteenth) and some of the accidents while riders are in a mass tow beggar belief. The annual dash along the main straight and heavy braking into San Donato at Mugello by a crop of testosterone-fuelled teenagers almost has to be watched through the fingers.

Some of the reckless actions and behaviour of certain eager runners was placed into a brighter spotlight during the period after Dupasquier's accident. Penalties for on-track actions became more frequent and the age limit was rightfully increased to eighteen. 'It's good, but there are still some riders that go full risk,' opines Florian. 'Maybe they need to punish those more so they understand quicker that this cannot happen. Just to have a long lap penalty in the race is not enough for some. They need to be stricter to make them think more.'

The urgency to make an impact, get a deal, show progression and not lose an opportunity to a following wave of talent is a heavy tenet of professional racing, sport even – Pruestel admitted as much with Dupasquier needing to show signs of evolution in his second season – but the combination of 150mph motorcycles and adolescent impetus means Moto3 can be a heady mix of fireball characters and unchecked desperation.

'Woah!' Florian reacts when I ask him about Moto3 racer temperaments. 'The thing is that when you talk to them then they're normal guys, but when they put the helmet on ...! Racing for me is fascinating because you can still go so fast but then you also need to fight rivals in groups and mostly in the last laps. In Moto3, we can have good qualifiers but this doesn't mean they are good racers. They need to have a strong mind and this fascinates me every time.'

The mind. The thoughts of repercussions of a crash at MotoGP or WorldSBK speed are kept somewhere in the paddock ether. It's not talked about. Except when a rider needs to highlight the hazards to enforce a point. I asked Jonathan Rea once about fear. His answer was quite surprising. 'I fear being lost in life,' he said after some thought. 'Right now, I have so much focus and dedication on my family and one particular thing [racing]. I think about after racing and what purpose I'll have apart from being a husband and a father. I want to contribute to people in any kind of way, and right now I get that satisfaction from making good race results or improving a bike for a manufacturer or enjoying teamwork with a group. So, I fear losing that purpose.'

Asolo, Italy. A small town of fewer that 10,000 people, west of Venice, on the first low ripples of the Dolomites. One side of the SP248 main road resists the tentative mountains. On the other, factories and premises for renowned brands like Replay, Diesel and Alpinestars line up rank and file. At the gate and main door of the original, modest two-floor building, the Alpinestars plaque is clear and clean, bearing the initial logo with the edelweiss flower that Sante Mazzarolo used to label and name his shoe company in 1963, with a focus on ski and mountain activities.

I'm here to interview Gabriele, his son, the owner and CEO of the company. Gabriele bought the business from his dad in 1993, having joined the firm in his late teens and established the American wing and subsidiary in the mid-1980s. Alpinestars is the predominant company in MotoGP for safety and protection, maybe even style.

I've visited Asolo at least three times. The Veneto region is a centre of pattern making and the textile industry. The quaint pockets of rural buildings, houses, winding streams and sudden small hills sit alongside frequent clusters of business parks and rectangular monoliths of industry. It seems to be a happy co-existence.

Gabriele is a motorsport obsessive. I'm used to seeing his tall, thin frame strolling around in a perfectly pressed Alpinestars shirt at MotoGP, MXGP and Supercross. He always stops to say hello. We've done interviews in the past, but not many. He doesn't speak publicly often and keeps a low profile. He's regularly on the move, between Italy and the USA, and many races and corporate events, as Alpinestars' output of products and endless new collections for road, off-road or lifestyle with sub-brands like Oscar is unrelenting.

The 2024 San Marino Grand Prix came at a good time. Mazzarolo would be in the office for a presentation to the team of sales reps and could squeeze me in.

First, friend and Astars' ever-energetic media manager, Chris Hillard, gives me a tour of the brand new 'R&D 1' building. The race department, where they service the customed-made suits, gloves, boots for their army of racers and athletes from across the world, from NASCAR to motocross, MotoGP to Flat Track, previously existed in the cramped confines of the original Alpinestars building. Now it is in the bright, airy splendour of 'R&D 1'.

We move through the glass-walled and clinical offices of the design teams (moto, auto and off-road sections) into the pattern department, where a crew of nine ladies is responsible for measuring and 'mapping' the sections of a suit. Everyone wears a lab coat. On two large white tables are irregular shaped piles of paper, labelled 'Bastianini'. Alpinestars take thirty-six measures of each rider for a suit. They are then plotted onto eighty pieces of paper that are used as the templates for printing and cutting the leather and other materials. The suit itself will be stitched and pulled together from 150 sections or components. This customized service is used by twenty-six riders. Chris opens one of the many cabinets. This one is labelled 'E–J'. Inside are individual hangers with the papers collated on each one: every hanger is a suit in the planning form and represents the body shape of a person.

I'm soon driven the five-minute journey back to the 'Jeremy McGrath' meeting room in HQ and Gabriele wanders in. He's as interested in the nature of the interview and this book as I am in his story and how he steered Alpinestars to the status it has today.

'My father was never into motorcycles or motorsport but he was a very good product person for footwear and always thought in an innovative way,' he begins. 'He was a big thinker. Alpinestars was a hiking and ski company, mainly using leather, but then plastic came in as a technology around 1964–65. A plastic injected boot was a completely different business for my dad.

'We had a small motocross track in the area and my dad went there one day and saw that the riders didn't have boots [specifically] for motocross. They had some with laces; they were for other purposes. He came up with a motocross boot that, in terms of DNA, is very similar to today's boot because it fastened at the side, had buckles and had a shin pad that was later replaced by a steel plate. The soles were smooth because the riders did not want to catch the ground, they wanted to slide. He was innovating but at the same time it was a product that addressed a need.'

How did a man who wasn't into bikes or racing end up at a motocross track? 'I never asked but he told me once that he had gone along with some friends. Maybe he was looking for other ways to expand the business and there was a group of young, wealthy kids from Padua that had money to spend on those bikes at the time. He spoke to them and made the boot, and, famously, people like Roger de Coster [five times 500cc motocross world champion] and John Penton [American racer and entrepreneur, known for helping establish KTM in North America] were at a high level and were looking for that kind of product.'

In contrast to his dad, Mazzarolo junior was obsessed by vehicles that moved quickly. 'I was crazy for motorcycles and cars. My dad went to some races and I would go with him, of course. My education came through those trips. I would talk to the racers and look after the boots. I still do that ... even though we have a lot more people now!'

It feels unusual to encounter a firm of Alpinestars' size and reputation with such a forceful hereditary and generational link. If Sante, who passed away in 2020 at the age of ninety-one, was the product master, then I'm curious how Gabriele sees his role in the story, particularly accounting for the massive expansion and widened scope, to the point where 700 employees are now on the books in five countries.

As he talks in his quiet, whispery tones about his dad, Gabriele starts to doodle on the lined A4 pad in front of him. By the end of the hour, the page will be full of black shapes, boxes and scribbles. 'My father had skill as a pattern maker and a footwear designer on a technical side. He could make things well. And had vision. I think I brought this also: a way to see how and why a product should be better,' he says. 'I did OK at school and I took a path on the scientific and business side, but I was interested in making something that would work for athletes. From the beginning, I thought motorsport would be an activity that would eventually be mainstream but there were needs to be addressed. It is easy to say, "We need safety", but it has to be safety that people want to use. A boot has to be protective but also flexible. I wanted us to be the brand that was loved by the racers; we'd always be the ones that represent their activity. That was how I saw it. And later, by being with the racers, we had something that was organic.'

The Mazzarolos travelled a lot. Sante would pile them into the car and head to places like Paris, Milan and Barcelona. With his fondness for racing and company activities, Gabriele was soon able to count athletes as friends. People like Randy Mamola, Kevin Schwantz, Mick Doohan, McGrath and Rick Johnson. He bought a house with De Coster in 1989. 'These were people that were friendly, open, could talk to anyone but had the drive to win, and win championships. I saw my mentality as a bit similar to them. We are a racing company and we think like a racing company. We are the only ones that top teams want across many series. Nobody else makes this effort.'

Gabriele founded Alpinestars in California and established a culture that was more international, far outstripping the green fields around Asolo. Father and son were close, so I asked Gabriele why he had to buy the company from his dad in 1993. It was a pivotal move because the business ripened further from that point. 'My dad lived next door to the factory and my mum – being super-smart – convinced him not to go in. Otherwise, he'd be there and wouldn't agree with anything! Until 1993, we only made footwear, and between 1988 and 1991 we made mountain bikes, which was how I was able to buy a part of the company. Our first jackets were in 1995. My dad wouldn't have done it and I know there are things that he thought would never work but he never stopped me from doing it. When I was younger, he was upset that I went to races every weekend but he did not stop me. He would tell me not to go but then he'd also give me the money to get there. That's how he was. He could not be a partner. It was one or the other.'

Gabriele is sixty. I'm still a little surprised by the earnest way he advocates for racing and athletes. There is a deep-seated enchantment with the sport. When we talk more business, it feels like we are talking more about sport. He is humble and repeatedly asks me to present his stories and comments in a way that credits his family and the people around him. At one point I feel I have to justify my questioning because his narrative and the personal investment of time and energy made into motorsport has led to the omnipresence of Alpinestars. But whether he likes it or not, he's the ringmaster. His narrative and personal investment of time and energy made into motorsport have led to the omnipresence of Alpinestars.

Gabriele, almost shyly, tells an anecdote about needing to measure the feet of rally driver Colin McRae at a competitive meeting but only having a metallic tape measure. He drove home and then returned to Monte Carlo, a 600km trip, because 'it bothered me like crazy that I had the wrong tools. I went back the next day with a soft tape and, to this day, I have one in my backpack because I always want to be prepared. It was already a lot that Colin gave me the time to get the measurements and I was so sorry to do it again. We became pretty close after that. Most of our athletes feel that we look after them. They don't have to force us or beg us. We do more for them than we ask.'

Alpinestars were able to kick up several gears with their innovations in the area of safety. The difficulty comes with the compromise between protection and practicality. 'Safety but safety that you'll use,' Gabriele reasons. 'It's the same for our street jackets. It might have protection but if someone does not want to wear it then it's just hanging in the wardrobe, offering zero. If it is hard to use or put on, or a rider does not love it, then it has no value. A racer is the same when he crashes: he wants more protection until he gets to a point where he forgets about it and then goes back to the minimum equipment, which is a good thing. Racers are intelligent people, otherwise they would not be that successful for so long. To be that driven when you are comfortable and having made money and so on – that is a form of intelligence because you must overpower the natural tendency that everyone has to take it easy and not work so hard. Nobody likes to be hurt but a racer also has the "pain" of losing championship points or positions. The goal of a lifetime. It's the same for the road. People in the city on bikes are wearing normal brands and not motorcycle brands and they can cost more! I was in Paris not long ago during fashion week and there were a lot of scooters and most of the riders were not in motorcycle gear because they wanted style. So, we want to give that style which also happens to be protective if they crash. They don't think about crashing, which is correct, and you shouldn't think this way, but style becomes part of safety and the reason why people want to use it.'

He gives me another example of testing and trying in MotoGP, something that fans never usually see, even the eagle-eyed ones.

'We made a system to cool the riders down on the grid for those ten minutes after the sighting lap when they are sitting on these hot bikes. It was a fan in the hump of the suit but then we took it out because we needed the space for electronics. We went back with a new system but the riders did not want it; for me this is clearly because the system did not work. How could they not want to be cooler at that moment when they need the most lucidity for the first corner?! We needed to help them, so we kept investing until we found something that could help them.'

For many motorcyclists, Alpinestars' longest and closest rival has been Dainese, also established in Veneto but almost a decade later and specializing in clothing, eventually purchasing AGV helmets in 2007. Dainese's main shareholder is the American investment company the Carlyle Group, who acquired the firm of a thousand employees and distribution network in 2022 for a fee touching almost 700 million dollars. I bring up the subject of the Italian competition. The only reaction seems to be one of familiarity and diplomacy. 'I've always said that any competitor can only help motorcycling look better,' Gabriele insists. 'If they make a beautiful advert of a product that makes people want to ride then this is not competition, it is good for everyone. Valentino Rossi was not with Alpinestars but he helped motorcycling in general. We create more interest in riding and then the best product will win. I don't see them as taking things away from us. We also do pretty well so I am not worried. Maybe I would see it differently if we were in a difficult position. I am happy to make the field bigger and then we can compete in it. I truly never had a problematic relationship with another company. Everybody is trying to do their best.'

There are several moments when Gabriele's composed and professional exterior cracks into a resonant laugh. The last of those comes when I ask about the future of protection and how the likes of Alpinestars, Dainese, REV'IT! and Ixon can keep on improving racer safety when the suits are already lighter, stronger and more advanced than ever. The helmets are more multifunctional, the boots more robust and the gloves hard-wearing. Alpinestars covers almost every practical inch of a MotoGP rider. For the Italian, the answer is quite clear. 'We started making a leather pattern in 1994, went to market in 1995 and began selling suits in 1997. Then the brief was we would try to make them in any material: Kevlar, carbon fibre, plastic, whatever … except leather. And we are still using leather! We are still at step one, literally. We are working on it, but to make a material that would not melt at very high heat means it gets heavier and less stretchy. High heat resistance is vital because a crashing rider slides on the tarmac for a short time before they start to tumble. Pedro Acosta crashed at nearly 300km/h for 5.8 seconds [in Austria, 2024]. At the moment, only leather can resist that [force] and for the right weight and the flexibility. So, we could make something safer but the riders wouldn't use it because there are more negatives than positives. OK, we cover the body, yes, but we are still at step one and it is very motivating. We have enough to do.'

FIVE

Orange Spirit and the Hardline and Hope

Crossing from Spain to Andorra involves passing through two stages of border control and threading through a dated customs checkpoint that makes you feel guilty even though you have zero reason to be. I look to see if there is a 'MotoGP Fast Track' option but no such luck. It's taken over two and a half hours to drive to the frontier from Barcelona. Maverick Viñales and his assistant Alex Salas told me they used to make the commute in just two hours from the airport. They must have learned the positions of all the speed cameras and taken their chances passing any trucks on some of the single lane sections.

Andorra, the 180-square-mile principality wedged between France and Spain, in the loftiest peaks of the Pyrenees, has been the European refuge for at least fifteen MotoGP riders past and present and their families. The 10 per cent income tax rate is the main incentive, but the ski haven is also renowned for first-class sporting facilities and draws athletes from across the spectrum.

I wind along the narrow road and through the town of La Massana. The last time I visited Andorra was in early 2017 to interview Viñales. We met in a gym complex and, as we talked, at different points, Jorge Lorenzo and

Alex Rins sauntered by to see what was going on, and I was left wondering if Andorra is the equivalent of a MotoGP country club.

The then-twenty-two-year-old told me that Andorra 'is quiet, and you can do a lot of sport. So for my career at the moment it is good to be there. Away from the track my life is about motocross, cycling and the gym.' But Maverick did not last long in the relative seclusion. He abandoned the mountains three years later when he met his wife, Raquel, and relocated to Girona, not far from his hometown of Roses. His turbulent final period as a factory Yamaha rider included being embroiled in the company's mess with fragile engine valves, a controversial motor blow-up that he instigated in protest, suspension, deletion of his Twitter account and then the mid-season split with the Japanese in 2021, ending a four-and-a-half-year relationship. All of which is documented in MotoGP's revealing but also half-baked TV series *Unlimited*. He was rescued by Aprilia after the Yamaha fall-out.

In 2017, I asked the grand prix winner in all classes if he was a sensitive soul, particularly to outside criticism. 'Yes, a lot,' he replied in his hushed English. 'And it is strange because when I'm at the track or doing something in MotoGP, I am not: I'm quite strong. But when I'm at home, I'm very different, very normal, and reading some bad media you get some bad feelings. But I try to use that stuff in a different way.'

In 2024, I'm visiting another breed of racer, one seemingly oblivious to the modern 'peripheries' of being an elite athlete. A KTM rider for ten years, he is a fitting symbol of their racing ethos: arduous, no-nonsense, direct, never compromising. KTM is the most prolific manufacturer in motorcycle sport with over 340 FIM titles in almost every discipline since their first in 1974.

Brad Binder's social media activity is perfunctory. His media profile comparatively scant. Sponsorship, endorsement and extracurricular duties? It's hard to think of any outside of his native South Africa. Yet he is a Moto3 world champion in orange, a multiple Moto2 GP winner and championship runner-up, and victor in MotoGP, as well as a KTM folk hero for delivering their first premier class victory in 2020 at Brno in the Czech Republic.

The twenty-nine-year-old might be described as 'old school', but he is also incredibly receptive and friendly. When you talk, he actually listens. He is that cliched description of being another animal altogether on the motorcycle: bustling, aggressive and far more of a presence than his small, slight frame would indicate.

Brad meets me outside his abode. It is on a near-silent street on the apron of Andorra's western peaks. The bulk of the country's urbanization flows like water through the gully of the mountainous range. As the territory became more populous at the turn of the century, the houses crept higher up the hills. There are a dozen similar-looking stony properties in the same close. Fifty metres away, a small crane cranks over another development. Brad and his wife, Courtney, married at the end of 2023, have been in Andorra for several years and have made it their home away from home and Binder's family roots west of Johannesburg.

He has ditched the ever-present Red Bull cap and is dressed in a black hoodie from sunglasses sponsor 100%. It must be ten degrees cooler in Andorra compared to Barcelona. Sweatshirt weather already in mid-September. The house is compact but tall and stretches up four narrow floors and therefore has an interior lift. The exterior is made from a dark grey rock that characterizes a lot of other buildings in the area and the country. Brad and Courtney bought the property from former Dakar winner Cyril Despres.

Brad's grey van is parked in the road and we have a quick look in the basement/garage at ground level where he has half a dozen KTMs for motocross and supermoto and a pair of GASGAS trial bikes. A mid-weight track racebike is propped on a stand. Some of his brother Darryn's motorcycles are here too. A few framed racing prints and paintings scattered around are the only clue to his profession. A trick-looking Felt bicycle hangs on the wall and is worth more than most small family cars. Brad is bothered by the dirty state of both his and Darryn's mountain bikes after their sortie that morning. He comments on the mud more than once and it's obvious what he'll be doing once I've finished occupying his time.

He talks a bit about life up here. His wide social circle involves other sports people – rally, enduro and MotoGP racers and cyclists. There appears to be endless opportunities to bicycle, train and be outdoors. Brad admits he struggles to sit still and will be pedalling most days around the nearby roads and lanes, so he's either fighting gravity or very much going with the flow. While we're in the garage, he points to the row of houses opposite and beyond and reels off the names of four or five MotoGP riders that could be considered neighbours. I ask whether it feels a bit much, living in proximity to competitors and people with whom he fraternizes inside an already intense paddock. 'We don't really see much of each other, to be honest.'

Upstairs, the living room is pristine, with one of the biggest L-shaped sofas I've ever seen. A massive television is set against one wall. A collection of books sits in the furniture underneath. I spot titles about Kobe Bryant and other sports subjects in Taschen-style publications. 'I find myself with a lot of time, especially in Europe. At home, in South Africa, it seems there are not enough hours in the day to get things done. Here, I was watching so much TV or the phone and then thinking, "Why are you doing that?" Reading is a lot better for you and keeps you a lot more clear. It was one of the main reasons to do it and I just dig it nowadays. Sometimes, I just like walking into a bookshop and seeing what looks cool.'

There are large photos of Brad and Courtney from their wedding day on the wall and barely any traces of his vocation. No trophies, keepsakes or mementos. 'I think I am pretty chilled and easy to be around.' He pauses, then laughs. 'Court might say different! But I try to keep all my shit in order.'

I first became aware of the name Brad Binder during his three seasons in the Red Bull MotoGP Rookies Cup from 2009 to 2011. His parents had made sacrifices from their home southwest of the South African capital to help a talented and very determined boy have a go at his ambitions. Trevor Binder had been motorsport mad and, after a dip at karting for his sons, bikes beckoned. 'Dad started his company when I was a kid. He didn't have a super amount of money but as we grew, so did his company. It specialized in heavy engineering works. Around 2012, I think, he was doing alright but he didn't have the money to just give away. My old man was always a bike guy and went to track days. When we were old enough, we joined him and that's how it started.'

Brad says he enjoyed sport – 'cricket, rugby, hockey … but I was so useless.'

While his mother, Sharon, was completely selfless ('my mum did everything for us. She runs around for my brother and me to this day. Whatever I need, I call her; she still does all my merchandise and all the packaging and sorts out things for us at home.'), Trevor instilled a willingness in his boys through a staunch attitude to life. 'He was always the first one up and the last one in the house and is never too tired to help, whether it was work on an engine or change tyres, pull suspension out. He was always down for something,' Brad reminisces.

'I was taught that if you do something then do it properly or not at all. Sometimes in my life it's gone a bit far the other way and if something doesn't interest me then I do nothing! As far as racing goes, I feel I never left a stone unturned. I've gone that extra mile or a good day is never quite good enough. I think it came from my old man, who is quite a hard-working guy and he installed that in us early on.'

The family used to gather on the sofa and watch MotoGP on Sunday afternoons. Brad's own career started slow, then saw him post some results, and swell in confidence and belief that he'd rise to be the cream of the crop. He had to deal with the obstacle of moving a large distance across the continents and knowing that a lack of progression would swiftly turn into a plane ticket back, for good. Non-Europeans have the cliched 'ticking clock' moving faster than their counterparts. 'Coming from South Africa is a bit tricky because it's a long way to chase a goal and to try to become a MotoGP rider when there is no written explanation of how to do it or which route to take. It was just my dad and I trying to figure things out on the way. Every day felt important.

'Racing in South Africa was a different story because there were not many kids,' he explains. 'Well, on the 50s there were, but then as soon as you got to the 125s the classes were small. There were ten guys if you were lucky. Mathew Scholtz, who is now in the AMA, and I were the fastest. So, we always had a step to the other kids. When I was twelve we came over to England for the first time. I raced in the Superteens series there and in my first race I came second when I thought I'd be thrashed. It was pretty cool but the rude awakening then came in the Rookies Cup. That's when I thought, "Shit, these kids are fast!" All through my career, I have never been the fastest kid right away. I was mid-pack or just cracking top ten, but I guess I was working much harder than the others and I figured it out in the end. In all the categories, I managed to get better and be where I wanted to be: MotoGP not yet! Got a bit of work to do there. In Moto3 I was thrashed, start of Moto2 I got destroyed. The start of MotoGP for some reason came right away. I mean, I was useless at the first test but …'

Breaking off the chronology, I ask what he means by 'working hard'. It must be more than just physical training because that seems almost a prerequisite for talented youngsters and professionals. 'The biggest part for me, mentally, is showing up ready,' he explains. 'I "sign" a contract with myself at the beginning of each year. Whatever my trainer puts on the app for me with the training peaks then that's the job that has to be done. It's non-negotiable, so I try to follow everything to the "T", do it properly, don't miss sessions. Of course, there are always days where you cannot train because you have media events or another commitment, but I always try to make sure I do my best to stick to it. Then, on the other hand you are looking at data, watching videos to understand what's going on [on track]. When you are shit in one area, you make sure the next time you go out you aren't shit there anymore! Now, if I arrive to a circuit and I am not on the pace then it really irritates me. I don't want to be there, and the only way to fix that is to fix what I am doing wrong.'

Binder's nationality cast him as a novelty rather than a preference in what was a simmering period for Spanish and Italian kids. After his Rookies education, a lot hinged on a first grand prix season in 2012, where he only scored points once until the final three rounds.

'I had two moments in my early days where I thought, "This is over",' he admits. 'Firstly, in 2012, for my first year, my dad had to pay a ridiculous amount of money to get me a ride. My parents had to empty their savings to put it together. We got to Valencia at the end of that season and I still didn't have a contract [for season two]. I knew the first year was just one shot: if I cut it then fantastic; if not, I was coming back home. I didn't have anything at Valencia and I remember a few GPs before thinking, "These might be my last races here … enjoy it." My final race was wet! But I remember feeling f**king great. I think I was fourth and I got overtaken for the podium on the last corner! From that performance, Ambrogio Racing reached out and offered me a ride. That was the step that kept my career alive. It changed my life. Then, in 2016, I knew I had to win in Moto3 otherwise I would just fizzle out. Through my career, I never wanted to just make up the numbers. Living in Europe now is a lot better but in the early days I hated it. Any chance I could I went back home. When I wasn't achieving then it wasn't worth being away. So I put big pressure on myself to perform or get out of there. After the championship in 2016, it was "OK, next step …."

'When you are younger, you take all those opportunities for granted,' he adds. 'My mum was in Europe with me; my dad was back home making the money to keep us there. I was a kid living my dream and racing in the world championship, but for them, there was so much going on behind the scenes to make it happen and that was the crazy part. Already in Moto3 when things click and you start taking podiums, some wins and then the championship, your life switches to how you think it is going to be. I was in Spain when I was eighteen and as soon as I had a driver's licence, Mum and Dad could chill at home and I could sort myself out. Things changed. I had to figure things out for myself. I was fortunate that in my second year, I had a little salary from the team so I was able to fend for myself and survive. That was cool! I've been really lucky with my whole route.'

Binder's personality and personal philosophy follow the values of his upbringing plus the awareness of his good fortune. Humbly, he credits circumstances rather than his own skills or mentality for where he is today. He comes across as a contrasting mix of resolute desire and endless appreciation, and it seems at odds. Maybe it makes him more rounded, or more unique.

Two Moto3 podiums came in 2014 and the career motion began. 'I think in my life I built things up to be too big in my head: to win meant doing everything absolutely perfectly, while the reality was that if you are the fastest dude over twenty laps then you win the race. It is actually so simple and I made a big deal out of too many things. But that is also cool in a way because it made me put in the extra work. In the smaller classes, I always thought, "If I can get one, then another one will come." Hiccups can happen but you just chase that momentum. Fighting for the podium becomes the norm and before you get to the circuit at the weekend, you know you'll be there. It's crazy how things psychologically just keep moving on and you are never happy. Never. Regardless if you are second or third. If you win then it's sweet for a couple of hours but after that you are like, "Shit … it's on to the next one."'

Four podiums were banked in 2015 when he joined Aki Ajo's fabled grand prix team and the beginning of the Red Bull KTM story. The Fin has a reputation for not suffering fools but also creating champions if young aspirants can follow his working system. Binder's transition was not so smooth at first.

'The toughest time for me personally was 2015 and my first year with Aki,' he says. 'I stepped off the Mahindra, which was actually a decent motorbike by the end of 2014, and I expected to make the step other riders had made when they went to that team. When I started with Aki, I realized I was still a rookie. I didn't know anything. The best information I had for my career and going forward came from that year and 2016.'

The interview so far has been littered with moments when Brad's self-effacing tendency means he laughs at himself. Talking about Ajo gets him animated further. 'You would ride in [to the pitbox] and complain about something and he'll look at the screen, look at you and then say, "But you're one second off … Help yourself before we help you. The bike is fine." Panicking and throwing your toys out of the cot – which was me at the beginning – would not work. He would come over and say, "Hey, that's not how we do it. Be calm, relaxed. If there's a problem, then there's no problem. You go out and do your job properly and the results will come." It took me a while! I was lucky, I got a few results. When things were clicking then I was fast, if not then I was really far back. It was difficult to find a good average! Aki taught me how to work through sessions, explain myself, work out what I could do differently or how I needed help from the bike, and look at the bigger picture. I couldn't come in and say, "The front keeps closing … fix it." He taught me a better idea of how to be a professional rider. Not just a rider, but to be more mature.'

Binder was a good and feisty Moto3 racer but he became a truly great one on 24 April 2016. He had grabbed three trophies in the first three rounds and looked accomplished and full of intent with used tyres all weekend on the KTM RC4 at the Circuit de Jerez for the Spanish Grand Prix. Being dumped to thirty-fifth and last place on the grid after he'd been found with a non-homologated mapping for the electronics was not quite part of the plan, but Binder shocked Ajo and staff around him, like data engineer and now MotoGP Crew Chief Andres Madrid, by claiming that he'd still win.

'The time I need to start dead-last was the time I put it all together!' The laugh again. 'I remember after warm-up, I was getting undressed and we were still waiting for words from the stewards. All that had happened was that the guys had changed my map filename to something else. It was the same as everyone else's but the change of name meant it was irregular when it was pulled up along with the other KTM guys. The penalty was for Le Mans and the following race but then Aki comes into the truck and says, "OK, so, you're going to be starting last." He didn't give much more of an explanation! He told me just to finish the race and that I had everything under control and then walked straight out! I didn't have much chance to think about it. I lined up, tried my best, caught the front guys and then I thought, "If I've come this far then maybe I can win this thing."'

It was a pleasure to sit, watch and chart Binder's elevation through the pack that day. He overtook names like Enea Bastianini, Fabio Quartararo, Pecco Bagnaia, Fabio Di Giannantonio and Joan Mir ('Now when I look at MotoGP then they are dudes I have been racing my whole life. Everyone just moves through. Shuffles.'). He took the lead on lap eighteen of twenty-three and won by over three seconds – effectively a mile in Moto3 parlance. It was a startling first grand prix feat, also outstanding considering the calibre of the opposition. Both for his ability and his tenacity as well as the distinction of his nationality – the Jerez win was the first of seventeen across the board at the time of writing and the first for South Africa since Jon Ekerold's 1981 350cc success at Monza (the 350cc category was discontinued from 1983) – Binder had reinforced his profile in the paddock and in the sport. Jerez bolstered his world championship margin: he won six more times in 2016 and delivered the title at Aragon (four rounds early), his country's first since Ekerold's 350cc crown in 1980.

'When I won my championship in Aragon, I had a few races

left that season and thought, "Now what?!" It was supposed to be the be all and end all and I woke up on Monday thinking, "This feels weird." It's still the same for me now: a good result like a podium or a win means a nice few hours but then you quickly want more.

'I did have so much more shit to do!' he says, after a brief pause. 'So many interviews. I went back to South Africa and had a full week of media stuff. I was like "jeez, this is crazy" but all of that becomes the norm. It's cool how it all progresses.'

As if to underline that so much in life and sport is about timing, Binder's championship coincided with KTM's announcement that they would enter MotoGP, and the Austrian's commitment to the premier class was followed by the swift implementation of a complete pathway for riders, from the first feeder series like Rookies with the same KTM-kitted bikes in Moto3, then Moto2 all the way to the MotoGP elite. The germs of what is now the KTM GP Academy had begun to ferment.

'I was super-lucky that things happened at the right time,' Binder comments. 'In 2016, I was ready. We had the best bike on the grid and all I had to do was put the results together. Then, all of a sudden, KTM wanted to have a Moto2 team so I could stay with the exact crowd I was with and move to the next step. Then, in Moto2, it was like "Wait, there's a MotoGP team!" It all fell into place.'

'I have always been a KTM guy,' Brad said. 'I cannot remember how many times I have signed now. They have really looked after me. I am happy where I am and that's a big thing. My crew: I would not change a single guy for the world. It's such a tightknit group and I love being part of it, especially at this stage.

'I always feel the need, however shit things might be, to rise to the occasion and perform. If you don't perform then you don't have a seat. So that has always been in the back of my mind. It might be that you are hurt, the bike is not working well or there is an issue: you still need to perform. I try to live by that and always try to maximize what is possible on the day. If that's a tenth then it's a tenth, and if it's fighting for the podium then that's what I can give.'

Herein lies something of the KTM paradox. Being 'in' the structure and in favour brings all the spoils and treatment of a full factory elite racer, and the affection and respect that entails. Being 'out' signifies short thrift. Compared to the onion layers of Japanese organization, the idea of the emperor hovering his thumb up and down over one of his combatants seems much more real at KTM.

An example came in 2022 when the KTM RC16 was not the easiest iteration of the bike in MotoGP and presented a quandary for the two standout riders from Moto2 in 2021: the Red Bull KTM Ajo pairing of Remy Gardner and Raul Fernandez. On paper, the prospect was mouthwatering. They had been first and second in the Moto2 championship and both were from the academy structure, Fernandez even more so with his Moto3 story beginning three years earlier with Ajo. Fernandez was contracted to KTM and wanted MotoGP action despite having just one year in Moto2 and being only twenty at the time. KTM, recognizing that the threat of losing the Spaniard to Aprilia was very real, enforced their contract with him and then had a talented and fast MotoGP rookie in a sustained sulk for the better part of 2022, counting the days until he could sign a bigger and better deal with the Italians. Moto2 world champion Gardner was dismayed by the difficulty of the RC16 and the size of the task to try to make it work for his style. He scored points in only four events until outspoken comments from his manager only added to the general disillusionment from both rider and factory. KTM were unimpressed with the Aussie's outlook, even down to occasions when Remy's slightly bohemian personality would clash with the basic level of acceptable presentation. Eventually, Gardner's future came down to mathematics: were the Austrians ready to invest another ten million (and change) to enter another MotoGP season with the Moto2 champion? The answer was no. In contrast, Gardner's Moto2 successor, Augusto Fernandez, entered the Tech3 framework at the end of that year with the kind of knuckle-down outlook that saw the Majorcan win the hard 'five riders for four bikes' dilemma midway through 2023. Fortunately for KTM, Pol Espargaró's injury setback from his smash at the Portuguese Grand Prix, the seven-round absence and then eventual willingness to accept a testing role eased the anxiety for 2024. Pedro Acosta was able to slide into place alongside Fernandez.

I ask Brad whether being a KTM rider equals more pressure because of the profound sequencing all the way through the company. He brushes off the notion. 'The way I look at it is that you are a MotoGP rider hired to do a job and if you aren't performing then they can find someone else,' he reasons. 'It is a bit difficult because you know, as a rider, that there are never any perfect moments. You are up and down and you are winning one weekend and crashing the next. It is hard to be super-stable but I'm lucky that KTM have always had my back. The first time they looked after me was when they kept me in 2015 for 2016. Then there were moments in Moto2 when I was shocking. I fell off at the beginning and I had a broken arm but they stuck by me when the results were not there. There have been moments when I haven't been at my best and they've helped me, and moments too when the bike hasn't quite cut it. But we've always managed to do things. We've had a good stint together.'

'Since I have known Brad, from the first day, he puts a massive trust in the group,' Andres Madrid told me. 'He will say, "Guys, this is what I need … I trust you with whatever you decide and we go 100 per cent." This makes our lives much easier. I've seen other riders much more involved in the technical side and it becomes more complicated because they think they know! OK, they know a lot because they see and feel things that we cannot on the data, but there are still other things that they don't. We have a much bigger picture on the technical side than them.'

'When the rider has a set mood then he transmits a calmness to you. They lead,' Madrid says. 'The calmness means that whatever decision we make, he will still make it out there. I've seen Brad like this a few times. It happened in Moto2 in his last season; in the second half, he started to win and make many podiums and I remember in Moto3 he was also very confident. I saw that same Brad during 2023, he just has more experience now.'

The combination of KTM's backing, the team environment and Binder's work ethic is summed up in that initial dizzying MotoGP period together in 2020. At his first MotoGP test in Valencia at the end of 2019, he was more than two seconds a lap off the pace. 'And I think that was the best thing that could have happened because I went home to South Africa and didn't stop watching videos to figure out how the f**k those guys were doing it.' Binder was much, much quicker by the time MotoGP restarted in the chaos of the pandemic at Jerez. By round three, he had carved that milestone at Brno. That year was the annus mirabilis for the KTM RC16, with Binder's breakthrough in the Czech Republic, Espargaró's fifth place in the championship (tied on points for fourth) and Miguel Oliveira's double in Austria and Portugal.

Binder couldn't have boosted his stock higher if he'd tried any harder in 2021. By taking the remarkable gamble of staying out on a wet Red Bull Ring track with slick tyres with four laps to go he teetered around, almost losing it on the final corner, and grabbed an emotional home success for the team and the company. It was a feast among times of famine, with KTM scampering for cast-offs from Ducati's banquet, like everyone else in MotoGP, and Binder searching for sustained consistency.

Whether trying for P1 or P10, the 'BB33' motorcycle is never boring. More often than not, the small South African is drifting, squirming and manipulating the forces bumping the RC16. 'Style is the last of my worries,' he claims. 'I'm not there for the show. And whatever works the best for me or my machine at the time is what I am going to do. There are different ways to do things of course but I feel my style is something that I am always trying to change. For sure, it looks a bit funny compared to the others. I always find when I sit on the bike, I throw my knee out really early into corners even before the bike is cranked over. The other guys are more like "one unit" before they hit that point of tipping in. I always feel I'm a bit flappy or loose on the bike compared to other dudes.'

I ask him if there is someone who he considers as a refence in the style-stakes. 'The guy who is winning is always the one doing it right, bud!' A big smile. 'You can drag your head, your knee, whatever you want if it's working. If it's what it takes, then do it.'

Binder's wildest expression came at the 2023 Spanish Grand Prix: his Jerez haunting ground. A Sprint win and second on Sunday came with ferocious spinning and sliding and awesome angle under braking. 'I saw it back afterwards and thought, "Jeez, that was a bit over the top . . ." But the reality is that I slide a lot as a rider, although it doesn't feel like it. It looks like I'm on the steering lock into most corners and I wonder why I am doing it, but I don't notice it anymore. It feels normal.'

When he says, 'I don't see how I am different to anybody I hang out with or any person doing a normal day job,' with a very serious sincerity then, like Jorge Prado, it's tempting to believe him. Almost. I point out that his day job is one that fewer than thirty people in the entire world can do. 'If you look at it this way then it's super-cool. But I look at it like it's been a lifetime of trying to get to this point,' he counters. 'A life of dedication, hard work and a lot of sacrifices. It is super-great but I don't think I'm different to anyone else.'

Dedication and resilience: Binder carries traits of his employer and the rise of a manufacturer that became the largest in Europe up to the point where overzealous expansion threatened the existence of KTM in 2024. Former CEO Stefan Pierer oversaw more than a decade of continual growth since he rescued the firm from bankruptcy in the early 1990s. Pierer came into KTM thanks to friend and Austrian motorsport icon (a former motocross world champion for the brand) Heinz Kinigadner. 'Kini's close tie with Red Bull is mostly responsible for the force that Red Bull KTM is today. Always smiley, Heinz's typically booming greeting of 'servus!' is only dwarfed by the bear-like grasp of his handshake. I often bump into him taking photos with his phone trackside at MXGP, like an unceasing fan.

Kinigadner may have laid part of the modern-day KTM racing foundations, as well as the Red Bull pulse for bike racing, but the architect of the orange track 'garage' is a German. Pit Beirer was thirty years old when he joined Red Bull KTM Factory Racing in 2003, and as one of the most high-profile riders in the 250cc Motocross World Championship. Less than six months later his life changed. Pit's accident at Sevlievo for the Bulgarian Grand

Prix happened on the approach to a table-top jump as he battled to arrest a slide from second position in the first four laps of the race. I was watching from the other side of the leap. I did not see the crash or the impact but vividly remember KTM team manager Toby Gustafson running to help his stricken rider and gesturing urgently for medical assistance. Beirer was airlifted to a nearby military hospital and had an operation to stabilize his spine before being flown to Munich where he was placed into an induced coma for three days at a specialized back clinic.

The next time I spoke to Pit was before the 2004 season at Mattighofen, in the small original race department. It was for a meeting with Kurt Nicoll, then KTM's Head of Motorsport, and Jurgen Weiss, the sport marketing assistant, about writing press releases for KTM in motocross that year. Pit, blond, frail and submerged into his wheelchair was, however, highly engaged and clearly adjusting to the next chapter at thirty-one. When Nicoll moved to the United States for KTM's American programme, Pit grabbed the handlebars and was able to apply his own ideals and beliefs to motorsport management.

His legacy in KTM's racing history is assured. After a rocky start with the factory motocross team (star signings Mickael Pichon and Sebastien Tortelli falling short in 2006) he then made key recruitments to enhance KTM's presence in Supercross, MXGP, the immediate breach of Moto3 and then the splash into MotoGP. Beirer's leadership, headhunting and policy of scouting and signing youth prospects to bring through the KTM structure paid off, as did an openness to collaborate with the likes of Aki Ajo, Herve Poncharal and even Red Bull Advanced Technologies to accelerate KTM's aerodynamic development.

Riders left their fingerprints. None more so than Pol Espargaró, who not only grasped the first podium Prosecco bottle by taking third in the rain of Valencia at the end of 2018 but then rose to fifth in the world in 2020. Miguel Oliveira also, showing the true latent possibilities of the RC16 fashioned by technicians like Sebastian Risse, Kurt Trieb and Wolfgang Felber when in 'satellite' team guise at Tech3.

By 2024 KTM's prevalence in MotoGP bulged in the balance. At one recent grand prix at the Red Bull Ring there were almost 100 Austrian bikes on track with the Red Bull MotoGP Rookies Cup, Austrian Junior Cup, Moto3, Moto2 and MotoGP. The reach was vast.

'KTM, compared to the other competitors in here – maybe Aprilia is similar – we have to find our budget from selling bikes,' Kinigadner told me over lunch at the German Grand Prix in 2024. 'We have no benefit from cars or other machinery. Bikes only. We are like the slogan "ready to race", and nobody else suffers like us from the "winning on Sunday and sell on Monday". We are budget driven. We have to know what we are doing with every single euro, and on one side this is good and on the other not so easy.'

In 2023, parent company Pierer Mobility AG made 2.6 million euros in revenue and sold over 381,000 units, but earnings after taxes were down by over 50 per cent. PMAG had to belt-tighten, produce fewer bikes and consolidate capital for 2024 due to what their business report cited as 'declining sales', 'high interest rates in the United States' and a 'volatile European market'. After increasing employment year-on-year, this was another area that had to be trimmed. Despite the tough conditions for the industry (Ducati were also manufacturing fewer bikes in 2023), KTM – or their race division – should be investing in the sport and MotoGP until the end of the 2026 season at least.

'This is an activity almost three digits in terms of millions of euros,' former board member Hubert Trunkenpolz said to me during an interview at KTM's superb Motohall museum/ exhibition in central Mattighofen. 'You have to justify this because with that amount of money, you can do many other things. So, when businesses come under pressure and the economy is not great then you have to question even more whether the investment is right. Frankly speaking, without the partnership with Red Bull then it would not be possible, and we're grateful for that and for the contributions of all the other sponsors. If you are on the top in MotoGP then the media value justifies it.'

KTM had doubled their turnover until the latter stages of almost ten years in MotoGP. Streetbike sales eventually outstripped off-road models. The investment had paid off, but over-speculation instigated restructuring in 2024. MotoGP was put on the line, and with the real threat that the orange zest for racing would be diluted and even removed for the future, ironically as KTM lined-up their most formidable line-up for 2025 in Binder, Acosta, Viñales and Bastianini; four of the top seven-ranked riders from 2024.

———

Appreciating some of the scale of MotoGP means being in the paddock after hours. For a moment, the panorama quietens. The races have finished, the fans, spectators and guests are filing out and away from the circuit. The engines are cooling. The PA has been silenced. There is gentle bustle, then a completely different soundtrack starts.

The teams are collapsing the pitboxes and prepping the bikes for transport. Some music pipes up. The race trucks slide in their compartments, and lockers, containers and sections are filled and closed. At the non-European grands prix, hundreds and hundreds of freight cases appear out of nowhere in pitlane.

The general hubbub of deconstruction ramps up. The beeping of reversing vehicles. Shouts between workers, the grind of forklifts and carriers. The rumble of trucks arriving from their distant parking slot in the nether regions of the circuit to hook and load. The hiss of brakes. The once orderly paddock lanes are jumbled. The map has been blurred and the spewed interiors of hospitalities lie in piles. Logistics teams whizz around each other. A multitude of people work in MotoGP. Only a few hundred are still going when Sunday dusk turns to dark: the ones responsible for pulling it down, and those responsible for writing or talking about it (although some of those sometimes also try to pull it down).

Sunday evenings at MotoGP highlight how a lot of individuals work damn hard and make heavy personal commitments to the sport. It also pokes the torch 'under the cushions' for the money to be in Grand Prix. The show moves around and seems to pop up almost automatically but there are thousands upon thousands of hours accumulated to make it repeatedly blossom into an ordered sprawl of a diverse technical tribe.

People. Good people, the right people, are the best and biggest outlay for teams to be in MotoGP. Yes, the bikes themselves may cost just over 2 million euros each to lease from manufacturers, but Dorna's deal with the independent teams, six of the eleven on the grid, cover these wallet-busters and the promoter ships all the freight containers around the world outside of Europe. The trucks, spares, tools, hospitality and other bills fill the teams' Excel sheets.

Sometimes teams don't even pay for the riders. Manufacturers will tie up the talent and then use the terms of agreement with their satellite squads to match names to saddles. Thanks to the technical alignment of premier class rules and cost caps, a 'satellite' team is no longer a plucky side-effort with which to develop young prospects or to use as mules for test parts. Anyone can podium from anywhere. The final top ten of the 2004 French Grand Prix at Le Mans was separated by thirty-nine seconds. In 2014 at Le Mans, it was down to twenty-three. By 2024, only thirteen seconds split the runners after twenty-seven laps. At the 2024 Aragon GP Sprint, the first five riders in the classification were from independent teams. When MotoGP integrated more controlled regulations for electronics in 2016 (single-make tyres since 2009) and then grabbed a rein on aerodynamics with tighter homologation, excessive expenditure was arrested and parity prevailed. There were five different winners in 2015. That number rose to nine the following season, dropped back to five for 2017 and, aside from Márquez's tour de force in 2019, has provided at least seven each year since 2020.

Only twenty-two individuals can compete in MotoGP. They should be a manufacturer or company's crucial expense. In some cases, they are. Marc Márquez's premature split from HRC in the autumn of 2023, when he still had one year left on his contract, cost up to 25 million euros, depending on who you want to believe. He was the highest earner in MotoGP by far. In spring 2024, Fabio Quartararo signed for two more seasons with the struggling but proactive Yamaha factory. His years of seemingly effortless glide with the M1 from 2019 to the last Japanese title-winning term in 2021 evaporated with the Iwata firm's bit-part status on the grid from 2022. The Frenchman had been assured by Yamaha Motor Racing and Yamaha Motor Corps management that the company was ditching the brakes to return to former glories. More staff, more Japanese engineers, a quicker attitude to change, more testing – all of this transpired during 2024.

Naturally, Quartararo was also persuaded with a fat new

cheque. Uri Puigdemont, a friend I first met when he interned at Dorna Communications department and later really earned his spurs reporting on F1 for Spanish daily *El País*, broke the story of a two-year, 12 million euros agreement in April 2024. A staggering amount that many wouldn't begrudge twenty-five-year-old Quartararo. Boy, was he earning it through 2024, with at least five private tests between the already extensive calendar of races as Yamaha exploited their new freedom under the concessions rules that permit them extra time and allowances with tyres and parts to try to catch the others.

Uri has crafted a strong reputation for news-breaking exclusives in motorsport, although the lack of transparency over factors like cost and salaries in MotoGP and the small community nature of the paddock means it's not an easy task. 'It's complicated with stories like those because it's sensitive information and nobody likes to have intimate info like their salary being made public,' he told me in the Alpinestars hospitality at Misano in 2024. 'When we're talking about important numbers like those for MotoGP riders then there are extra elements, like their privacy, fiscal status and so on. I think it's also the case that salaries are indicative of status. This happened with Marc when he signed a four-year deal with Honda that was hovering around 20 to 25 million euros a season, so that's 100 million and the most important contract in the history of MotoGP. It was known by various sources and I would only write a story with information like this if the figures were accurate because I think it represents a plus for the sport.

'After Marc left Honda, Fabio Quartararo became the highest-paid rider on the grid,' he added. Bagnaia is apparently on half of that base amount, bonuses excluded, and Márquez himself went to a fraction of Fabio's rate for 2024, never mind what he used to file into the bank. 'This means other things, like the depth of Yamaha's commitment to the sport. Ducati has the bike, but neither Pecco nor Marc will earn what Fabio is at base level.'

Uri is an efficient newshound. His friendly character and almost ten years with the sport's biggest website mean he is ingrained in the paddock. The Quartararo story was just one of a glut of exclusives he'd unearthed, although he has to be careful with the figures he uncovers, due to the already mentioned lack of transparency over factors like cost and salaries in MotoGP.

'I had to be really sure, even if there is always a small window of variation with the numbers when you are talking about 10, 12, 15 million,' he explained. 'But more or less, I knew the ballpark. You get to that number by learning who Fabio's people have talked to and why, and you have to open and close a few doors to arrive to the figure.'

Just after the article was published, I was with Uri in Austin at the Grand Prix of the Americas when we bumped into Quartararo heading to the media centre. 'I was expecting … something,' Uri told me later. 'One of the fears journalists have is public denial of news. Sometimes they [riders] deny because they have to, not because they want to. I had a conversation with him and there was no denial. I said to him, "If I put you in an awkward position then I apologize." He said I hadn't, but he wanted to know the source. Of course, it's information that I could not share! I thought in the context of the renewal with Yamaha it was important to reveal he was the best paid rider on the grid. It gives credence to how much Yamaha are convinced by their future. Fabio took the gamble to stay but they had to pay for him to roll those dice. It is a big sporting and economic decision.'

I asked Uri if he thought 12 million per year was too much. He paused for a long time. 'No, I think … it's a complicated question because these are important numbers, but you have to take into account the sport and the spectacle,' he eventually replied. 'These "animals" do something very unique and specific. In Fabio's case, there were some key factors like Yamaha passing through a moment that is not their best, he has been world champion and is recognized as one of the best riders. MotoGP is growing, growing and growing. Yamaha consider him an investment. And I see no evidence against that.'

───────────

To get some expert insight on rider contracts, I cornered Wasserman Media Group's Executive Vice President of Motorsports Bob Moore to ask about the agent's side of MotoGP life. 'I know it sounds simple but, in reality, it comes down to a handful of people that want to make a deal happen and have the ability to do it from a marketing perspective. You try to get to a limit that makes everybody comfortable. You are never 100 per cent happy with every deal because you always want more but I'm sure it's the same for the other party.'

Bob's principal client is Brad Binder, as well as his brother, and the likes of Moto2 rider Aron Canet. To date, Bob is still America's last FIM Motocross world champion. The Californian was a 125cc West Supercross winner before beginning a decade of competition as a grand prix rider and won the 125cc title in 1994. The next phase of his career embraced representation, working for Wasserman and starting their business in MotoGP. He's been in and around the paddock for almost twenty years. He has at least half a dozen notable 'rivals' in MotoGP. 'Contracts can be flexible, especially in the other classes like Moto2 or Moto3,' he explained, as we sat in the air-conditioned confines of Brad

Binder's race truck office at the 2024 Austrian Grand Prix. It was dark and ordered and most of the space was taken up by the large table we were sitting across. Brad's friend and assistant Bjorn had sorted out some boots in the corner.

'MotoGP is where all the riders want to be and it's where you start making money as a rider. Until you get here, then the athletes will be OK but not making a really good wage. It can be hard to educate guys about that. Knowing the levels and knowing the numbers, it's an advantage in trying to get the best for your guys. It's my job to know what everyone else is on as well.'

Moore has moved through the end of the tobacco wave of cash, the 2000s financial crisis as well as the pandemic. I asked him how those jolts of business turbulence affected him. He grinned wryly. 'I remember when I put together my business plan in 2005 for Wasserman because I really wanted to come into MotoGP. I did all my due diligence and found out what riders were making. I won't go into specifics but a top intermediate class rider, 250s then and Moto2 now, was close to mid-seven figures. The upper end guys. That was mega. All I had to do was put together a few slides and show that we only had to get a few of these riders and one or two in MotoGP and we'd be rolling ... but then everything started going the opposite way and it made it more of a challenge! I'm really lucky to have the guys that I do right now and, from what I am seeing, I think the next five years will bring an uptick. We do so much sponsor-related analysis and data and we have never seen results like the ones that are coming out. It will take a couple of years for that to happen.'

Is that because of the Liberty Media acquisition? '100 per cent, because it is a different vision of MotoGP. I'm not saying anything negative about the series now because MotoGP has done fantastically, but these outside corporate companies have a different view of what it should look like. If you see what Formula One has done in the last six years, then it's a different game. We will never get to the level of F1, but we should not be 15–17 times less on sponsorship deals than they are. We have a really attractive programme here, very good racing, very good coverage, as long as we can get a few little things going then it will blow up, I think.'

Márquez's HRC breakaway and Jonathan Rea's similar scenario at Kawasaki in WorldSBK show that some riders will prioritize their competitive instincts over the hustle to make money during the short spell of premium contract offers they will receive in their careers. But these are two exceptional cases, the elite of the elite and financially set. More often than not, a grand prix rider's initial goal will be to earn professional status at the highest level. In other words: get paid well to race in MotoGP. The flames of ambition then start to flare when they find the right environment. They settle, find routines and compartmentalize their day-to-day requirements of the job. Then try to match that framework with dreams of sporting achievement. The compartmentalization is normally assisted by people like Bob, who not only takes care of the haggling and the opportunities but all the other aspects of their career, from residence, commercial deals and publicity to safeguarding the black and white in the PDF which means his client cannot be pushed around. I remember early in 2024 there was talk of Binder potentially being placed in Tech3 for 2025 if Márquez could be snared to race alongside Pedro Acosta. I bumped into Bob at a race and mentioned the gossip and he flashed that lopsided grin and said: 'He's a Red Bull KTM rider …'

I wondered how much Moore has to 'go into battle' for his clients. I imagined he was incredibly weary of Jerry Maguire-style references but I can only imagine how a hardball negotiation phase with the likes of Pit Beirer, Lin Jarvis, Massimo Rivola or Alberto

Puig must go. 'It's what I live for. I'm a racer at heart,' he laughed. 'I literally put myself in a "race" and I want to win for my guy. I try to be as pleasant and professional as possible but sometimes there are deals that just won't work and there are others that will. I'm "yes" or "no", and I'm happy to say no, while I've also heard thousands of them! If I get to a certain level and I feel I can achieve it then I've won. I'm winning for my guy and I really love that part of the job, but the contract side of the business is perhaps 10 per cent of the work because you only get a short amount of time to go in and negotiate. Once you get to these key owners, management or bosses then it can be a short and sweet conversation.'

Managing expectations must be part of the gig. If Binder wants 'X' but KTM are offering 'Y' then where does that leave Moore? 'Fortunately, I have the best guys now and I am able to say to them, "You won't get that [amount]." I can ask for whatever they want. And if they are set on an amount that won't work then I can easily say to them, "It'll be a 'no'." There are always things, such as if a certain company really wants a rider because of a nationality or because he's a team player or a hard worker or whatever, you can always milk that … but there is a point where you will get a "no".

Maybe the rider then thinks he can get his fortune by using another mediator? 'Hey, I've accepted that,' he said, holding his hands up. 'I look at myself as someone who is here to help, here to work for someone else. I'm no different to a gardener: if I'm not cutting your grass well, tidying the yard and doing a good job then fire me. That's why I have the easiest contract in this paddock: if Brad walked in here and said, "Ciao, Bob, adios" then thirty days and I'm done. It keeps me on my toes.'

One area of curiosity is a rider's social media activity. On the track, only one of twenty-two can be champion and not many will win a series of grand prix races. So how valuable is their 'presence' away from the motorcycle? There is a slight undercurrent to the subject because Binder's ruthless commitment to racing means he is not the best at this part of the job. It's simply not a priority for him. But should it be?

'OK, it depends on how fast the rider is,' Moore underlined. 'Every case is different. Some are much better at social media and that does have value. We have guys [on the WMG books] that you might not have heard of [for results] but they make fifty or sixty grand a month on their social media. They are rolling. They could never get that on the racing side. It's all about the individual and the character. We have a really good structure around our company that is educational, and we give these guys everything they need from top to bottom. I never force them to do this or that, but I do tell them that they are leaving money on the table if they don't do something. It's up to them, but if you educate them and give them the tools then some go crazy and take off and are very successful at it. At the end of the day, everyone is looking out for that next winner and someone who can go out and be on that top step.

'You have to understand the character of the person, right?' I sensed he was alluding more towards Brad here, or at least riders that neglect the presentation side of the job. 'You cannot force something that is not there. You cannot say to someone like Raul Fernandez, "Become the next Travis Pastrana." Everyone will know it's not real. I give Liberty Media a lot of credit for allowing F1 drivers to have access and use content and that has allowed it to blow up. If they do the same thing here, then it will work because there are some awesome characters in this paddock. There needs to be more stories than just, "Here's the next Spanish kid coming into MotoGP" or "Here is the next Marc Márquez". There are more stories out there and they need to be told.'

Moore's remit is to facilitate sponsorship. As one of the few Americans in grand prix, he was a connection point for Monster Energy. He also has some views on the commercial position of MotoGP. 'I've been fortunate to have been sat across from a lot of big companies, names you will easily have heard of, and our sport just … isn't there yet, in their opinion. Will it be? I'm hopeful. Though it's frustrating because you see it all here and you think, "You don't even have to spend half of what you might in Formula One, spend a tenth!" and they would kill it.

'There is an unbelievable tool here. I see the value and I said the same thing to the head of Monster Energy before they were even here. I said, "Marc [Hall], I have a sport that is five times the size of supercross and motocross and there's only one brand here: you gotta come." I was lucky enough to bring him to Mugello, got him on the back of the scooter and we drove around. He said, "Who's that number 46 guy? That's the guy we need." I said, "Yes! I know! Let's go." Once these guys get here and see it then it's different. The CEO of one of Brad's big partners in South Africa, the Checkers Group, came to Austria and it's so nice when you can get him in the garage and around the track, to show that it's helping his company sell product.

'I brought Microsoft to several races because they were a client with Wasserman,' he said. 'This was before the system was installed for the track limits and it would have been a perfect fit for their software, but I didn't know at the time that Dorna were already working with some universities. You must give these companies something to do in the sport. Amazon came in with their AWS [cloud solutions] and they are making a lot of money on it, but they are also advertising and spending a lot of money. You have to give back to a company like that. It's tough because those deals where you say, "I'll put your logo here and provide a few passes and you'll give me ten million" have gone. You have to integrate everything – athletes, social media and there has to be a charitable component in there and other factors. Otherwise, a proposal isn't worth it.'

———————

A greater American presence might have been part of Yamaha's conviction for the weighty Quartararo deal. The team's title sponsor, Monster Energy, has spread into the MotoGP 'room' like the sweet aroma of one of their drinks. The Californians first placed that big green claw into AMA Supercross and cherry-picked certain athletes. With the establishment of their European base towards the end of the 2000s, they started to think more globally. Of all the companies that have entered MotoGP this century, few have invested as largely and as quickly.

'When I came along, I think we had a much smaller presence in MotoGP because we were a much smaller company.' This was Mitch Covington, Senior VP of sports marketing and the man behind some of the big associations Monster have created with the likes of NASCAR, F1, UFC and more. I've known Mitch for more than ten years. His son, Thomas, moved from amateur motocross in the US to MXGP, winning several MX2 grands prix and finishing fourth in the 2017 world championship, and I was always quite impressed that Mitch could wear two hats so well when he was in the MXGP paddock. When he watched Tom race, he'd also cast an eye on MXGP and a series that Monster have title-sponsored since 2010. Mitch was by no means a traditional 'motocross dad' and to see him frequently enjoying the sport in a semi-professional capacity and being overjoyed when Thomas did well was one of the more heartwarming stories. Covington junior was Monster-backed, naturally, but his career had genuine promise while he lived in Belgium and raced for Jacky Martens' renowned team, putting to bed murmurs of nepotism. His best season came while he was a Rockstar Husqvarna athlete.

Mitch is connected for a call from an office set-up in his garage at his home in Florida. We had bumped into each other on the grid at the 2024 Catalan Grand Prix, a Monster signature event since 2014, but he was speaking to me while I was at Misano and it looked like there was a rack of fishing equipment behind him as he explained some of the Monster and MotoGP story and how energy drinks, namely his company and main rival Red Bull (both brands are close for sales in North America and shift three times more than the next nearest product), came to fill some of the void left by the smouldering butt of tobacco money.

'I think MotoGP registered with Rodney [Sacks], the CEO, near the end of the decade and it became recognized as the face of our brand outside North America because of the reach and the exposure and then because of the culture. It fit our brand better than any other sport on a global basis. Even though it wasn't as big in North America, we could cover North America with other sports,' he said of the catch.

Monster is distributed in more than 140 countries and also creeps into the music industry, video games, music festivals and mainstream youth culture thanks to the clever branding (they barely advertise), licensing and presence of an alternative image. 'MotoGP is aggressive and more blue collar than Formula One. The sport fits the demographic and who we are as a brand much more than F1.'

They logged 6.3 billion dollars of net sales in 2022 and have recorded thirty-one consecutive years of increasing sales. Monster is a *monster*, and this rate of growth was reflected in their MotoGP spread. And by reeling in one racer in particular. 'Monster signing Valentino Rossi had a huge impact on our company and opened our eyes for the potential of MotoGP because he transcended the sport so well,' Mitch said. 'He became a key ambassador right away and also taught us the value of those kinds of athletes. We've done deals in other sports, like with Tiger Woods. We're not into golf but he's the greatest of all time, like Valentino in racing. Signing Valentino was a milestone in the company.'

Rossi and Lewis Hamilton were the only racing stars to have had their own drink flavour. Rossi's 'The Doctor' beverage had a citrusy and fruity tang and was released in 2014. Monster backed Rossi's VR46 Academy and then looked even wider. 'Having races and the naming rights was just an evolution of our company growing and being in a position to do that,' Covington said. 'We always started out in a sport with an athlete or some athletes, and if they performed well and we thought the sport was growing then we tried to get a team. As the company expanded, we were able to afford that. It was a big moment for us when we could sign Pro Circuit in Supercross and we elevated to title sponsorship of the series. It was the same in MotoGP. We could start with Valentino and others with helmet deals and finally we could have a team, even if it was not as a title. Then it was a whole team and then a whole race where we could do key promotional activities: you cannot really do it on a big scale unless you have entitlement. It's something we're known for now.'

'Owning' a grand prix can cost several million euros and comes with all the branding, activation and passes and access and customization of a large section of the VIP village structure. MotoGP is beamed live to more than 200 countries, spreading to almost the entire world. There are more than 110 media partners and in 2023, the sport produced over 50,000 hours of footage.

There is also an official community of 120 million followers on social media channels. Monster dabbled with the French and Czech grands prix and have since settled on Catalan and British rounds for the last few years. In 2023, that meant reach to almost 300,000 at both races. MotoGP counted nearly 3 million people through circuit gates in total in that year.

'It's been successful in several ways,' Mitch outlined. 'One is with our retail partners. We can bring a high-end VIP retail partner to races and they are hopefully blown away by our presence. We give them what we call the "campfire" experience, where they get to watch the race at the closest quarters and with the hospitality. It's a huge opportunity to entertain our trade guests. From that standpoint, it's been really good. From an exposure standpoint, you cannot watch the race without seeing our logos everywhere, so it really ties us to the sport, even in the eyes of a casual fan. Just seeing fifteen minutes of one of our grands prix on TV will make you feel that Monster is really into the sport.'

Conversely, Red Bull have been part of MotoGP since their days backing Peter Clifford's WCM Yamaha team at the end of the 1990s and into the millennium. They dallied with HRC and Márquez and have been KTM's singular badge since Moto3 impact in 2012. Events-wise, the US grand prix from Laguna Seca in 2005 bore that bright red, blue and white livery. They now vie with Monster and brands like Oakley, GoPro and Qatar Airways as the main non-motorcycling industry sponsors.

'We've invested hugely in MotoGP and we think that's a good thing, to race against our competitors,' Covington said. 'We built the company on racing, music and girls and it kinda hits all of those. It is a young, cool demographic.'

My fifteen-year-old could feel the vibe at the 2024 Catalan Grand Prix. He travelled from our home in the centre of Barcelona on the train with two friends to Granollers and made the short walk to the track. Jordi has been to MotoGP before but by entering the paddock with me and he hadn't sampled the event as a fan. He also loves MXGP and taking photos trackside, but his excitement with mates at the Circuit de Barcelona-Catalunya was noticeably animated from a placid, discreet boy. On a sidenote, his older brother by two years, Alex, preferred to do interviews and text. In 2018, I asked Cal Crutchlow if he'd give him ten minutes while in the Catalan paddock. Alex was twelve. It was to be expected that Cal would claim Alex's questions were better than mine. Perhaps there has been no better piss-taker on the MotoGP grid. When Alex's final poser was 'Do you like crepes?' and Cal answered '… now you have ruined me.' I saw a flash of alarm on the poor kid's face. Cal does like his snacks. He said that he'd have to go back to the motorhome for a scoff. Gotta love kids, and the big ones too.

I'll admit that there is a hint of bias when I say the Catalan Grand Prix is one of my favourite races of the year. It is a small annual joy to be able to work at a round of MotoGP and still sleep in my own bed. But I think the race has other merits. The gem that is Barcelona is twenty minutes down the motorway. Food, beach, nightlife, flights. The weather is usually great. The atmosphere is lively and the venue busy. The layout itself has a wide mix of corners, even if the riders deplore the eternally slick asphalt, which is a consequence of the locally mined stone and the hard resurfacing necessary to deal with all the events and track days the facility accommodates. There have been very tough sporting moments, like the Salom crash that brought an alteration to the track momentarily with a pithy but necessary chicane, and some unforgettable ones, such as the Rossi–Lorenzo last lap spat in

2009 – one of the best final corner moves in recent memory, although both Andrea Dovizioso's and Alex Rins' muggings of Marc Márquez in 2019 at Austria and Silverstone have to rank high.

Aside from being Dorna's home race, at least for their operational HQ, Catalunya is one of MotoGP's prevalent and persistent sites. In 2024, it was the host for the thirty-third consecutive time since opening in 1992, after the Generalitat (Catalan government) decided that the region needed an established motorsports home due to the obsoletion of the public road course of Montjuic Parc in the centre of Barcelona.

'The Circuit de Barcelona-Catalunya is run as a public company with the Generalitat holding a percentage and then other partners like RACC [the Catalan AA] and the local council of Montmelo implied. Around 85 per cent is public funded. Moving structures like this has its difficulties and requires a passage of steps that can also be slower,' explained Circuit Director Josep Lluis Santamaria, in place since 2020 and who has to silence his phone when we first started talking through a Zoom call during the 2024 24-hour race, a screaming F1 car noise alerting him of a message.

The circuit has benefited from a 30-million-euro cash injection up until 2024 for improvement of the installation. This includes even more of a push to sustainability ('I think we're at a level with the best in Europe,' he says. 'The Middle East is another step. We've made upgrades and now have a very sustainable site. In 2008, we were the first circuit with the ISO 1400 certificate and we have more than six thousand square metres of solar panels'). The circuit has to rely on the support of politicians and their agendas to make grands prix work.

'It's like starting a new school! With new schoolmates or

new teachers and the processes must be explained,' Santamaria joked, regarding the changing landscape and Catalunya's active preoccupation for political activity. 'We have the advantage that we know the sector very well but we still have to explain it all to politicians. For example, this installation is the biggest sport facility in Catalunya, and we can say in all of Spain also because of the capacity for more than 125,000 people.'

While I didn't expect figures to be forthcoming, I pushed him a little further on the breakdown of prices and why a motorsport circuit has political significance. 'There is the set-up cost and then the operating costs of a grand prix, the latter being doctors, marshals, officials, workers, hospitality staff, car park personnel. We have income from ticket sales, hospitality and from companies that come to the grand prix but there are also benefits for the region with people filling hotels, restaurants, using gas stations, supermarkets and so on. This does not really bring anything directly to the circuit but has its own importance. For a period [each year], the circuit generates an impact of around 400 million euros and from this economic generation around sixty are taxes recovered by the local and central government. When we talk about the government paying most of the fees, they recover it afterwards, also through tourism in Barcelona and the surrounding areas. They are big numbers, and if you only look at it through the earnings and losses of the circuit then it has losses ... but, overall, the circuit brings a lot of money to the whole territory.'

Character, culture and logistics mean that Catalunya is very much a home fixture for the power brokers in MotoGP (although you could also count COTA as well, if Liberty Media enter with intent) but the local venue doesn't get preferential treatment. 'Even though there is a Catalan "base" to Dorna that still doesn't mean it's easy!' Santamaria smiled. 'Of course, we have good and strong communication, but the standards [for MotoGP] apply to all circuits. It's quite a regular contract and, compared to other motorsports, quite simple, but then there are clear demands with subjects of security, the paddock, general organization, hospitality space.'

The Circuit de Barcelona-Catalunya is one of six tracks that MotoGP shares with Formula One (at least in the 2024 schedule), which means both FIM and FIA (Fédération Internationale de l'Automobile) inspections and feedback for modifications. They also have a sliding scale for the budget. 'The prices are different,' Santamaria understated. 'Higher in Formula One. The public habits for each race are different too. MotoGP sees a lot of hotel users and campers and people visiting from southern Europe, while F1 has more non-European spectators, more high-end hotels and for longer stays. A general package of travel, hotel, tickets and costs for F1 can be around 1,500 euros. For MotoGP, it is half that. We have a lot of Dutch, British and French for F1: mainly because France doesn't have a GP and the Brits tell us it's cheaper to get a plane and hotel to watch here than go to Silverstone. MotoGP is more from Spain and France. We've noticed a surge in F1 in the last few years and that has also helped MotoGP.'

For the Catalan Grand Prix to happen, teams have to inch their immaculate half-a-million-euro trucks into the paddock. Of the eleven teams in MotoGP, six are 'independent' and, at the time of writing, have signed two five-year deals with Dorna that ensures their presence on the grid and as part of the championship. Administered by IRTA, Dorna supply the teams with financial and logistic support (sometimes surplus backing for a particular rider, as was the case with Joe Roberts and the Trackhouse Racing saga in 2024). Dorna also gatekeep. Any new brand, such as, say, BMW, will have to buy into one of the existing teams, unless one of them bows out, and the next contract window expires at the end of 2026.

One of the oldest on the grid is Lucio Cecchinello Racing. The former 125cc rider founded his own operation in 1996, one year ahead of fellow countryman and competitor Fausto Gresini. Lucio's second season in the 125s as a racer was Fausto's last. Gresini set up shop and is based in Faenza, near Imola, and a few miles away from the old motocross grand prix track, which has now been bought and renovated by Andrea Dovizioso. LCR is split between San Marino and Cecchinello's base in Monaco.

The squad with the longest history in the premier class belongs to current IRTA President Herve Poncharal, whose Tech3 Racing competed with leased Yamahas from 2001 until their transfer to KTM in 2019. Gresini jumped into MotoGP with Honda in 2002 and adopted Aprilia factory status for seven seasons before returning to independent roots with Ducati from 2022.

LCR went 'up' from 125 and 250 success in 2006, most notably as a single-rider effort and with the outrageous potential of an Australian rookie called Casey Stoner in the Honda saddle. To this day, Cecchinello has maintained ties with Honda and since 2015 has kept a strong identity with sponsors like Castrol and Givi.

In the paddock, LCR has one of the tallest, brightest and friendliest hospitality set-ups. I did an interview with the diminutive Italian during the team's pomp when Cal Crutchlow was winning grands prix (2016 was the team's best season to date with two victories and four podiums) and asked him about the expense and necessity of splashing out on corporate entertainment. He told me a story of how a businessman had walked into the unit, liked what he saw, asked for a meeting and became a substantial sponsor. 'You never know what will come through the door,' Lucio said, both baffled and amused at the rhyme and reason of running a race team.

LCR have always tried to be a bit different. Their rider signings were a little 'leftfield' – all the way from the punt with Stoner to Randy De Puniet, Stefan Bradl, Crutchlow after he had bailed on Ducati after one season, Toni Elias for one year, Alex Rins, and Honda appeasement with Taka Nakagami and Álex Márquez. They ran their own glossy magazine, would introduce one-race title sponsors, like *Playboy*, invited guests onto a special viewing platform in the pitbox and would try to do something alternative with the image of the squad. In 2022, I spent a day in a tatty former factory workspace in the centre of Barcelona hosting and filming the team presentation video, interviewing Márquez and Nakagami as they walked around the gallery room and spoke about a number of photographic prints of themselves growing up that were perched around the space on easels. It was a cool concept.

Accelerating to 2024 and speaking again with Lucio, the malaise of Honda's competitiveness had darkened the mood. The quest for results had been replaced by the grind of laps and constant testing-while-racing.

'I feel very lucky because despite experiencing a very difficult moment, the passion is still there. It's the same,' he almost sighed. 'And the excitement to come to the races, to work with my team, my riders, follow the sessions, follow the races and to try to improve. However, I don't need to hide from you that it is a bit frustrating, especially when you are permanently at the bottom of the ranking. I feel that we have made improvements though and that is important for everybody's motivation.'

Ducati are the principal force in MotoGP because they convinced independent teams like Rossi's VR46 and Gresini to field their machinery and riders and doubled the cast of their net of data beyond the factory squad and long-term satellite Pramac – up until 2025 anyway, when Yamaha will regain some of the pie by acquiring Pramac, and will hopefully learn from the indifference they tended to show to Tech3 in the past and then lost the French team to Austria.

LCR get copious support from Honda as the sole line-up outside of the official HRC tree, but they still need sponsorship to survive and that means results and exposure. Wouldn't that be easier with a different brand? Cecchinello seemed to read my thoughts as we spoke.

'I feel that Honda is seriously committed and concerned about the situation,' he said, managing not to simply sound like he was toeing a party line. 'They have made so many compromises since August 2023. They have dramatically improved their commitment to MotoGP with more manpower and more engineers and much more budget on the development side. Difficult to say a number but this has never happened in the past. OK, it's thanks also to the concessions ... but Honda never changed the engines two to three times in a season. Honda have never produced so many aero packages or brought so many Japanese staff to the track. They are seriously looking to take engineers from other teams. They are doubling their testing programme. I feel relieved. I am sure with this mentality we can catch our competitors. It is difficult to see when, but this is the organization to do it.'

Still, LCR have felt the repercussions of the drop. 'In truth, we lost four sponsors from 2023,' Cecchinello admitted. 'But on the other hand, we tried to carry on our programme and were very pleased to reach an agreement with Castrol to take on title sponsorship for 90 per cent of the season. Yes, a lack of results is very bad for sponsorship motivation and some that needed visibility decided to leave, but there are some that are involved in the motorcycle accessory business and the fact that Honda is the biggest motorcycle manufacturer in the world in terms of sales represents a big asset for us as LCR. For companies like Castrol and Givi to be associated with Honda … the name is important. You have to consider that Honda sells around 20 million two-wheel units and this means they can count on a couple of hundred million Honda users. To have a Givi or Castrol logo as part of that, even just a very small percentage, is marketing. It's an asset and that's a form of leverage that we use a lot to convince the sponsors. We say: "Your brand is part of the Honda racing programme," and Honda themselves make a lot of publicity around the world about their racing. And LCR is part of that. It is a big promotion that influences the customers. This helps us but we need to improve our results and when that happens, it will be even better.'

Cecchinello counts on a steady flow from motorcycle industry companies. This has undoubtedly given the team its backbone. He was one of many inside the paddock who watched the Liberty Media news with interest. 'What is missing at the moment in MotoGP are the blue-chip companies,' he said. 'The big companies and corporations. Those of high tech and communications. The Fortune 500s. Most of them are from America and I think Liberty have a lot of knowledge and access; they know how to promote, how to leverage and how to enhance MotoGP. The series has incredible assets: it is extremely spectacular and extremely visual and exciting. Especially lately with the Sprint races and the introduction of the technical rules that help every team to be competitive. The ranking is squashed and that means we can have a lot of winners and a lot of battles.'

There was some truth but also some wishful thinking from Lucio here. Ducati riders have profited but only Rins in LCR colours, Aleix Espargaró and Maverick Viñales have won for other brands since the start of 2023. In the opening phase of 2023, the levelling-up of MotoGP was a sizeable talking point. I spoke to Espargaró about it in Jerez and we debated whether the lack of clear superiority in MotoGP might be disorientating for new fans or the unpredictability of who might win every grand prix was a dream scenario. 'It's difficult and there aren't just one or two riders who are a lot better than the rest anymore and who can make the difference every single week in any conditions,' he reasoned. 'Now it is a lot more open, but it depends on the character of the person when it comes to rivalries. Sometimes it seems like people want one hero but when you look back to when Valentino or [Jorge] Lorenzo was dominating, then the races were not fun. This is my point of view.' As if to prove that motorsport can flip on an axis, the Bagnaia/Martin dynamic then began to play out, with Márquez toiling in the wings and other manufacturers treading water and trying to work out the boundaries of the race rubber.

'Dorna have done an incredible job to make the sport so spectacular and to make it very interesting in many factors. With Liberty, I think we can make another step forwards,' Lucio said. Interestingly, he believes MotoGP's efforts with sustainability with non-fossil-based fuel and recyclable material in the Michelin tyres could be a route of attraction.

'We need to focus even more to develop technical rules in line with where the world is obliging us to go, in terms of being greener, being safer. Yes, we are going to race with sustainable fuel, which is a very good plus, and soon I would love that we race with recycled lubricants and wish we are going to race with tyres with more than 50 per cent recycled material. I wish we would have a mandatory amount of parts on the bike that have come from recycled material. These are things that can be very beneficial for technology because we can develop it and then deliver these greener materials to production and society. By doing that, we can enhance the perception of MotoGP and show that we are not just crazy, brave, wild people on motorcycles who don't have respect for their own lives.'

In 2024, Formula One managed twenty-four grands prix. MotoGP could be edging the same way to keep the sport relevant and in people's 'feeds' all year round. F1 has many more resources. The entire LCR Honda crew would be a mere section of a car racing counterpart. Lucio might need to find more people and more investors to meet the demands of a longer series. 'I think MotoGP is ten years behind F1 but I think we are following them,' he opined. 'Why are we ten years behind? The business and turnover and the economic interest in our industry is much lower. That's the reality. We cannot compare the motorcycle industry with the car industry. Dorna, of course, is looking to listen to every promoter and I will not be surprised if we very soon have twenty-two races and then even more. In that case, we should maybe reduce the tests; if not, then we should start to have a second team. The people who work around the team, it is very hard for them to keep this kind of pace. Then again, I think most of the people who work in the paddock are driven by passion and that is like a powerful internal combustion engine itself. People might complain but they still come back.'

Or others want to get in.

Trackhouse, the NASCAR team located in North Carolina, is owned and run by former race car driver Justin Marks and Armando Christian Pérez, also known as the rapper Pitbull. Marks visited Red Bull Ring in the summer of 2023 on a reconnaissance mission for possible expansion and entry to MotoGP. The collapse of the RNF Aprilia Racing team at the end of 2023 opened a gap; Marks had a route into the sport cleared by Dorna, and quickly stepped in. Trackhouse were on the grid for 2024 and retained most of the RNF staff roster but still had to reorganize and establish their own framework for how the team would be, what it represents, the budgeting and logistics. All within a two-month period. So, 2024 wasn't so much an exercise in getting their feet damp but trying to stop the waves washing overhead while bobbing optimistically in the middle of the Atlantic.

They managed to hustle to be ready for a team launch in Los Angeles. I bumped into Miguel Oliveira in the hotel gym and spoke to Raul Fernandez in the reception area of the accommodation just off Sunset Boulevard. Then-team manager, the affable and always approachable Wilco Zeelenberg, did an interview for the *Paddock Pass Podcast*. After driving back from Anaheim, the team's hard-working PR crew of Jeremy Appleton and Maria Pohlmann had lined up Justin for a slot, shortly before the bikes in question were unveiled in the rooftop bar with some notable American VIP guests, CEOs of companies and ex-riders like Kevin Schwantz, Wayne Rainey and John Kocinski in attendance. And, ironically, Joe Roberts.

Ignoring some of the noisier guests in reception, Justin had the time and mental space to talk to me about MotoGP. Now here was a real grand prix rookie. He had created Trackhouse in 2019 after twenty years racing and another two building a business plan. 'We were going to create something in motorsports that was different. Something that was brand-centric, and we could be exciting storytellers and engage with the fans in ways that teams and brands had not done yet,' he recounted. Following success off the bat, with the team almost winning NASCAR in their first year, the forty-three-year-old was 'thinking about how to scale Trackhouse into a truly global brand and to find exciting motorsports opportunities around the world that are compelling and where we can put our personal touch.

'I went to the MotoGP race at Red Bull Ring just to see what it was all about, how they engage with fans, how the teams operate, and I started asking a lot of business questions: how do the economics work? How do the independent teams work? What's the global reach? What's the cost to compete? I immediately recognized that there was a massive opportunity for Trackhouse.

'I got to the point where I wanted to talk to MotoGP about what it would look like if a company like ours jumped into the championship, and originally my plan was to enter in 2025 and spend a year learning the sport, planning, going to races and understanding the value proposition for sponsorships. But, due to some circumstances on the grid, there was an opportunity for 2024 and that was pretty much the only time the door would swing open. It was really a "ready, fire, aim!" situation for us. I just decided to go for it and we've had to figure out how to build a MotoGP team in the space of four months.'

Marks is not just a businessman and an entrepreneur (although the impending Liberty Media deal during 2024 meant that it was a very shrewd time to become an American team owner in MotoGP) but is also moved by motorsports. Team Principal Davide Brivio would describe Trackhouse to me as a 'racing company' and Marks was enamoured when he got up close and identified elements of the appeal that hooks millions of others. 'People want to see other humans doing things that they cannot do,' he said. 'NASCAR is some of the most competitive, if not the most competitive, racing in the world and what they do is incredible on these high-banked ovals at 200mph pushing each other. It's a spectacle. But watching these riders banging elbows and come off corners and manipulate body weight and make saves when they lose grip is an incredible thing to watch and something that fans connect deeply with.'

Trackhouse absorbed the RNF headcount and was already relying on European staff to marshal a unit that exists on a different continent and in a different time zone. When it comes to setting, managing and hauling a motorsport team, Marks and his committee are well-versed with the drains and the intricacies of being on the road, even if it is just between a couple of borders.

'NASCAR is such a machine because we have thirty-eight races in forty-two weeks. It is such a logistical lift. We have full teams of people that never leave the shop and full teams of people on the road,' he explained. 'We have fifteen sponsors that all have different deliverables and needs and different ways they are using the company to promote their goods and services. In MotoGP, we have fewer than thirty people and in the NASCAR team we have 170 and each team has two vehicles on the racetrack. MotoGP is so international and is going around the world, so you have to be very efficient with staffing and how you do the whole exercise. But in NASCAR, with simulation and engineering and machining and fabrication, it is truly an army of people. At the end of the day, it's racing, like anything else, but one weekend we'll be in Georgia and then in California the next, then New York, then Florida and everybody comes back to the shop between every single race. It's very, very demanding. MotoGP is the same but they also have it very dialled with how they manage their international logistics and packing. One of the big differences is the work that happens on the bikes takes place at the track – it's where they are serviced and rebuilt. There isn't too much of a workshop culture. At Trackhouse, every Tuesday and Wednesday, all 170 people are in the race shop and turning the cars around and re-loading, prepping cars for two weeks later, filling trucks that do tens of thousands of miles every year. I've been doing it now for three years and I am no less impressed than on the first day.'

The enthusiasm for MotoGP is not a novel subject. Excited anticipation is common through all the teams pre-season. Expectations strained at the limits of realism. But Marks' emotions are coming from an earnest and uninitiated source. He is playing MotoGP 'Fantasy', even if the odds are daunting for the inaugural attempt. As with every new toy, there is always a risk that boredom or distraction sets in. How long will Trackhouse be around for? How serious are their intentions? 'It is vitally important that Dorna supports the independent teams in the way they do,' he said, both as a plea but also a gesture of gratitude. 'It's an expensive endeavour and it's a difficult sponsorship landscape. Dorna have been great about being patient with me and supporting me. I think we are important to them, but I also think they are big believers in their product and they see the value of factory teams and healthy independent teams.'

Red Bull Ring, 2024. Seven months after our last conversation and Justin was in Austria again. I wanted a catch-up perspective. Quite a bit had happened. Brivio, the man who brought Rossi to Yamaha, managed his affairs, reinstalled Suzuki as grand prix winners and worked for three years in several roles with the Alpine F1 team, has been fixed as team principal. 'I try to explain what I think, what I see, how it is,' the Italian offered. 'Maybe "educate" is a strong word but, of course, we get many questions about MotoGP from the US. We try to explain everything and that's why it is a learning year for Trackhouse as an organization.'

Aprilia have provided Oliveira and then Fernandez with 2024 spec motorcycles. The highlight of a fairly barren passage was the Portuguese's runner-up finish in the German Grand Prix Sprint. Trackhouse was then at the centre of a month-long turbine of speculation that Joe Roberts, having a strong term in Moto2, would be their ideal rider recruitment for 2025, with Oliveira tempted by the new Pramac proposition with Yamaha. Jack Miller's deal was also closing at KTM and the Australian was seen as another racer that provided an ideal choice for Trackhouse in terms of PR and experience for Aprilia.

Raul Fernandez was buoyant about his chances of another two-year Aprilia deal while speaking with us at the Catalan Grand Prix at the end of May. It was still surprising that the first rider 'reveal' by Trackhouse was a re-up with the Spaniard who smashed Moto2 in 2021 but had failed to follow up that potential since, and his crash at the 2024 Sepang shakedown that caused him to miss the rest of the test with injury was looked upon as a rash and foolish mistake.

'He's very hungry,' Zeelenberg rationalized to me at Aragon later in the summer of 2024.

'Aren't they all?' I replied.

'Yes … but some go further than others,' he said. 'If we talk about a rider who is hungry then we look at Marc Márquez. He is always trying the maximum and challenging himself and the limits. Not everybody can do that in MotoGP. You can injure yourself very easily with these bikes, so you have to be very strong. Raul is eager to perform and go over the limit.'

The Roberts link dragged on while pressure was closing on Brivio's head from Dorna and TV broadcasters, and even commercial temptation with rumours that the American would bring in extra sponsorship. Roberts was riding well, with an outside shot of the Moto2 championship, and is good looking and marketable. Trackhouse then plumped for quietly spoken Japanese Ai Ogura – a decision that made sporting sense as the former Asian Talent Cup star was one of the best riders in Moto2, but from a PR standpoint it confused many. Trackhouse had wanted to be an alternative, visible and accessible race team, but seemed to have done a 180 when it came to rider selections that would have enforced that view and ensured people would have spoken about their representatives whether they were winning or not. Fernandez and Ogura, both twenty-four for 2025 (Ogura being three years younger than Roberts), were a duo that screamed 'potential' but, unfairly or not, would struggle to generate column inches without some serious work on the presentation side.

The signature of a rookie was also a quandary for Aprilia who were losing Espargaró, Oliveira and Maverick Viñales, and badly needed mileage or continuity for the motorcycle.

'They need a year or two,' Zeelenberg admitted to me. I couldn't help but feel that Ogura, backed by Honda his whole career and the most obvious replacement for the ageing Nakagami, might be back in his HRC-supported confines by the time his two-year Trackhouse contract ends and once the company were back in the hunt for results. 'Pedro [Acosta] was outperforming in the beginning,' Wilco said by way of justification. 'I thought it was not possible in this championship any more to do that and of course he crashed a couple of times and lost some performance. Those finishes outside the top ten lately have been more "normal". This championship is very hard at the moment. Everybody's pushing.'

Brivio was in demand for his media debrief at the Red Bull Ring, hours after the news had been made public. 'We decided to go in a different direction. To go for a young talent, to start a new project,' he explained on Ogura. The second question was immediately about Roberts. 'We considered him, and then we made some evaluations, more from the potential sporting performance point of view. [Is it] right or wrong? I will tell you in a couple of years whether it was the right or wrong decision. But as I said before, you have to take a decision. So, we made our analysis, and we decided that Ai was a better choice for our project. Regardless of the passport, let's say.

'We always talk very closely with Aprilia, and they were aware, but, at the end, to be honest, this has been more our choice than Aprilia's choice,' he continued. Brivio admitted there had been peer pressure over one of the few free MotoGP saddles on the grid and for a team with a lot of topical spotlight but felt that 'if you look from Dorna's perspective, they should have some reason to be happy because an Asia Talent Cup rider finally joined MotoGP.'

Trackhouse were the main talking point at the Red Bull Ring. One person at Dorna said to me that the team were not flavour of the month in the promoter's paddock offices. Meanwhile, in the dark Trackhouse hospitality, Justin Marks was feeling jetlagged, and our second meeting was slated on the basis of the cordial understanding that he wouldn't be grilled about Ogura. Instead, I was chasing any discernible differences in his sentiments about MotoGP through the (at times) bumpy baptism and the looming veil of Liberty, whose arrival had been in the final throes of the confidential paper shuffle when Trackhouse was laying out the burgers in LA.

'While racing is racing in a lot of ways, there is also incredible nuance to motorcycle racing at this level and we're learning that,' he said looking athletic, lightly bearded, youthful, cap in place. 'At NASCAR races, there is a lot of people asking about it; either just general interest or from a technical point of view, like brake suppliers in the US asking about the bikes. I also get asked about the experience for fans and the hospitality experience. There is a lot that's different over here.'

Over half a year on from the LA launch and Trackhouse still don't have a title sponsor, but the team is making baby steps and Marks' tone of voice seemed to indicate that the set-up could soon be running. 'We've been on an awareness building campaign,' he claimed. 'MotoGP is primed for big sponsors to come in from industries that are not in the sport right now. It's so compelling. Big consumer brands belong here. We're educating some big brands that we have on the NASCAR side and we're saying to them, "There's this amazing global property over here." We weren't able to go to market for this season because everything was so late, so we've been using the time to introduce our eco-system to MotoGP and those who don't have exposure to it yet.'

In the fifteen-minute talk, we didn't mention the riders, but at the Red Bull Ring there was a large (helmeted) elephant in the corner of the hospitality. 'It's not just them, it's the personnel we put around them and the way we work and drive Aprilia,' he alluded. 'There are a lot of puzzle pieces. What's exciting for 2025 and beyond is that we have one of the most diverse athlete rosters in the industry. In the company, we have racers that represent Mexico, the US, New Zealand, Spain and Japan. I love that, and we want to tell the story. That's the strategy in NASCAR and it's the strategy in MotoGP.'

The final feedback was bullish. 'I am trying to take the long view on this, the three-, five- and ten-year view, and to make decisions and manage the operation this year for the long-term. It has been an incredible experience and I remain as passionate and excited about it today as when I first came here, maybe even more so. I think we have a great future in the sport.'

Marks selected Brivio as the conductor for his orchestra. The sixty-year-old has decent history with developing young riders: Viñales, Rins and Joan Mir all converted from debutants to MotoGP winners under his watch at Suzuki. His acumen for establishing a winning culture at teams is also prominent.

Brivio did not start 2024 in Trackhouse. He was a late conscript for a mission that was already tight for time. 'One of the first problems we had was not so related to the sport but the general organization. For instance: the hospitality. When I arrived it was in Qatar, 19 February, and we didn't have a plan for hospitality yet because there was an idea to bring a unit that would have been too small. We were not organized with catering. I thought, "We cannot go to our first MotoGP race unorganized." You need a proper hospitality. We found some solutions that we thought were reasonable but at a good level. Of course, it can be much better but you can imagine that it is not a 10 or 20,000-dollar budget! I ended up explaining my point of view and what was necessary for MotoGP, and very quickly we took a decision to go for it. This was very good for me because they trusted what I said at the time. I knew it was a very expensive thing but we really needed to go this way.

'Justin is learning more and more about MotoGP so I expect very soon he will have his own ideas. That will be great because we can have a discussion, and he doesn't only have to listen to me! Maybe we have different ideas and that's what makes the team grow up. That's how you improve.'

Davide spends a lot of time on Zoom dealing with Trackhouse's administration. Almost all of his previous experience in MotoGP meant setting the clock the other way. Moving from Japanese to American cultures must be an engrossing drift for him.

'Different world,' he said. 'But ... also hard to describe the difference. I worked with the Japanese by working with the factories. Their main job was to design, develop and build the bikes. In this, they were very good because they had a system in place. They have a very well-organized group. I felt we gave them a lot of help with management of the bikes and the logistics, the technical organization at the racetracks and where, maybe, quick decisions were needed. There was a cooperation where the Western people were taking care of logistics. Once the bike was designed and produced, it was being put into the hands of the Western group, which is what happened with Yamaha and Suzuki. Now, as an independent team, we are in a different situation. Aprilia fill the role of the Japanese with the equipment and, with Trackhouse, managing things together. And the Americans are more like Europeans in solving problems: logistics, management and business. It is not a big corporation like Yamaha or Suzuki. It is very easy going and, for instance, everybody can talk to Justin in our team. You cannot talk with the president of Suzuki or Yamaha all the time!'

Davide, who smiles easily and has always been one of the more approachable senior management figures in MotoGP, laughed: 'I'm still trying to learn!' It's easy to see why he embraced the role. 'There will come a time when we start planning the future and the first things we have to decide is our position and our target and can we make this target in terms of organization,' he said, over a month before the Ogura signing would cause ripples and float the idea that Brivio was pulling more Trackhouse strings than many think. 'The people have to buy into this and then follow the Trackhouse strategy or idea.'

MotoGP staff habitually work to two-year contracts, but burnout and turnover exists. Even supposed 'cemented' sponsors are not a 'given' in MotoGP. In 2024, Repsol trimmed their support for HRC, which resulted a bizarre black and multi-coloured livery for the Hondas. During the summer, the impending departure of the petroleum giants, who only a year before were waxing lyrical about their work with MotoGP for sustainable fuel, was confirmed and a thirty-year association, stretching back to the midst of the Doohan domination, was over. HRC have raced without a title sponsor before and could again in the future. Perhaps they have their own failure with the motorcycle to blame and the exit of a name like Repsol in the sport can be seen as a loss for the marketing and presence they bring to certain markets. On a personal note: good riddance. The arrogance or indifference of the company at the HRC team launches in Madrid was detectable. Media were made to work on the foyer floor and the coffee bar was guarded for 'guests' only. I'll fill up at Cespa instead, thanks.

The threat of the bottom line and then being able to hit targets is arguably more pronounced in Moto3. These teams run at a fraction of the budget of MotoGP but that doesn't make their year-to-year existence any easier. Moto3 is even closer than the premier class and while that can be devilishly teasing it can also be frustratingly distant. Less than half a second a lap and without the skill for towing mean mid-to-rear pack obscurity and oblivion.

This frat pack of fraternization and chaos is the home of MotoGP's only British team. MLav Racing is also one of the newest squads on the grid and was born from ex-racer and TNT Sports commentator/presenter Michael Laverty (brother to WorldSBK race winner and former MotoGP rider Eugene) feeling like he had to take action against the dearth of Brits in grands prix. There was no direct pipeline to Moto3 for native UK riders, against the endless waves of Spaniards that set the bar in the Rookies Cup and JuniorGP. Even springboards like the British Talent Cup hadn't had much bounce when it came pinging potential to the world championship.

'Weirdly, I had no great desire to run a team, but through the TV gig, I talked a lot about a lack of a British team and how that needed to be fixed,' Michael told me at the beginning of a very honest and forthright chat at Mugello 2024 and in the bowels of Alpinestars' ever-accommodating hospitality. 'Someone approached me and said: "Aren't you the person with the contacts to do that and look at the youth development side?" I'd run some tuition and instruction days for the kids that were riding at our kart track and ended up starting a minibike academy team during lockdown. I was introduced to Simon Marsh, who owned VisionTrack, and was passionate about trying to do something similar, and he stirred up the idea in my head and pushed me in the direction. From there, the initial junior team in the UK was really hard in terms of getting any funding or support, so I thought it would be easier to build it from the top down. The idea was to get a Moto3 team running, bring the funding in and make the rest to create the lower rungs of the ladder.'

Michael's description of the chronology and the methodology to enter MotoGP is like a *Dummy's Guide* to grand prix racing. It seems both quite easy but tremendously hard work: a process of mining contacts, hours of planning and fortuitous improvisation and securing costs in the space of seven days to make the 2022 grid. 'Basically, I needed 1.5 million euros if I wanted to do Moto3 for a season and Moto2 would be 2.2, but that was ballpark or baseline. I'd probably need a bit more for Moto2 and it depended if I was taking on riders' salaries or they would be development riders [placements for manufacturers]. After a few conversations, we made it happen and it was around ten days from dreaming about it to having it all coming to fruition. It was a mammoth task to get the team together for the first test in February but we got there.'

I couldn't resist asking how much a Moto3 rider would empty the bank. In 2024, Columbian/Spaniard David Alonso was clearly the benchmark. 'You could get a potential top-five runner for under 100,000 euros,' Michael said. 'You will get some fast riders that come to you and say: "I have 2–300,000 of sponsorship with me," and that's a win-win. If they are fast and come with money, then that's the dream: 50,000 would get you a good rider, 100,000 a top rider. It's not big money in comparison to MotoGP or even Moto2, but it's what you need to target.

'Money can get you most of the way, but you obviously need the knowledge of how it is all put together and the contacts to get the manufacturer contract, so either KTM or Honda,' he explained of the rest of the set-up. 'At the time, I wasn't given the choice because the championship was losing two Honda teams so we had to go with them. I needed to get an agreement with Honda, and Carlos Ezpeleta was helpful there. I knew a few guys from Honda but not the actual person for the Moto3 side. Carlos and Mike were the key people but then Johan Stigefelt helped a lot and I wanted to try to pick up some of his staff as the team was folding but ended up building it from scratch.'

Michael then detailed the process of recruitment, based on recommendations, synchronicity and opportunity. So much of it seems dependent on timing and availability. The location of the workshop was the next task, with Brexit influencing the geography and administration. The truck splits time between a place in Barcelona and southern Ireland. 'With a GP team, you work at the shop a few weeks in the winter and then you come back in the summer and restock and that's it until Valencia. It's like a travelling circus, and you're not at the workshop that much. So, once you have the base, set up the company, get the material, sourced your partners, put all the sponsors in place, sign the riders, bought your trucks, then you're ready.' Sounds like a breeze.

Laverty is not only a team owner but also a principal, which means he must try to dictate the culture of the team and that also funnels through the staff. 'We did a great job of putting the team together in year one: two good and experienced crew chiefs, and we had seven people in the team. Eight is the maximum you need with the eighth being the truck driver/tyre technician with a data guy in the middle. I looked at all the Moto3 teams to see which would be best and six, seven or eight people seemed right. Some get away with six! We're actually now around nine because we invested a bit more this year with having a track engineer between our crew chiefs – just different things as we try to evolve.'

The team stretches into the JuniorGP with four riders and support from Dorna (they pay 50 per cent of the budget) and also the British Talent Cup to be the premium British pipeline. This extends to the spanner wielders as well. 'I didn't just want to give riders from the UK an opportunity but mechanics as well … but to bring in someone with no real experience at this level was the wrong decision. I got it slightly wrong in year one. It was a good idea but with the British Championship team and JuniorGP team we can send any promising guys that way.'

The British angle was the primary motivation, and it's become a stipulation from Dorna that helps Laverty implement the structure from national to grand prix level, but it can also be a bind for the Moto3 operation that needs results and attention to confirm sponsorship to continue. For 2024, they lost VisionTrack as a title backer and were obliged to give Scott Ogden another opportunity, even if Michael is forthright about how the team and rider had difficult moments matching their goals. 'Losing VisionTrack was a tough pill to swallow. I knew it was happening halfway through 2023. I knew that keeping British riders for a third year in a row was not interesting to them and I had to change and I needed a potential front runner. I was told by Dorna in a roundabout way that I had to keep the British theme going, which I want to, but it gets appealing when I have some French riders with sponsors in tow. Immediately, it costs you much less money but you are taking the French rider because of the sponsor. It's an easy fix. But we toughed it out for another year, trying to keep on the British train.'

It feels ironic. MLav Racing was created to elevate Brits but if none are on the horizon or can make the grade, then the team needs some spur to survive and thrive to be the springboard for the next 'Marcus Marqueth' who comes along. It has to go foreign.

The forty-three-year-old spoke about his three-tiered set-up like it's a garden project. The weight, the work and the pressure for the father of a young family doesn't sound like it has made him world weary, and he still carries on with his fulltime TNT position as well. He told me about his fastidious approach to admin and booking all the team's travel to save on budget where he can. In the first year, he even drove the 7.5 team truck to some events. 'In year one, I put a lot of personal money in. Year two, I put the same as VisionTrack. This year, we lost VisionTrack so it is back to square one, but in 2023 I took on a business partner and sold 25 per cent of the team, which was a good move to offload all of the financial risk from my shoulders and also the business admin, as well as gain the advantage of someone with a different business outlook.'

He is chained to the Excel sheet. 'I dream of the day when I can have a line in there where I can pay myself something rather than putting my own money in!' he laughed. 'I'm working around the clock but hopefully it should level off and we get a bit more support. If I have an extra 50,000 then I have to do X, Y and Z with it and without cutting cloth and doing it right. Sometimes the boys might have to take a Ryanair flight instead of British Airways but it's not horrendous and most Moto3 teams do this. I also don't book shit flights. I don't think I am a control freak,' he added, before contradicting himself, 'but I like to take care of this …'

Sponsorship for a British grand prix racing team: I already knew the answer before posing the question. 'Really difficult.' Again, the smile. 'I had a lot of contacts and did smaller deals but MotoGP sponsorship is more expensive than, say, British Superbike, and fifty grand in BSB will get you a lot and you can take your clients to Brands for the weekend and be home for Sunday night. [Moto3] is a bigger commitment for British companies. Some are really into it but I have been banging my head on closed doors. However, if you bang fifty then one will open.'

Results have been hard to come by and haven't been helped by the superiority of Austrian machinery for the most part in 2023 and 2024. Yes, Jaume Masia won the 2023 title for Honda, but the podium has been routinely full of KTMs, CFMOTOs, GASGASs and Husqvarnas. Laverty had to use Japanese equipment but support increased for 2024 and the crew could count on more liaison with reigning champions Leopard Honda. What's also enlightening is how the team buys the hardware then recycles the parts through the series.

'Moto3 is quite good because there is a price cap,' he said. 'A rolling chassis costs a maximum of 87,500 euros. That's the limit and, funnily enough, it's what a Honda costs! And probably a KTM too. You have your parts list from Honda and that's quite expensive, but they are all prototype parts. You'll have the same for your Talent Cup bikes, they are almost identical, but Moto3 is four or five times the price! Sometimes they are the same, just marked up. A bit frustrating. The good thing about the rules is that there is a three-year development freeze, so when we buy all the bikes for 2023 then – in theory – they are only refreshed every winter and we don't need to go and buy two more 87,500-euro bikes. We just put in a new frame, a new swingarm, new tank and replace every nut and bolt when it's up to mileage. I remember in year one, we didn't have the bikes but we had the parts case and we could have built them up anyway from that! That's how most teams are now: you don't actually buy a physical bike but rather all the parts.'

I looked at him and we both uttered the same thing: 'Trigger's broom!' in reference to the *Only Fools and Horses* skit.

Like every team, MLav Racing needs hospitality. Michael called it 'a necessary evil' but invested anew in 2024 and didn't hesitate to justify the outlay. 'Businesswise, we needed to attract customers and clients through the door, so we invested in our own unit and outsourced the catering. Having your own space to network: I can already see the use. The team might have preferred more salary, especially considering that we lost our title sponsor, but it is already working for other sponsors and I'm hoping all the smaller deals will also feed into one big one, and the conversations come off the back of the hospitality. We need and want to get people to events and to come and enjoy the weekend at races.'

Watching his riders should be the best payback. Similar to Justin Marks. But I got the sense that Michael had a lot more on his plate. Such as when he talked about influencers and acknowledged that he still needs to get creative to investigate every means to spread the word and instil MLav Racing for the long-term. 'I used to get eight-to-ten grand a year when I was racing from the Northern Ireland sports council if I went to Europe,' he said. 'I still don't know if that's a "thing" but there are other opportunities out there, other avenues. Tapping into those is the next step. Until now, I'm chasing sponsors in the usual way: using contacts and the network on LinkedIn. It is awesome when someone wants to get involved and then bringing them through the door and giving them an experience in the paddock for the weekend. A lot of them aren't fussed about the logos too much, they just want to be there and to feel like they are helping the next crop of British riders or those from UK and Ireland.'

Will MLav be on the grid in 2026? Will there be a Brit to push on the way and to chase the shadows of Jake Dixon and Sam Lowes in Moto2 and then Cal Crutchlow, Scott Redding, Bradley Smith or the Laverty brothers to the premier class? Dreams in racing have been built on less.

SIX

The Salsa

I arrived in Barcelona in early 2001, aged twenty-four, to work for Dorna. I'm still grateful to Ana Cortes to this day, the assistant to then-Communications Director Paco Latorre, who helped me obtain residency and a bank account, as well as find an apartment in three days. Spain loves a bit of drawn-out bureaucracy.

I jetted to six of the first seven weekends of the season between MotoGP and MXGP, populating motogp.com with content. I then went into Paco's office and asked if I could avoid round four of MotoGP in late May in France on account of the amount of work and travel. The request was met by a shrug and the feeling that I was being in some way unreasonable. 'Bollocks to this …' I thought. Latorre had offered me a meagre salary with the mitigation that 'life in Spain is 30 per cent cheaper than the UK'. Maybe, but Barcelona is still a prominent European city. I had twigged that Dorna then were a firm that recruited people trading on their interest or passion for the sport. I wasn't naïve enough to realize this might be the case for many other companies or institutions, but, from my chair, Dorna did not have the biggest team nor were they flush with native English-speaking journalists queueing up to move across Europe. Yet, the attitude still seemed to be 'if he or she won't fit then there will easily be another one'. It didn't sit easily with me, and for a guy trying to adapt to a new country and lifestyle.

There was one thing that stopped me in my tracks from moving on. I watched her walk past my desk to the printer every day. She had (has) a natural unforced beauty and a character that attracted people. Maybe it was her smile. Perhaps the kindness and lack of cynicism. For sure, the intelligence and the open mind and the vibe of creativity, as she was a graphic designer. Nuria felt well out of my league (she still does), yet, although her level of English was bitty and my Spanish pathetic, we had a connection. We had a date in the park and from there I soon came to realize that I was standing at a large life crossroads and the sign was big and flashing in only one direction. By the end of the summer of 2002 as a soon-to-be freelance writer, I was landing at Barcelona airport, flying parallel to the city and spellbound by the sunset, and it was starting to feel like home.

Moving around and working in racing became part of our day-to-day and Nuria will always have my endless respect, admiration and affection for managing time when I was away and our boys were small. I was wholly aware of the absenteeism and made sure that when I was back I tried extra hard. Alex and Jordi arrived in 2006 and 2009.

From a distance, as the noughties progressed, through Nuria's job, I saw a small, patriarchal company explode as MotoGP inflated with popularity and the broadcast deals increased. Dorna zealously safeguarded their video and TV production material, and it became the goose that expelled larger and larger golden eggs, as Valentino Rossi drove MotoGP closer to the mainstream in countries beyond the 'homers', while racers like Pedrosa, Lorenzo and Márquez kept the home lanterns lit.

Dorna initially filled only two floors of five in the building in Sant Just Desvern, located in an industrial park surrounded by TV studios and next to a chemical factory that pumped out soapy smells each day. It's a suburb better known in the last few years for the new, epic Ciutat Esportiva Joan Gamper, FC Barcelona's sparkling training complex. Dorna now occupy their entire office structure and even spent considerable time converting the basement into a high-class TV production den.

Dorna have set the tone of grand prix motorcycle racing since a small conglomerate of influential Spanish businessmen, promoters and entrepreneurs recognized the potential of a sport that filters into the general consciousness in their country and is based around a vehicle that is part of daily life, ridden by all age groups and demographics. Dorna signed their first deal with the FIM and took control of grand prix racing for the 1992 season. In 2024, they inked another FIM contract to extend that story all the way to 2060.

The first visual sign of change in the early 1990s came with the erosion of the designatory number plates – green, black and yellow – for the classes. IRTA was founded, Carmelo Ezpeleta became the 'Eccelstone figurehead' for the series and dictated the shape of the sport for the teams and riders, the territories, the circuits, the broadcast deals and how Dorna could promote, while also trying to bring the manufacturers and other 'stakeholders' of the sport onto the train.

Dorna drew investment and flowered. It then tried to stay the course through the metamorphosis of the media (print to digital, free-to-air to subscription, video and OTT), consumer habits (merchandise and licensing) and motorcycle industry trends (two-stroke to four, electronics), while navigating global events like terrorist attacks, volcanic eruptions, financial crises, wars and the costs of transportation and pressing environmental pressure. There might have been around a hundred people employed (counting the freelance cameramen, as Dorna were taking their

TV crew around the world by that stage to ensure the high standards of the production) when I first started there. In 2024, they are close to 600. In more than two decades, they received cash influxes from CVC and Bridgepoint investment groups, and reached a valuation of billions as opposed to millions. It is a fantastic story of strategy and prosperity.

Dorna, in turn, poured money in some critical areas. For example, their library of footage stretching back to 1992 is treasure in tape, and the R&D they made with onboard cameras, installed in collaboration with the teams and the riders, was industry-leading and brought TV viewers closer to the challenges and thrill of motorsport than ever before. Their quality output became a reference for other championships. Formula One arguably lagged behind MotoGP in this respect until they were able to unveil the driver's eye-view cam in 2021, following a trial in Formula E and refining it down to a 9x9mm lens embedded in the helmet liner. MotoGP's response was to gather the potential of Sony's auto stabilizing lens to unveil the shoulder cam.

Towards the end of the 2010s, Carmelo's second-born, Carlos, became more of a figure in the paddock. He assumed responsibilities for sporting matters, was a link between Dorna and IRTA and was installed as an MD. I interviewed him in 2020, when journalists were carefully allowed back into the paddock among masks, distancing, controlled tests and health certificates. I found an intense guy who was already putting his energy into Dorna's reinvention, his conviction emboldened no doubt by his name and an outgoing, confident personality.

'Spreading the sport is the number one target of the company,' he insisted. 'I have this constant attitude where I question why we do things and how we've always done them. I got told off in the beginning when I came into the company full-time for trying to change everything on the first day! The attitude is important because that's how you improve.'

His older sister, Ana, has directed schemes like the Asian Talent Cup and other aspects of the Road to MotoGP programme, and is implicated in Dorna's preoccupation with a gateway for riders into the MotoGP kingdom. In 2021, Carlos became chief sporting officer and is now the ringleader of MotoGP thanks to his say on what happens on track but also in the commercial and organizational affairs. He was the face of the Sprint concept introductory presentation in 2022. He was integral in the recruitment of New Yorker Dan Rossomondo in early 2023 to spearhead Dorna's new commercial desire. If he hasn't quite lit a fire at Dorna's existentialism then he has certainly piled on a lot of wood, dowsed it in (partially non-fossil) gasoline and is impatiently flicking the flint of a lighter in its direction. Dorna are trying to eclecticize their team, overhaul their sponsorship integration policies and review their content creation, and will rebrand MotoGP for 2025.

———

August 2024. The rebranding is three months away and will be presented at the final round. I've been privy to the process because Nuria, as senior brand manager, has been flat out and cracking the whip.

The taxi ride from the station to Dorna's Madrid office took fifteen minutes. When I left the car, Carlos was already waiting outside what is quite a dated and modest building, although in quite an affluent and 'businessy' neighbourhood north of the centre and what transpired to be a twenty-minute walk to Real Madrid's Santiago Bernabeu stadium. He's dressed in a smart jacket, tailored white shirt and sockless shoes. We walked a few minutes up the road to get a flat white, talking football and children. His son, Carmelo (could MotoGP be overseen by another Carmelo Ezpeleta?), is almost one year old. Conversation was easy. Carlos is friendly, animated and convincing. We both speak Spanish but we talked in English. We inevitably chatted about MotoGP and travelling; his latest topic for debate was the recent trials with radios in grand prix and how riders will soon carry this tech. He frequently returned to Dorna's impending push for change in MotoGP. I've played football with the guy a few times in the usual Thursday evening games we organize on the eve of races, and I already know he is someone who likes to lead and is accustomed to being front and centre.

The Dorna office interiors are beige and non-descript, except for the MotoGP memorabilia in almost every corner. We went upstairs to be confronted by a large Monster Energy Yamaha M1 on the landing. Dan Rossomondo's area is dark and uninhabited. Carlos' space, by contrast, is bursting. There are helmets everywhere. A commemorative, personalized golf bag sits in one corner with only a putter inside. Framed covers from the old official magazine obscure the walls and one half of a Ducati fairing has been mounted on a frame behind his desk. Halfway through the hour we spent talking, Carmelo wandered in, smiled, said hello and offered a hand. He said he needed to talk to Carlos when he was free, but the younger Ezpeleta didn't show signs of hurrying.

His English is fantastic. His parents sent him to British primary and secondary schools in Madrid. 'There was more … practicality, and I'd say maybe 10 per cent of us were Spanish,' he said. 'We spoke English all the time. We listened to American music, watched American shows. My Spanish friends called the school "the UN" but I think it helped to have an open mind, in terms of religion, culture and everything, and also knowing that if you want to build something global, it has to be global within. It's a big part of who I am.'

A month before this meeting, in July 2024, I was in a windy Sachsenring, Germany. Dan Rossomondo is a man on the move – seemingly forever connected and in two places at once. An individual with a spinal curvature fashioned by a business class plane seat. Rather than trying to line up conversations with both Carlos and Dan in Madrid, I had decided to target the American – Dorna's first non-Spanish senior management hire – at a couple of races. He had fifteen minutes for me in Germany before having to dash into a meeting about what would become the calendar adjustment to replace Kazakhstan with another grand prix at Misano.

Dan's enclosure in the Dorna 'carpa' is situated to the left of a narrow corridor. His semi-circular desk is flanked by a large monitor showing the grand prix sessions and a few photographic prints on the walls. A large air conditioning unit sits above his head. There's no need for it at a brisk Sachsenring. The layout of the desk makes him seem (appropriately) like a casino card table dealer.

Light-eyed, presentable and wearing a light hoodie over his Dorna shirt that gives him a more youthful glaze, Dan, in his early fifties, is engaging. He speaks effortlessly, articulately, self-effacingly and sometimes quietly, with one of those 'cool' east coast accents, rather than a splurge of west coast dialect and slang. We had interviewed him at Mugello in 2023 for the podcast, where he still had a wide-eyed 'where am I and what's going on?' expression, but now, well over a year into the job, Dan has racked up enough miles to creak open the cave door to MotoGP in his homeland and is pushing his ideas with force. MotoGP's new look has a lot of his willpower and enthusiasm behind it; the variation on the TV package in the US and the 2025 pre-season teams presentation being talked about in the late summer of 2024 are his brain's offspring.

By his own admission, Rossomondo knew little about MotoGP. His slight naïvety about a compact sport and industry could have been a thin twig to beat him with, but that external standpoint and the near two-decade spell of selling aspects of the NBA is exactly why the Ezpeletas chased him. His business vision for how MotoGP has to peer through new windows could shape how the sport shifts and the activities it undertakes in the coming years. And for all the talk of nationalities and the effort to dilute Dorna's southern Europeanism, Rossomondo's passport was surely a coincidental taster of Liberty Media's impending arrival and their own agenda for how MotoGP could change and become more worldly.

On the Monday after the 2024 Red Bull Grand Prix of the Americas, in April, Rossomondo had sent me a WhatsApp. 'Am I correct in saying, "Holy shit, what a race?"' He evidently has a hard crush on the sport. It reminded me of that feeling of ripe fandom, that honeymoon period of exhilaration and curiosity, whether it's an activity, a band, a TV series or even a new partner. There is an impulse to share the emotion. I thought it was great.

Dan's transparency makes him likeable, as does his tendency not to silo himself in Dorna's offices at grands prix. I've seen him talking to wide gamut of people, even some characters where I think, 'Mate, don't waste your time ...' And he has created some fresh, passionate MotoGP fans in his family. I was shown a video of his eldest son, on the brink of university entry, at home, jumping around the room and going crazy at one of the grand prix battles in 2024. Both of Dan's kids have taken part in our

MotoGP football gatherings and it's funny to see how competitive the three of them are and how they bicker.

Fifteen minutes at the Sachsenring vanishes. We reconvened at the Red Bull Ring in August. Outside the same office it felt like the paddock asphalt was melting in the summer heat. There was also hot ambition pumping out of Dorna's hive in the paddock. Carlos and Dan are two of the principal generators of Dorna's transition from a family affair to a more modern, better-equipped sports promotion company. Carmelo Ezpeleta is almost an institution in international motorsports and an architect of modern-day motorcycle racing. His story is easily bookworthy. But all his skills with diplomacy and management are being turbocharged by people leading the next gear-change for MotoGP.

'Growing up in Spain and in the paddock, it was fairly obvious that he was someone important,' Carlos said of his dad while we were in Madrid. 'The sport was growing a lot when I was young, especially in Spain with [Alex Criville] winning in 1999 and then Dani and Jorge. The business was growing. You could tell at home that things were going well. He would get recognized more often. Once I started with a real job and having real importance within Dorna, then it was also important for me to detach myself as much as possible.'

Carlos had unbeatable access to grand prix racing but he also understands the power of the sport and the allure it has because he was also infatuated. He studied and worked with the end goal of finding a place in the paddock. MotoGP did not acquire Ezpeleta junior, it consumed him.

'I would be very surprised if someone grew up in the paddock and became detached from the sport,' he explained. 'There is something about it that makes you want to be involved. It captures you. I was quickly in love with it and into what the riders do. I wanted to make a space for myself in the championship while being very fortunate to grow up learning a lot about the business itself and being around conversations about it. Of course, it gives you foundations. I'm sure a lot of jobs are cool, don't get me wrong, but if you work in an office in an accounting role then maybe you don't have the same kind of attachment to it that we do.

'Business was interesting to me, and I studied engineering at university because I believed it would give me a good foundation for any industry. I started doing things in the paddock when I was sixteen and grew to learn what the departments in Dorna did. Being with Carmelo and at races, we'd talk a lot about the sport and the teams and the circuits. That's where I thought I could be of more use. It is a much more professional world now, the sporting industry in general and MotoGP specifically. I think Dorna, years ago, didn't have a hard organization where there were specific people for specific things. Competent people just ended up taking more responsibility. I wanted to take a role that would help make the rules and affect the design itself.'

The name was a help but also a hindrance. 'Of course, that's always in your mind,' he admitted. 'You know you cannot afford to f**k it up and you also have to live with the fact that people will say, "He's there because of that [his surname]." I really liked MotoGP. It's really fun and also to learn more and more every day: when you are in a position when everything is new, decisions are happening or you are in a room where really interesting conversations are being had. When I was younger I'd be a plus one with Carmelo at meetings or at F1 or meet characters around riders. To be able to then execute on problems and solve them is a really cool job.'

Carmelo Ezpeleta is almost eighty years old but endures in the job and is vigorous, while Carlos has the same approach. 'You can tell the apple has not fallen too far from the tree, even by the way they walk!' Rossomondo told me in Austria. 'Carlos has wisdom beyond his age and Carmelo has energy of a guy half his age. It's an interesting dynamic.'

'I would say in many ways we have similarities, but in others we are very different, and we argue quite a bit, to be honest,' Carlos said. 'In the end, he's the boss and that's what matters. We have very distinct personalities and there are times we don't see things on the same page, more in terms of style than in terms of targets.

'For me, the process, the explanation and the narrative is always very important for what we do and some other things for Carmelo is just about the end product. He is very visceral in defending his views and – this is a contradiction – is very open to new ideas, which is great. That's the reason why he's good at what he does: he's surrounded himself with younger people because he knows the world has changed a lot. Carmelo is already an icon, and when you are seeing a prime minister or minister of state or high-ranking officials, there is this baggage and respect that comes with him and it's very impressive.

'I think he created a character and a personality that is very valuable for Dorna and the business,' Carlos continued. 'I'm different in the way I manage things. One of the things I have from my childhood, deep within, is this responsibility that Carmelo has embedded into Dorna and towards our teams, our riders and our fans, and it's not only as a business but it's more profound. Particularly in terms of the 3,000 families that live off the paddock. To me, it's a sense of being one more person in the paddock. It's not like it's a monarchy or anything. At home, we love the sport so much that it's this ingrained responsibility that we want more people around the world to feel the same.'

The Ezpeleta family dinners must be interesting. He smiled at the notion. 'As soon as I became involved in the business, it became clear that we could not speak about it around the table or my mum would have gone mad. There was a "no business" rule! We tried very hard. It was good for us too because this is a job where there is no off button. There is constantly stuff happening.'

Aside from the radical movement with the Sprint in 2022, the rebranding and the acquisition, I asked Carlos what other impact he's proud of, particularly on the sporting side and before his influence filtered more 'upstairs'. 'The Long Lap,' he replied. 'We had a genuine problem where we were handing out these time penalties. It was terrible. Ten three-second penalties after a race, or a "drop position", which we couldn't even monitor because someone in fifteenth wouldn't have the cameras on them. I remember being at the FIM Congress in February and doodling on a napkin in the coffee break. There was a MotoGP test in Qatar after that and I wasn't meant to go, but I went with Loris [Capirossi] and drew the Long Lap at Lusail with a scooter and a piece of chalk! The marshals were looking at us like we were out of our minds. I was hanging off the back of the scooter and we were drawing. Stuff like that is really fun and a cool part of the job. I've lost some of the intrinsic sporting part now as I am more and more focused on the business.'

Business. And sport. Dan Rossomondo's tale appears to be one of those set from birth. 'I grew up in New Jersey. To say sports was important in my youth and to my development is an understatement. I played everything. I am competitive in everything, and my wife and I are like that all the time. I think I had a shirt in high school that said: "If I can't win, I don't want to play." I was probably a bad sport.'

Rossomondo's father worked in sales for Estée Lauder and travelled a lot. Dan was attending the 1990 World Cup in Italy, followed football, basketball, the Olympics. He got a job at Madison Square Garden and the corporate sponsor group that sold for the teams and also the television network implicated with events and sports at the facility. 'I was on the revenue generation side and that was always competitive too,' he recalled. 'I liked making deals and putting partnerships together. It also fed my intellectual curiosity a bit because you had to go and talk to other people about their businesses and work with them to help them solve their business goals. I thought sales was like a four-letter word at first, but then at some point, I decided it was like winning, which I like doing,' he grinned.

Rossomondo was already gathering a perspective in the sports industry while he was still studying. 'I would say that sport, in many ways, is recession-proof. At least in the United States. Actually "proof" is perhaps the wrong word. Maybe "resistant" is better because people watch it. It's the last thing that people will cut out of their budget. One of the best learning experiences I had was not during a bust but during the dot.com boom in the 2000s, when anybody could sell anything and there was stupid money flying around everywhere. You could tell it wasn't real. It was like the crypto bubble of a couple of years ago. I learned a lot by trying to judge who would be around longer term and would fulfil their obligations. One example was when the Yankees brought in a Japanese pitcher and a senior boss at the Garden came into one of our meetings and said, "I want us to sell this guy … anybody who does it gets a bonus." I was a junior and not a full-fledged salesperson, but I went out and found a Japanese beer company – Asahi – and sold him for 45k on Yankees radio in 1997. The plug would go out every week and I remember getting the recognition … and the cheque.'

Rossomondo came out of business school a few months after September 11. 'I was in NYU when the towers fell. The world was a little weird. I found my way into IMG, and the guy who helped me get there went to the NBA and then he hired me again. At the NBA, I realized I was around really smart people. I knew how to sell and talk and to work my way politically in a company. I found my way.'

But it did become all-encompassing for almost twenty years. The NBA is a recognized brand around the world. It's the defining standard of one particular sport. 'Sometimes people say to me: "It must be easy selling the NBA, it's so popular." It is, but not for the price or the way we had to sell it. There was a certain level of sophistication that you had to bring and that the company required. There were also certain revenue targets that were audacious. Anybody could sell the NBA for $50, but we were doing deals for 10, 20, 50 million. Different dynamic.'

Rossomondo had a good grounding for all the factions he'd soon encounter in MotoGP. 'The basketball eco-system is very complex. There are teams, owners, players, union, broadcast partners, sponsors, local sponsors, national, global. A lot of people, so you have to prioritize, and the problem is that people burn out because it gets exhausting: summer league, summer meetings, draft, pre-season, season, Christmas, all-stars, play-offs. It always spins.'

I asked how a New Jersey guy bouncing around the US suddenly found himself packing a suitcase for Europe and a sport he'd never heard of. 'I was having one of those days,' he recounted. 'I was still partially working at home and at lunch I told my wife

I was going for a walk in the park near us. I had a WhatsApp call from a UK number. It was a recruiter who said he had a European rights holder and wanted to know if I was interested to talk. Sure. I had to sign an NDA [non-disclosure agreement] and then, wow. MotoGP. I said to Carlos and Carmelo several times when we talked, "This might be the conversation where I lose interest, or you do." I mean, it was based in Spain, I didn't know a thing about it and I'd never been a huge motorsports fan. My wife didn't believe it was real and then I was in the kitchen at home when the offer came through on the phone. She looked at me and said, "It's good …?" And I said, "Yeah! Enough to have a real conversation." She turned white, and she's very tanned! Sometimes, you just know. And it was the people: Carmelo, Enrique [Aldama, CFO] and Carlos. I had lunch with them in Madrid in February and had a good affinity. It was something new. Let's go.'

'I was very involved in the process,' Carlos said of the Rossomondo enlistment. 'Before the decision, we spent some time talking to Dan and, without being all romantic, it stood out clearly that Dan was a great person and an excellent guy. We're travelling together, eating together; there is a personal part which is important. What also stood out is Dan's capacity to create business and his passion. It was very aligned with Dorna. It had to be an international person, and that personality and global perception is already starting to rub off on the paddock.'

'I tried very hard not to make assumptions,' Rossomondo said of his MotoGP 'apprenticeship' through 2023. 'I think a lot of my initial reactions have been borne out. I think that this company has done so well because of a) how good the sport is and b) the sheer will of Carmelo and Enrique has dragged everybody along. I think there are some legacy or institutional challenges because when they do things, it's because they have always been done that way. That's hard. There has never been a [proper] marketing department, and we have sixteen people. Some of the F1 *teams* have upwards of seventy-five. I think there is a realization that things could be done another way and there could be some hard conversations when people realize that perhaps they can't ... but I think everybody's heart is in the right place. The business has been built to this size and it's been an unbelievable success, but if we want to go to the next level then it cannot happen organically.'

For Carlos, any public criticism or persecution of Dorna involved an extra personal note. 'I remember criticism when changing from two-stroke to four-stroke and being completely hammered in the media, but it wasn't really a problem and you could see that Carmelo was very sure about it,' Carlos claimed. 'The decision had been taken and time would prove the critics wrong. When accusations get more personal and stupid then it affects you, and when you are younger you get more worried. But as you get older, you realize you are better off just not listening to it. I think we are much less exposed at the management level than the riders are, let's say, and it's important not to read much of the negative stuff.'

Dorna have also been bashed over issues and changes with the calendar and individual grands prix. High-profile deals for the collapse that was the Circuit of Wales, the twice postponed Grand Prix of Kazakhstan, and the complications of organization and payments that plagued what was otherwise a pretty successful first visit to India in 2023 have animated the keyboard warriors. They are just some examples, as well as the persistent presence of four, sometimes five, rounds on the Iberian peninsula, even though the grands prix tend to draw the crowds and there is demand.

I brought up the matter with Carlos. After seeing how inexplicable some MXGP events have been over the years (organized for cash or a promise and very short-term) and learning how different groups and companies can test the flexibility of agreements or suddenly find themselves in cash holes, I have some sympathy for promoters who also have to work to budget projections. Companies like Dorna not only have to cart a sport, infrastructure and live TV production around the world, but then also invest to improve it and find ways to make it bigger while making their money. They need a backbone of solid contracts and partners and can then take a chance on a new territory or alliance. And those don't always come off. Late changes can carry negative implications but how many deals in business collapse? Dorna's predicament lies in how public their every move is.

'The Circuit of Wales wasn't even a leap of faith,' Carlos insisted. 'We had three GPs organized and paid by these guys at Silverstone. It was bizarre but the funding was there. When you are in a business where there are governments in the middle – and changing governments – that sort of stuff happens. You also think, "Why would a country like Kazakhstan go to all of this trouble and not do the event?" But it happens. It's unfortunate and it sucks, but at the end of the day, there is a deadline where you have to publish a calendar and you are working on it all in the background. We don't want to make any changes but, to be honest, the room to manoeuvre is smaller every time. With F1 having twenty-four races, us having twenty-two, Ramadan, logistics – there are choices you can make but they are finite. It's not that flexible. Teams used to prefer doing triple headers, now they don't that much, but then if you talk with the riders, they like triple headers because it is done and dusted! Everyone has an opinion and no matter what calendar you publish, people are going to criticize it and you have to learn to live with that.

You'll listen to feedback and adopt a new philosophy the next year and still get dumped on.'

For a loud, environmentally 'awkward', resource-chewing series tallying a carbon footprint that would give Greta Thunberg a seizure, Dorna has also been proactive with attempts at sustainability, such as the quest with Michelin to develop tyres made from recycled material, greener fuel (100 per cent by 2027) and better carbon accountancy. Then there are the millions spent by Ducati and Dorna on MotoE and the ceaseless drum-banging by series Director Nicolas Goubert for the electric contest to be given more credence, despite the wavering situation in society generally for electric mobility. Under the FIM's guidance, the noise limit will also fall in future seasons of MotoGP.

Dorna's prioritization of safety will be one of their best legacies. Again, critics can point at the levelling of machinery to increase entertainment potential and contain costs for the manufacturers as well as the fact that the last three fatalities have come from contact in close quarters. But the system for response and treatment, the pressure on circuits for alterations and the total open-mindedness for any solution that can help with rider safety are constant offsets to this, while accepting that racing motorcycles is hazardous to health. Dorna's established Safety Commission is also a means to put the ball into the court of the people twisting the throttles and ensure not only an easy forum for concerns and action but also a healthy dialogue and collaboration between the two factions: promoter and participant.

Dorna also bank a lot of goodwill and power in the paddock through their support of the teams. Without their funding system, the sport could be far more unstable. 'We benefit from a very healthy relationship with the teams, and they have been very supportive during these three decades of Dorna's vision for the sport. They put on a great show every weekend,' Carlos said, sounding diplomatic, but then also hinting at the shifting sands to come. 'That collaboration will only get stronger with time: a full commercial and promotion collaboration, not just one based on sport and the racing fees, event fees and the freight. Those discussions about tyres, capacities, engines are going to become more and more about how we promote the sport in different countries, how do we do more for the fans. They are the biggest ambassadors of the sport – the riders and teams – much more than we are. They are the faces and what people see. When we present the rebranding in Valencia this year, it is our job to involve the teams as much as possible. Fans need to be much more aware of our targets and our personality and what we want to do – and that includes the ambassadors. That relationship is much closer every year.'

'It wasn't that long ago that we were fishing around for MotoGP teams,' he emphasized. 'Now the foundations have been laid. There is incredible demand for new teams. There are independent teams winning now and fighting for the championship. I think we have high standards in many things and we will continue to work on the sport because it is the core of our business, but I think now we're ready for the next era for attracting new people. That's where success lies. What we have is good, but we can re-think what we are doing, why we are doing it and who we are doing it for. I would not say I've had success in creating my own thing at Dorna because it's not mine, I've just contributed and I'm one more person in the company.'

Change. It's coming. The idea of MotoGP being described as a 'product' might make hardened fans recoil but, in the middle of the third decade of the century, what sport is now *just* a sport? To hammer home the fact that MotoGP is evolving to be more than a race series, the new logotype doesn't have a checkered flag 'component', and is the result of a long overdue makeover of a design made at the end of the last century and last revised almost twenty years ago. It's a very visual example of where grand prix is heading. The polemic subject of rider radio communication is another. The benefit of augmenting the live TV production is clear (it will initially be teams talking to riders but inevitably will become two-way), but then the added dimension in terms of information for safety and track conditions does have merit. What else could be brewing?

'For the first year, I was in evaluation mode and now I am starting to break shit, to be frank,' Rossomondo said. 'That means we are creating stuff: a new department, a rebranding, new campaigns, concepts like Fan Vision, which we started last year. I just have to be mindful that this organization is only a set number of people, not counting PROmotor [the firm that takes care of MotoGP logistics], and we are putting on twenty-two high-class events around the world each year. Those have to get done.

'We know the sport and can tell the stories but are we too close to it?' the American continued. 'How do you talk to the uninitiated? My sons are a good example. They got inside the bubble very quicky because of their access, but for a seventeen-year-old kid in New York, are we feeding him the right content? Are we reaching him in the right way? Do we even know how to approach him? We know how to tell the story to hardcore fans and we do a great job of it. But in order to monetize this business we need to bring in new fans. That's the trick.'

Personally, I find all this signalling, and the rallying cries, refreshing and proactive. I would also like more people to know about MotoGP. Package it as a global entertainment product if necessary, but if MotoGP becomes more popular through securing more widespread TV deals, a streaming series, cool online content, embracing well-known ambassadors, big-time sponsors or whatever … then bring it on.

One quandary for Dorna lies in the exclusive broadcast contracts that bring in a hefty wedge of the cash. These hamstring the footage that can be spread by other entities on social media (or they did, historically) and involve smaller, paying audiences. MotoGP would gain easily more than a million viewers per race when it was shown on the BBC over a decade ago and that number would triple for significant events like the British Grand Prix. Allegedly, TNT Sports are fighting to get near the same total per event, even if their comprehensive coverage with a top-notch team of talent means MotoGP fans will not want for quality broadcasting if they sign up and pay. Assuming that live TV will still be the way to accrue the most views in the next five years anyway, Dorna might be placed in a position where less lucrative deals will lead to bigger audience potential, which they then need the marketing and commercial chops to sink their teeth into and reap the profit. What will they do?

'The easiest way to divide Dorna's business is in three major buckets: media, promoters/circuits and sponsorship, with hospitality and licensing and all that,' Carlos explained. 'There is growth projected in all of them … hopefully. There are different ways to grow but I think we are very mindful of not being shortsighted. Of course, there is always a lot of criticism in terms of the platforms and pay TV and the visibility of the sport. I think right now, all major sports are on some sort of platform. It is just the way the world is, and without that, I don't think we would be able to sustain the paddock the way we do.'

I could tell it's a subject that perturbs Rossomondo: 'There is not a day where I don't think about the cost/benefit analysis of where we are broadcasting our sport,' he said a little wearily. 'Meaning, we are taking money from great partners in the pay cable space but we are limiting the distribution a little bit. It happens, that's the reality, and you are making decisions based on a lot of factors. The opportunity from these devices [holds up his phone] and social media is that we can talk directly to people and we have to do that. The challenge is there but the problem is that discovery is so hard, there is too much stuff out there. Every sport. Sport is the thing that gets people together. I'm not asking for a lot – a Sprint is twenty-odd minutes – then Sunday as well. An NFL game is three hours.'

'We are very proud of the sport we have and are not afraid of people getting into contact with it and then not liking it,' said Carlos, with full-bore sincerity. 'We feel that there is genuine value in us saying we have the most exciting sport in the world. We know once people touch it then they'll like it as much as we do. Pay TV platforms are an intrinsic part of the sport and we have to leverage our fanbase to go to those platforms either directly or indirectly. In every market, we have a different approach. In more mature markets that can stand and in others we'll take an investment in order to have much more visibility to then grow the fanbase and have a better deal a few years from now.'

I asked Dan how his meetings with possible new partners and sponsors have been going. 'People have been very receptive but I have not had as much success as I would have liked in closing things,' he replied, very openly. 'It's very unknown in the United States, where most of the deals are coming from, and it has very low resonance in the UK, where a lot of deals are coming from also. The two biggest commercial hubs are the US and the UK and we don't have great penetration there. That's hard. We've been good at selling signage and hospitality, track presence and VIP tickets, but sponsorship doesn't work that way anymore. They want ideas, solutions, so we have to adjust. We've recently hired an activation team and they are there to do two things: firstly, help our existing partners fill their deals with unique and cool ideas, and, secondly, then bring that to new partners! We have a small team of five people on that now.'

Fees to promoters and circuits for staging grands prix should be another consistent source of income, even though – as mentioned – this can be a patchwork quilt. 'The way I see it, you negotiate a deal with the promoters and the moment you sign it then you have to be happy,' said Carlos. 'There is no way you can look back and say, "That promoter is not paying the fee that we want." Some promoters have a higher fee, others, lower [Brno, in the Czech Republic, apparently paid 6 million euros] but the goal is to make every event the best it can be because we're in a marriage now. I think it's known across motorsport that there are different territories with different values. Maybe it's not the hosting fee but the TV deal or the sponsorship. Once you have twenty races or more then you try to slot everybody as close as possible to their requested date and then look at how you promote it to get as many spectators as possible. Qatar, for example, have it in their agreement that they start the year. They won't in 2025 because of Ramadan and they didn't last year because of circuit construction.'

As for the commercial side, Dorna undoubtedly have to make upgrades to try to court 'outside' companies, but this is where the large wave of Liberty Media could make a splash in the coming years. Assuming the final deal goes through in 2025. 'It's the question everyone wants to know,' Carlos said, but understandably details can't be laid out. Dorna is already going through a period of transition before the final contract is sanctioned and gets locked away in a virtual safe somewhere.

Rob Gray/Polarity Photo gets creative with Australian Jack Miller on the Red Bull KTM. Miller, one of the more popular riders in MotoGP, had a tough 2024 but has career podium trophies with three different brands in the class.

ABOVE: The force of red. Factory Ducati machinery is lined-up and warmed-up at Mugello. The Italian circuit has provided MotoGP top speed records in recent years, with the radar beam breaking at 225mph. Up until 2024, Ducati and KTM have the fastest bikes on the grid.

BELOW: MotoGP football! A spread of Premier League aspirants from the paddock, drawn from Aprilia, Ducati, KTM, Alpinestars, Trackhouse, Dorna and media. Spot the riders?

ABOVE: Brad Binder checks the coast is clear before exiting the pitbox at the Sachsenring. Somebody in the background has forgotten their earplugs: a must-have next to the howl of modern-day MotoGP machines.

BELOW: View from the pitlane of the sumptuous Red Bull Ring Media Centre, where journalists are somewhat spoilt.

ABOVE: Marc Márquez rarely takes to the track without a camera send-off. His gamble to leave a lucrative HRC contract for a year-old Ducati in the satellite Gresini team achieved the desired effect in 2024: a two-season deal in full factory red.

BELOW: The back of the famous old steel monolith grandstand at Le Mans on a Sunday night in 2024, when the paddock is in deconstruct. The teams' rigs have already pulled out, and the show is noisily dismantled for travel to the next grand prix.

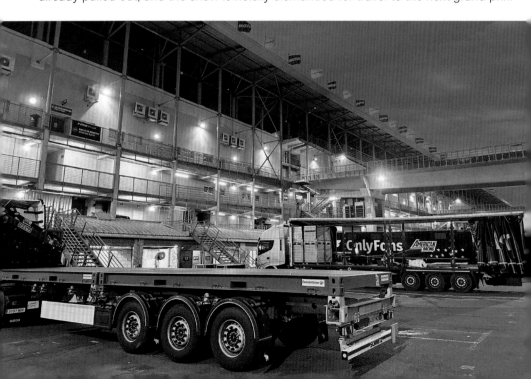

ABOVE: Double world champion Pecco Bagnaia swings a leg over the GP24 at Jerez. The bikes are custom fitted down to the last millimetre for riders, and then configured further for optimum feeling. They will be near lap-record pace by the start of their first lap.

BELOW: Jorge Martin is submerged by media on Saturday at the season-closing 2024 Barcelona grand prix for the post-session (or post-race) 'scrums'. Not the most efficient of systems for press.

ABOVE: Trackhouse Racing launch their maiden MotoGP effort from the top floor bar of a fancy joint in Hollywood.

BELOW: Looking ahead. On the grid at the 2024 Catalan grand prix. Pre-race expectation is tangible; guests and media mix with team personnel as other formalities take place.

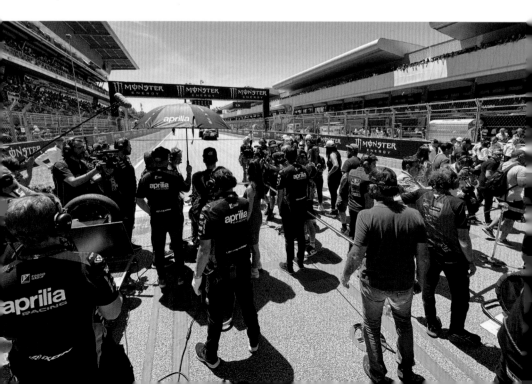

ABOVE: Official MotoGP press conference. Find space where you can. Rooms at many circuits are now no longer big enough for the amount of material needed for these events on Thursdays and Sundays. The broadcast set for TV is located elsewhere in the paddock.

BELOW: Well-drilled German marshals drag a damaged Alpina airfence away from the scene of some 'abuse' at the Sachsenring and the notorious Turn 1.

ABOVE: Sparks on show. 2024 world champion Jorge Martin enacts the full shoulder scrape at the Circuit de Barcelona-Catalunya. British rider Scott Redding even dragged his head on the asphalt once for a prank. [Photo by Rob Gray/Polarity Photo]

BELOW: Thirsty goat. The last drops of glory for arguably the most recognized motorcycle racer of all time, surrounded by that unmistakeable yellow. [Photo by Rob Gray/Polarity Photo]

I quizzed him on some background of the deal that involved ten figures. 'The conversation was very long. It was goosebumps, and very secretive. There were times when we were adamant it was going to happen and others when we thought it was off. It was up and down, like any negotiation, and there were things in our control and other things that weren't. We're extremely happy because we have this feeling of responsibility to the sport and we think it's the best thing that can happen, by far, for all the partners that we could have.'

'I cannot take any credit for the deal,' said Rossomondo. 'I was part of it when they came to us and I imagine it gave them some comfort that there was a guy that "spoke their language" inside the company. We've landed on the fact that MotoGP is the world's most exciting sport and I will keep saying it until everybody believes it. Will we ever get 500,000 spectators at Silverstone like F1 does? Probably not but we can create a very rich fanbase. We have 500 million fans around the world and I'd love to increase that by 50 per cent in five years. That's a good goal. That will auger a good revenue increase and permit more investment into the sport. We have to bring the rest of the paddock with us and that's really hard. Another key measurement for three to five years will be how far we've been able to get into mainstream culture, and not in just Spain and Italy. Keanu Reeves came to Germany, Jason Statham to Silverstone, Will Smith posted about Jorge Martin – these are all cool cultural entries. I want Pedro Acosta's riding style to be a thing!'

2014. Kegums. Latvia. The weather was dark and ominous in late September. I was there for the annual Motocross of Nations: the biggest team motorsport fixture in the FIM's canon. Usually, there are more events and press conferences at the 'MXoN' compared to a routine MXGP grand prix. One of the formalities in the media centre involved a presentation by a silver-haired, smartly dressed Portuguese outlining the reason for his departure from the role of FIM vice president and his vision and candidacy bid for the big chair. Jorge Viegas wants more prominence for the FIM and more unity; to rely less on promoters and to be more proactive with more women's racing and other schemes. 'It's like we are sleeping,' he said. A former racer, he had been part of the federation system since 1990 by heading the organization in his home country, followed by three terms as VP at the FIM. He believed there was enough political momentum behind him to run against friend and incumbent Vito Ippolito. If he didn't get the vote on 22 November, then 'I will be completely out of motorcycling,' he said.

2024. Mugello. Viegas is sat at the desk of his presidential office within the new FIM hospitality unit inside the Italian Grand Prix paddock. He is trying not to get distracted by the MotoGP free practice session that is being beamed on a monitor behind me. I mention our first meeting at Kegums and a small interview I did with him after the presentation. 'Ha! 2014. I was completely alone, abandoned and there was a lot of double-crossing. People who said they would be there for me suddenly forgot.' He didn't win the vote.

After a two-year hiatus in which he became a judge for the Portuguese Arbitrary Court of Sport, Viegas returned, ran for president again and triumphed, and has been the face and leader of the FIM since 2018.

The Fédération Internationale de Motocyclisme, or FIM (initially called FICM for Fédération Internationale des Clubs Motocyclistes), began life in 1904 with ten federations as founding members, but it wasn't until 1912 that its first sanctioned race was held – the event which is now better known as the International Six Days Enduro. Ten member bodies would triple and the FICM would cement the outline for disciplines like enduro, motocross, speedway and trial. The 'clubs' system was dropped to reflect the much bigger international scope after the Second World War, leading to the creation of the FIM Grand Prix World Championship in 1949.

Today, Viegas presides over a big operation. 'There are about 400 people working for the FIM,' he explained of the governing body and the co-rule makers. 'Around fifty have a salary, another fifty are paid and then we have about 300 that are what I call non-paid professionals: people who know what they are doing but we only pay the expenses, like those on commissions, the doctors, lawyers. We have around seventy motorcycle disciplines. But what people normally don't know about is the work we do with Brussels and the United Nations for the laws that touch motorcycles, the driving licences, the configuration of the bikes. We lobby the authorities in order to protect motorcycles: this is the third pillar of the FIM and the second is the tourism, which is growing and growing, all the gatherings and events.'

Viegas is not camera shy. In fact, his ability to pop up at FIM racing events on a global scale is relentless. He is not coy with his opinions and, in total contrast to his predecessors like Francesco Zerbi or Ippolito, who apologized for their weak English and barely registered on a PR scale, Jorge perhaps even goes a step too far with his input and revelations behind a microphone, such as unnecessarily alluding to FIM MotoGP Safety Officer Tome

Alfonso's second surname of Ezpeleta at his unveiling in Valencia in 2022 (he is Carmelo's nephew).

In his office, I wondered aloud about the depth and breadth of the FIM president's role, when former incumbents seemed very passive. Perhaps they were political animals or worked very well behind the scenes, as one might expect of the number one role.

'One of the things I have achieved, I believe, is to give more transparency to the FIM,' he started. 'To put us closer not only with the fans but with the riders, the journalists ... Everybody knows what the FIM is doing more or less, and that we are open to talk to everybody, and this is not something that happened in the past. It used to be a very closed institution. In March 2019 in Qatar, I did a presentation for MotoGP as to who was working and where, and I did the same in Superbikes, Endurance and motocross. It was something I wanted to do and also to motivate the other officials to do the same. We are all part of the same family and we all want motorcycle racing to go up because we are very small still in the sports business, even if you did see through the numbers of the Dorna sale to Liberty that we are not so small as people think. I think we are [going] in the right way because we have somehow kept the same crazy spirit of motorcycle racing, even if all this is so professional. I have tried that everyone follows this spirit. We have our duties, and I think we are doing quite well.

'I could have been like previous presidents and stay home, go out once a month here and there,' he continued. 'In one year, I have been to events for forty-one weekends and I love it, but it's very tiring. I've been to FIA conferences. It's important that the FIM are present in these events and I have a great relationship with the president of the FIA; they are our partners in some things. Together, we have to be stronger because we face other sports. I was able to redesign the job of president and I'm really happy with the achievement. The first thing I had to do was form my team and then you see it for real. When you can concretize your ideas then this is the best that can happen.'

Those ideas have been coming thick and fast. The FIM have a new logo, a new building and are converting the old site into a new, flash, interactive museum.

The FIM and Viegas' duties go hand in hand with the promoters of each series: the companies pay a fee for the FIM stamp and the code and rules that come with the official affiliation. The FIM's bond with Dorna is an example of a comfortable marriage. The story with Feld for Supercross was far rockier and ended in divorce, motivating Viegas to double-down on World Supercross instead with newcomers SX Global, who have paid up but still not delivered to an effective standard.

'I tried to have good relations – and I don't mean submissive relations – but more like partnerships with the promoters,' Viegas said. 'Obviously, Dorna is by far the biggest but we are working with sixteen different promoters, which is amazing. Some are quite big, the second biggest is Warner Bros. Discovery: they have two disciplines with Endurance and Speedway and I speak with them on a daily basis.'

Jorge headed off on a tangent about Supercross and it's clear there is little love lost for the Americans and for Kenneth Feld in particular. He was then distracted by a crash in the MotoGP session. 'This is the best thing we have enforced,' he says as the slow-motion replay clearly shows an airbag deployment. 'So many really serious injuries have been avoided by the airbags. We have enforced it in the rallies and they need to move for motocross.'

Part of politics is credit and prestige. Viegas said he gets mad at ambitious people taking advantage of what the FIM has achieved. He also claimed: 'I want to do more but we are limited by finance.

Compared with the FIA, we are very small. One of the things I like more is that in the first mandate I could increase the budget by 50 per cent and that's not bad …'

That's interesting. It also broaches a subject I wanted to ask about, regarding the FIM's funding to pursue all the projects and ensure all the presence of staff and organization. Obviously, a large slice comes from Dorna. 'I can imagine it's a pretty high percentage,' Carlos told me coyly in Madrid, but then Viegas has been active boosting the FIM accounts. 'By renewing contracts,' he explained 'The helmet [homologation] programme is also amazing. We sell the small stamps for four euros and in 2023 that brought in 800,000 euros and it's improving. Now we go for airbag homologation and boots and gloves. We want the riders to be more safe. So, we are working on more programmes of homologation with a university that makes the tests.'

The backscratching and the politics involved in bartering for power to get things done must be a tricky weave of judgment and trust when it comes to the FIM and all the nationalities, cultures and personalities. A mini FIFA. 'The fans don't know what happens behind the scenes and federations are political, obviously, in any sport,' he said with a knowing gesture.

'I have tried to show that the FIM takes decisions to benefit motorcycling. For instance, the FIM here in MotoGP didn't really exist. You never heard about the FIM being involved in anything. Now there is no decision [made] without us. Sometimes we take the initiative and present new things; for instance, the FIM did not have any engineers working for us and now we have five, and each is in a technical commission related to one discipline. The new MotoGP rules for 2027 were established with us and we are leading the commission for the new fuel. It is much more complex than you may think. It's a long story. We are also working on the noise level and new limits will come before 2027 because we cannot hide from the world. We know all these questions of energy transition, sustainability … we are too much exposed. We are a showcase. Even if our carbon print is [relatively] nothing [to the wider world], people still look at us for what we do. We are really committed to this direction. We have a lot going on and I'm proud when my people say "Please! No more ideas!"

'Communication, finance and legal are three departments that depend on me. I am an executive president so, unlike all my predecessors that were not running the show, I am taking care of a lot more than just politics. I am like a CEO, even if I have one, and a deputy who are fantastic! This is what changed a bit from the past.'

With Liberty set to enter MotoGP, Viegas enthused on the repercussions. 'We can do something to bring the youth back to this amazing sport because you see a lot of older people in motorcycle sports. I was a bit afraid of the departure of Valentino but this is now all coming back.'

He will be in charge until 2026. 'I don't know yet if I will do a third term,' he said, almost with a sigh. 'My conditions are that I'm in good health because it is very physical to travel all the time. Then I need to know that I can still make some ideas; I don't want to just "be there". This is not what I am about at all. I want to leave the FIM with a good team, with a healthy financial position and things like the museum, the new head office, new competition, the new logo.'

'It's a commercial relationship that is very healthy and the sport benefits from it,' Carlos said of the wrap with the FIM when we were in Madrid. I wondered what he perhaps really thought but he quickly added, 'I think we are grateful to each other. I'm not just talking shop here.' Maybe he saw my reaction. 'If it wasn't then we wouldn't extended it to 2060. I think there is room for the federations to have a non-commercial role and be impartial. I think Dorna is always impartial but someone without a commercial interest? There is a role.'

The changes to come. After the interview with Carlos in 2024, I was walking through Madrid's wonderfully straggling Retiro park back to Atocha station for the fast train to Barcelona: where the whole MotoGP adventure really started for me. The sun was beaming. I weaved between catchments of shade. The wind picked up and rustling leaves and branches through the green treetops provided one of those soundtracks only possible in city parks. It is hard not to think about the fresh air that will undoubtedly be blowing through MotoGP soon. What sound will it make?

SEVEN

The Reason

A typical day at MotoGP for a journalist starts with a guessing game and a hike. MotorLand Aragon is one of the more curious and winding racetracks on the calendar and the traffic into the facility is normally light, but count on a half-hour commute from whatever accommodation you might have been lucky to find in the many small hamlets dotted around a picturesque region.

The situation is similar at Mugello and at Jerez, you are rising before the sun, otherwise the motorway sliproad, adjacent to the circuit, becomes an exercise in restrained patience.

In Phillip Island, don't be alarmed by the kangaroos that will happily bounce in front of the car while you're doing a decent speed along the rural roads from the centre of Cowes.

Be wary of roundabout traffic at the top of the corner into Mulsanne (straight) at Le Mans, but also contentedly let your imagine wander as you gas down the open stretch of public road flanked by guardrail and little hallmarks of motorsport history, and then marvel at the loaded campsites as you thread into the heart of the famous complex. Cut through the early-morning mist crowding the green fields on the fifteen-minute glide from the sleepy town of Seckau to the Red Bull Ring.

Silverstone offers up a tang of history; like the drive over the

'Daily Express' bridge of what used to be the old dive to Woodcote.

Quite often, I enjoy the morning drive to MotoGP. I think of Dad. After all the years of bumper-to-bumper frustration and flooded grassy parking lots, he would have had a small kick from being able to travel in with me, through the control points and to the relative comfy and exclusive confines of Parking 1.

I relish those parking areas at circuits that mean a walk. It's a moment of calm before what can be a long day. Gather thoughts, think of the work ahead and ideas.

Getting through the door (into the circuit, even) means qualifying for media accreditation. Until recently, Dorna had a bizarre and unfair protocol of making digital media pay for passes. I suppose the policy had some sense in the early days of the internet and when the owner of random websites like www.ilovebikeracing.com could apply for a pass on the grounds he was a new-fangled blogger. But the truth is that there are so very few print-only titles now. In fact, I'm struggling to think of one while writing this. Perhaps that's why I'm writing this.

The meander into a MotoGP circuit means passing people, saying hello, fleeting small talk, a 'good luck' or a moment of banter. I'm usually carrying a heavy rucksack containing a laptop, back-up iPad, podcast recorder and mics, a big bag of dried fruit and nuts and the indispensable noise-cancelling headphones that serve two purposes: one, listening to the superb live feed commentary from the likes of Birty (Matt Birt, a Leicester City obsessive and therefore a fellow football sufferer), Louis Suddaby (Hull City) and reporter Jack Appleyard (Bradford FC), with Simon Crafar's input being nothing short of indispensable up until 2024. The guys not only augment the show that MotoGP provides through the TV but their research and information act like a crib sheet for us hacks at keyboards listening to their data.

Secondly, putting the headphones on is the equivalent of a 'do not disturb' sign in the media centre. Actually, there is a third purpose. The proliferation of podcasts in the last three years means that Saturday and Sunday late afternoon and early evenings produce more and more jabbering from Brits, Spaniards, Germans and Italians into their laptop screens or around a couple of mics. The headphones are antisocial but help to get things done.

Media centres vary greatly. Older enclosures at Jerez, Valencia, Mugello, Misano mean staring at outdated monitors, elbowing for space and hoping that friends and altruistic colleagues will have arrived first and reserved some seats with a decent view of the screens. Including team PR staff, there can be 200 people or more in these rooms. Traditionally, the first races in Europe – Jerez, Mugello, Valencia – are rammed.

King of the ring though has to be the Ring. The Austrian Grand Prix media centre is on the fourth floor of a modern marvel of shiny construction at the Red Bull Ring. It looms opposite the paddock and on the other side of the start straight. The zone not only has enough screens to put a large sports bar to shame but a comprehensive catering service, five coffee stations, blink-of-an-eye internet speed and a magnificent view over 70 per cent of the track. A wicked thunderstorm early Sunday evening in 2016 ripped advertising boards from the track and sent debris tumbling along the grid. We watched the bedlam from our floor-to-ceiling-windowed perch. In 2024, similar adverse conditions on Saturday afternoon meant the circuit 'disappeared' below us into a thick cloud of rain and hail.

You can take the lift from the ground floor and a mini Red Bull museum collection of race cars, bikes and a large Scalextric set, but it's better to walk off the strudel and cappuccinos and plod up 104 steps and seven flights to arrive breathless at the top.

Now, if this sounds like a first-world problem consider that the paddock is located through another 'tunnel of Legends', although far wider and more comfortable than the subterranean passage that links the paddocks at Sachsenring, complete with MotoGP graffiti on the white walls.

A Grand Prix gets fast from Friday. Thursday is media day. It's the only time that riders will offer one-to-one interview slots – and the more in-demand he is, the earlier you'll need to ask. Appointments with team managers, other management and figures can be done through the rest of the weekend. Thursday afternoon is also the start of the media debriefs: a system where a rider will answer questions from the press for five minutes in English and then his native language.

Access to people is important. It's the best (and some would say the minimum) provision that teams and manufacturers can provide to the media. There is no need to listen or talk to every rider on the grid every day … but the possibility should exist to ask a question to any of them. It's a system that Dorna still need to refine, although the efforts of Media Manager Frine Velilla and Sandra Bañez have tried to implement order to a melee of timetable clashes. External Communications and Press Senior Manager Fran Wyld's dedication to hearing and filtering the grumbling is also steadfast. She has a look that can freeze you but also a contagious giggle.

They used to call these debriefs 'scrums' and the description was quite fitting, thinking back to, say, the old state of the Lusail International Circuit and how everybody would try to huddle around Rossi or Márquez, hopefully jabbing a recorder or phone in the rider's general direction for a hint of audio, or perhaps cursing the nearby departure of a helicopter that made the whole endeavour pointless. Even now, some of the spaces for these occurrences on Thursday through to Sundays and post-race are laughably tight: Le Mans, Mugello, Misano, Catalunya are the worst offenders, where riders cannot even see who is throwing them a question.

Naturally, TV comes first. Print journalists' time and needs will often be at the mercy of riders' duties for the broadcasters. In press conferences, we inch and scramble around cameras, tripods and light stands. I recall one particularly vocal Spanish colleague telling me upon closure of the Thursday presser at the 2024 French Grand Prix, when we were wedged at the back behind equipment, team staff and hangers-on who didn't need to be there: '*Somos la mierda del paddock*' – 'We're the shit of the paddock.'

I sometimes look at my colleagues and think, 'What a disparate bunch.' A decent span of ages, a mix of cultures, nationalities and personalities. One person obsessing about tyre performance, another quizzing riders about their personal lives. Some questions leave you looking at the ceiling in boredom or disbelief (what do you expect these guys to say in their second or third language?) and others open a thread of opinions that are fascinating and provoke ideas for stories. There are some masters of the game: Mat Oxley, Michael Scott, Oriol, Jaime Martin, Emilio Perez de Rozas, Paolo Ianieri, Günther Wiesinger, Borja Gonzalez, Michael Turco, David Emmett, Neil Morrison, Mela Chercoles, Manu Pecino, Tom Baujard, Markus Zorweg and others. Simon Patterson is a serial Tweeter.

At the track, as a journalist, you watch MotoGP through a screen. The thirty seconds or so of a start might be enjoyed through the media centre window, but otherwise the app is open at your desk or you are craning your neck at the monitor, making notes, writing updates.

Close-up viewing from the circuit road is a perk, but one of the best feelings in the job is wandering down pitlane or standing at the side of the track and a germ of an idea sliding into your head. Then being able to speak to the relevant people to get a few quotes or information to flesh it out. The process of splurging it onto a blank document and getting a point across with some credibility never gets old or staid. Then, no matter how many people might have read or seen it, just one person commenting that they liked it is enough to check a box and move on to the next one.

———

In MotoGP, there is the action, the state of the motorcycles and the technical 'race' in the pitlane. Add in the competitive element of groups of people endlessly searching for ways to outdo each other and it's like reporting on a fun, niche 'conflict'. I've heard it said that we who work and find stories in motorcycle racing can hardly be classified as real journalists. Perhaps that's true compared to investigative work exposing corrupt institutions … but I'd rather be writing about Pecco Bagnaia's latest Ducati modification than Keir Starmer's latest pointless press conference or following Trump around from one rally to the next. If someone reads an article, any article, and even a spark of mental reaction is formed, then surely it was worth it?

In sport, excellence is always captivating, whether it is sustained or a momentary flash. When Fabio Di Giannantonio turned up to Qatar for the penultimate round of 2023 and said in his Thursday debrief to a handful of journalists that he would be going for the win even though he'd had only one podium finish in almost two years of MotoGP, Birty and I turned away from the table stifling a snigger. *Good one, Diggia.* He should have been laughing at us on Sunday after a mesmerizing performance and a victory that reignited his career and led to a VR46 contract for 2024 and then the next two years afterwards.

Media hysteria can be over the top. MotoGP 2015 and the Sepang clash was both the zenith and the nadir in this sense, and splintered opinion in almost every quarter. Journalists sided with either Márquez or Rossi after their latest bad-tempered spat; the slinging of words allowed writers to indulge in the mudfest and warm it nicely with reams of comment.

A collision of titans? Or multimillionaires getting grimy with playground tactics? Distasteful or delicious? It's still mentioned and stoked by figures ten years afterwards. Cal Crutchlow's 2016 Argentina win was clouded by Marc Márquez's overt brainfog and the contact with Rossi that caused the Italian to crash. In the post-race press conference, Crutchlow's first comment was to despairingly ask 'Where is all the media?' as the fuss to chase the latest fall-out episode between number 46 and number 93 ignited post-race.

There have been many instances where a rider has had his words twisted to suit an agenda. Or there are media that rip off the work or the exclusivity of others. I always enjoyed interviewing Bradley Smith because he was very thoughtful and articulate, not only on motorcycle racing but life as a motorcycle racer and trying to find a place in the elite. One set of reverent comments Brad gave me about Valentino Rossi for a *Daily Telegraph* story in 2018 was picked up and used by other news outlets out of context, as if Smith was insinuating that Rossi was past it and Dorna were just milking his profile. I was a little shocked at the way it was spun by the likes of the *Daily Express*. I apologized to Brad at the next grand prix for the escalation and he gave me a gesture as if to say: 'Welcome to the game.' For the life of me, I cannot fathom why journalists and writers would feel the need to publish something that is patently untrue or total fabrication. If it's only about clicks then what's the point?

Foraging for greatness and its cause is something that media and fans love. It's why we angle on the likes of new Spanish generational talents like Pedro Acosta or David Alonso and how they are formed. We also love comebacks by athletes we perceive as greats or needle-shifters. We celebrate those good sportsmen who get their day to shine and bask in the full 'fifteen minutes'. Writing about everyone is impossible but everybody will have an engaging moment or moments in their career and that's when you gravitate towards them. Though this is also the slightly superficial part of the job that is awkward to deal with, and naturally builds suspicion or cynicism from the athletes. The whole 'Oh, so *now* you're interested in me ...' notion.

More experienced sportsmen know that the media is like a weaving 'S' curve on the track: some can take it smoothly and quickly and pick the cutest line to use the bends to their advantage; others detest the challenge and just want to hurtle straight onwards. Some bounce from barrier to barrier on their way through. Journalists, like fans, will always be drawn to those that can negotiate the path with aplomb, both for style and decorum.

In his later years, riding for Pramac, at Mugello, Danilo Petrucci broke off from one of his debriefs on an uneventful session as we were standing around him by the race truck and dejectedly said, 'Guys, why do you come to listen to my bullshit?' The timing was perfect. Danilo is an example of a rider that garnered a lot of goodwill for his humble and inclusive nature. In a fifteen-minute interview slot with him, you'd need three, four questions at most. He would also answer in a way that made you feel like you were getting an exclusive reaction or inspired moment of thought ...

and then you'd read a similar comment in another article. A skill in itself, I suppose.

Since the 2020s, Luca Marini has become many press men's 'go-to' rider. The Italian's ability to open the window on what he does has increased his stock vastly as a member of the MotoGP grid. He managed to repel most of the nepotism finger-pointing over being Valentino Rossi's stepbrother with six wins and fifteen podiums in Moto2 and then gathered two podium finishes and a gaggle of top five results in three years with Ducati. 'Ay, this is bullshit,' Uccio told me in Sepang. 'If you are in the top five in MotoGP then it's not because you are Valentino Rossi's brother. It is not like this.'

It was a small surprise that he made the ballsy move to go to HRC and their rudderless effort for 2024, with the RCV motorcycle clearly uncompetitive and very much a work in progress. MotoGP in 2023 and 2024 was a humbling position for Honda for their lack of results, and when considering their size and record in the sport. It was a gutsy call from Marini, who effectively turned away from a winning bike for the challenge of transforming the company's fortunes. It also sidelined him slightly as the questions around his career became very samey. Losing a second a lap must also be the biggest test of a rider's motivation and professionalism, even if many whispers in HRC speak in glowing terms about the way Marini has embraced the task.

I've spoken with him a few times. In 2023, I felt like I had to ask why he made such effort engaging with media when the same activity for his teammate, Marco Bezzecchi, looked as much fun as removing one of his tattoos. 'I like to answer questions well,' he told me calmly but firmly, with his angled face and almost sleepy blue eyes. 'I like looking at interviews from other riders but also from other athletes in other sports. I feel that I want to understand more from what people are saying. I love to learn something new or something from the "inside" of sports that is impossible to understand from only watching TV. I like to give this to fans, to the journalists and to the people that want to know more about our job and our sport. In my opinion, this sort of stuff is interesting … and I don't mean just in MotoGP but in football or whatever. I don't want to be a rider that answers just "generally" – sometimes, yes, you need to – but if I can do something more then I like to, because the fans of racing are very passionate. Maybe telling them more about it will increase the passion? From the television it is hard to take in everything.'

Interviews take place on a clock, and they rarely run over fifteen minutes, but the possibilities for discussion and insight with athletes like Marini give substance that very rarely comes through a TV equivalent or even a podcast (those mediums require more of a performance). There is more nuance and subtlety to a written article, and arguably more storytelling. Luca spoke with me in his second language and his general enthusiasm to ruminate on the minutiae of MotoGP gives writers a reason for being.

The evaporation of magazines and outlets for long-form material is a gnawing frustration in MotoGP. There are constantly stories to be told, and not solely to stuff a website for clicks or to bash out lines to service SEO protocol. Therein lies another 'rub': dwindling readerships mean it's not always easy for writers to acquire a tiny block of a rider's day. It's a matter of priorities. Understandably, teams must comply with a sponsor's ambitions for visibility and that means mainly TV and lots of eyeballs. A racer will have minimal time for promotion in a grand prix schedule that involves the track sessions, preparation, team meetings, guest and fan engagements, commercial duties and physio. If a team's PR crew then want precious minutes for him to dress as a panda and produce a humorous video for TikTok or social media where it will gather hundreds of thousands of views and lots of interaction then it's clear that the humble journo with a drastically smaller audience will slip down the list. We're lucky that press officers still value the contribution of specialist 'print' media and that analysis and perspective can co-exist with other 'output'.

The Catalan Grand Prix in 2024, round six of the series, and Luca Marini was yet to score a point. There had been rumours in the Italian press that he wanted to break his two-year contract and escape the results-and-performance limbo. Apparently, Marini was pissed off. Not an apt time, then, for another one-to-one chat. Luckily for Luca and me, Honda's woes were not really my subject on the table. I was more interested in his genesis than the company's regeneration. Why MotoGP for him? Especially with a name like 'Rossi' a permanent part of his shadow. Due to his family and his connections, was MotoGP and motorcycle racing some sort of pre-ordained path? Sitting on the top floor of the wobbly HRC hospitality, I watched the eyebrows raise as he jostled on the edge of the armchair in his white HRC shirt.

'I was just trying to do what I like,' he explained. 'Sport was one of the most important things to me because I believe it can teach you many good things for life, and motorbikes was the sport that gave me the most emotion. I tried to understand my feelings and to enjoy the whole process. When I was a child, I never thought I was different. I was doing what made me happy. If I was not happy to be in the disco then I would be at home watching races or thinking about school – because I *had* to be good at school. I wanted to be on a track, on a bike and trying to improve myself every day.'

But where did that come from? 'This I don't know! My parents never told me how to do something. They gave me a lot of love in their ways, for sure, but my father told me – always – that the day I wanted to stop with the bikes then no problem, be free to do whatever you want, and I really appreciated this on one side but on the other side I would have liked to have been pushed more by my father to improve more when I was younger.'

Luca was twenty-seven when we spoke. He had recently married Marta, his partner of seven years, who he met while they were in primary school together. They were expecting their first child. Marini would end up as one of seven fathers on the grid. He was talking from a position of reflection and hindsight, but it is still unusual to find someone who wished he had been urged further. 'Yes, because I saw many riders that were forced more by the parents.' I brought up Jorge Lorenzo and the fractured relationship with his father/coach Chicho as an example of the other extreme.

'Extreme maybe … but he won five world championships!' Luca reasoned. 'So, it depends on which side you want to see it. I think he is enjoying his life now and with time, everything passes. I think you have to thank your parents because they only want the best for you, and they love you in their ways. Also, my mum let me be free in every way, not just bikes. She just told me: "Keep focused and don't worry."'

Marini might not have been coerced to race but, like all of his peers, he was backed. Support in some form or another seems to be essential. On the 2024 grid, Jorge Martin, Miguel Oliveira, Augusto Fernandez, the Márquez brothers, Raul Fernandez, Brad Binder and Pecco Bagnaia all had parents or siblings in their corner to call on.

'My parents saw I was fast and I was enjoying motorbikes and could have a career,' Luca went on. 'It was just the flow, following the flow. I was a rider and I was enjoying myself, so we looked to see if we could continue because I had problems of money as my dad was paying everything. He is a psychologist so not a rich man. I had to find sponsors and also my brother sometimes helped me and that was great. I was growing a lot during the years in the [VR46] academy and everything was getting better. I was enjoying it more and more and continued with this flow. I was loving what I was doing.'

Remuneration was apparently one of the reasons for his HRC choice. Understandable enough for a factory rider with a sizeable job on his hands, but Luca felt like he had to offer some perspective because sportsmen at his level have another type of determination and motivation. He stared into space, thought and then tried to express himself. 'The thing is that money is not what you are *looking* for when you are a rider. Yeah, we earn a good amount of money but it is never enough! It is for this that people go to Andorra. And, in the end, if you focus on that it is never enough. I focus on enjoying my life and doing something that gives me emotion, good feelings and trying, obviously, to earn as much as possible!'

He pointed at his personalized but blank cap on the low coffee table in front of us. 'But, as you can see, I don't have a sponsor so I'm not a guy who is pushing as much as others to have them because unfortunately it is not my target here. I think I am smart and clever and when I stop this career I will find something that can help me earn more money than here. I am just trying to enjoy this career and the only way to do that is to fight for victories and this moment I need to find fun in a different way.'

Marini's mentality switch from a race-winning motorcycle to

a machine, team and company in flux was one of the running themes on the grid during 2024 MotoGP. His career choice might still turn out to be inspired, didactic. His predicament could be very temporary, for the better or the worse, but it does provoke questions about the role of psychology.

'It is a super-powerful tool but, trust me, everybody uses it a lot,' Marini confided. 'You cannot see it clearly but it [MotoGP] is more about this than the physical side on many occasions. This sport is super-difficult and dangerous sometimes, so you have to be focused when you are riding. We have trained a lot since we were children because most of us started when we were four or five years old and we are ready to do everything.

'I am in my best moment and mental shape,' he insisted. 'It means when I arrive in the paddock, I am happy and calm and ready to do my job in the best way. But then we start to struggle with the bike on track! When you miss the speed then you cannot be … happy. I want to be fast, and I want to enjoy riding the bike, but at the moment, without the results, it is a little bit difficult. However, I'm also satisfied to work with all these engineers and Honda.'

———

Cal Crutchlow liked to talk and occasionally prod at journalists, and was unreserved with his views on the world and MotoGP, but sometimes found his words being misconstrued, and that bred a vein of mistrust. He tolerated us though, even when I knew he couldn't really stand the presence of some. Cal's debriefs around the rectangular white table in the LCR Honda hospitality, his team for six of a ten-year MotoGP career, were normally the longest, the funniest and sometimes the most baffling, with contradictions and power-statements that couldn't be fully backed-up because it meant revealing confidential information. I remember being surprised by his alarm over a stray cat wandering around under the old huts at the Lusail International Circuit, when it had the temerity to brush his leg during a debrief. Cal is not a cat lover.

As a rider he was fearless. I first met him at Valencia in 2009 when he had been freshly crowned as World Supersport champion. He was decked out in Yamaha Motor Europe gear and was clutching a poster of Valentino Rossi that he'd had signed. After one decent year in World Superbike, in which he grasped a couple of wins and appeared on the podium half a dozen times, he was racing against the Italian in MotoGP. Cal entered the class at the time when satellite bikes were just starting to keep pace with their factory counterparts and towards the standardization of the machinery in the middle of the decade. A difficult rookie season for the twenty-five-year-old was an obstacle to jump over but he was already grabbing the first of his nineteen podiums by his second term.

In Valencia one year, he requested that we stay behind after one debrief. He asked us our helmet sizes and proceeded to present us all with a Crutchlow Arai replica from a large pile of boxes he had in the LCR office. I was shocked at the gesture and, to my embarrassment, asked if he was taking the piss somehow, which made him smile. The helmet is still on the shelf to this day. This completely unnecessary gift was typical of the man I came to vaguely know; underneath the occasional surliness and the direct, sometimes frosty exterior was a kindness and a consideration. The way he would build and nurture a team environment around him was also in contrast to the 'suffer no fools' demeanour. I recall him once claiming that he didn't have a bad relationship with a single person in the MotoGP paddock, and although it was a statement made in that somewhat cocky style of his (which you had to embrace because it's how a motorcycle racer should be, right?) it was also true. He seemed incredibly well connected, apparently liked his fancy watches and had a deft hand with the stock market.

MotoGP riders do not get a mountain of time on the 2-million-euro race bikes. The first pre-season test in Malaysia (always the opening laps of the year because of Sepang's warm but not unbearable climate in February) is the biggest shock to the system of speed and forces after what is normally a docile winter break from December through to the end of January.

'On the first lap, we are up to 330kmph almost immediately, that's 200mph,' Cal told me during an interview in which we focused on the physical sensations of grand prix racing. 'It feels like being on a rollercoaster. But within three laps, you then feel nothing. After the first run of the day, you might complain that the bike is a bit too powerful or too fast and your eyes won't be up to speed, but once you are used to it and you get your head around it, then by the second run the bike isn't fast enough! We always want more power. The acceleration to 200kmph is where you really get the g-forces. It doesn't have that much effect on your body when you are tucked in but it hits you coming out of the corner and from other factors like the wind.

'There are some moments when you get off the bike and you think, "Ufff, that was fast,"' he said. 'Mugello is one where afterwards you think, "That's ridiculous." Places like Jerez and Turns 7 and 8; we go around there at speeds that you cannot imagine. I remember thinking, "How does this work?"'

'People think we are mad,' he reflected. 'They think the speed is mad, but if you don't want to go that fast then team managers will always find someone who does.'

Crutchlow told the press on more than one occasion that he did very well out of contracts for the factory Ducati team and then the HRC connection from LCR. He was also tied closely to Monster and Alpinestars. It was recompense for a marginal first-year deal in MotoGP with Tech3 and Cal was always proud of the fact that he bet on his own career and turned down bigger and better offers to stay in WorldSBK. Racers like Sam Lowes and Jake Dixon followed in kind. He was clued up with paddock politics and liked to remind us that we knew very little about the tactics that went on in negotiations and contracts in MotoGP, while keeping schtum and discreet in the same instance. If he ever publishes his own book and decides to 'tell all', it will be an essential read.

Generally, Cal came across more of an athlete or warrior than a motorcycle rider. Reluctant brilliance on two wheels. I once quizzed him on his profile and motivations for roaming limits. 'To be honest, I love riding my bicycle a lot more than riding my motorbike,' he confessed. 'People will find this comment strange but I don't really like riding motorcycles. I love my job. I love racing and the competitiveness of it and trying to improve but I don't really enjoy motorcycles. We are so on the limit here, and you are always trying to get that extra inch. It is so difficult. Sure, when you are winning and you are in that zone you love it, but most of the time it's difficult. I love what I do but I don't have a motorcycle outside of the circuit. If I rode any other bike now it would be a scooter. I understand 100 per cent why people love riding, don't get me wrong – the freedom, thrill and the smile it gives you. The sport is great fun … but you are constantly "at it". You cannot cruise in MotoGP. Any biker would love a day on my bike but that's because they don't have to work and strive to find that last tenth [of a second]. I never throw in the towel. I'll always go down trying, and that's always been my style. I'm not the most talented – I'm not exceptional – but I know I am good riding a motorcycle.'

When Cal retired from racing at the end of the pandemic season of 2020, his time had come. He looked weary with the routine of MotoGP. He and Lucy had a daughter, Willow, who was growing up fast, and he also seemed to be wearing all the hard hits of grand prix. From 2017–2019, he crashed fifty-three times trying to re-shape the RCV that, arguably, was already becoming a Márquez-only motorcycle. Perhaps the worst was the broken right ankle at Phillip Island in 2018. In his last two appearances at the hallowed track as a full-time racer, he was either in the hospital or on the podium; the last silverware of his career was earned there in 2019.

He tested and raced for Yamaha after 2020 but the physical problems did not stop. A particularly nasty infection in his right wrist shelved a lot of his 2024 duties. The joint looked swollen and immobile when I saw him last at Silverstone for Monster's inimitable Trackday of Legends during the summer.

'There are points of your career where you think, "I'll never miss this …" but deep down, you know you will,' he admitted in the interview. 'I won't miss the politics or the status of being a MotoGP rider because I'm not in it for that, and I'm not being unappreciative of my position by saying that. I will miss the team, the bike, the speed and the competitiveness.'

While constant travel is perhaps the biggest gripe inside the MotoGP bubble, it is a necessity that has to be swallowed.

Leaving home and the family means a switch of 'mode'.

Clicking the front door shut engages the mind to work. There are some races that feel easier to attend, maybe due to the accommodation, the general set-up or the vibe. The Grand Prix of the Americas being one. In 2024, I was passed by a pick-up truck, driving alongside Austin airport on the way to COTA, and saw 'Gas, Grass or Ass' plastered on the back. As bumper stickers go, that one tickled.

Flying long distance is an obvious drain but, for example, Malaysia's fandom for MotoGP is infectious and being part of a 'happening' is always invigorating. The sharing sensation of being in one place for one significant purpose is like the positive communal feeling people have at music festivals, concerts or other mass gatherings. A grand prix is a single annual fixture. And I guess we are only ever going to be around for a certain number of them.

Atmosphere or gimmicks: there is usually a hook to each and every MotoGP event.

From 2007 until 2022, and then again in 2024, the Lusail International Circuit in Qatar has given fans their first fix of a new season. The championship's sole appointment in the Middle Eastern region is also the only grand prix to take place at night, illuminated by the Musco lighting system with 3,600 sources (or bulbs) and 500km of wiring, calibrated for specific spots in and around the track so as not to affect the riders' vision. The site underwent a massive overhaul and facelift in 2022 in preparation for both MotoGP and F1 hosting duties and, in terms of infrastructure, is now the leading venue on the calendar.

The Lusail paddock is a striking sight of high-tech and of a budget with no bounds. Entering the new paddock 'avenue' between the doors to the pitboxes and the two-storey buildings used by the teams for offices and hospitality is like entering a fancy shopping arcade. Landscaping and giant second-floor LED screens arch overhead and beam riders, moving bikes and team insignia, getting brighter as the evening beckons. As the sun dips and the decorative illumination brightens into a cocktail of soft gels and fluorescent shades, the paddock becomes a place of 'chocolate factory' wonder – about as far removed from the spit, oil, fuel haze, tools on the ground, fag-ends and half-dressed women imagery of the sport from decades past as it's possible to be.

There's not much outside the gates apart from more site work, desert and wind, stadiums, facilities and debate. Doha sits just fifteen minutes south of Lusail by car, and is an ever-changing and ever-rising density of man-made monoliths of steel, glass and neon. The obsession with construction and legacy and the utter scale of the cost and effort hide the fact that Qatar is a country in perpetual motion, with questionable domestic and foreign policies.

Nevertheless, MotoGP has an established twenty-year home here, and the bond with Qatar extends to Qatar Airways being an official and valuable partner for freight and logistics as the sport moves around the world.

The physical (and ideological) isolation of Lusail at least allows you to sample MotoGP in its simplest and rawest state. The service road adjacent to the track on both sides is desolate, aside from the passing media shuttles. Marshal posts near the corners are manned by two or three staff wrapped up against the sun and then later the falling temperatures and a stiff breeze. When the bikes are not howling around the flat course, the silence is both eerie and relaxing. There is no PA commentary or announcements because there are no people beyond the main grandstand (which has been full for recent editions of the grand prix) and the new

Lusail Hill Turn 1 enclosure. The ground around Lusail is gravelly and stony. The wind is warm as it brushes the face and transports the fierce echoes of MotoGP bikes throttling out of the pitlane somewhere. The setting sun provides the many photographers circulating different points of the service road with 'golden hour' shots that can only be enjoyed in Lusail.

When darkness falls, the floodlight network makes a 'bath' of white. The effect never fails to impress. The endless rows and rows of different heights of pylons, poles and pillars are immense. It is a metal, humming 'woodland' of technology and power.

Sand blows in. It is barely noticeable on the ebony asphalt – only when a rider slows and cruises off the racing line, then it plumes like motocross roost from the rear tyre. The new race fuel, 40 per cent non-fossil origin since 2024, smells sickly sweet from some of the Ducatis and the KTMs. Lusail had been resurfaced as part of the general remodelling and the grip levels are, by all accounts, phenomenal. Speeds and lap-times were already surging for the 2023 grand prix in November and before Fabio Di Giannantonio enacted his wizardry. The state of the asphalt was good but the age-old issue of Lusail and its unique location prevailed: the breeze, the sand and the dirt. The problem became chronic in 2023 when Jorge Martin's tyre choice created one of the defining moments of the championship as TV viewers watched the irate Spaniard repeatedly shake his head as he dropped to tenth and allowed Pecco Bagnaia to breathe a little easier going to Valencia's title decider with a bigger points margin.

Qatar's usual position as the opener means it is the source of nerves, hype and conjecture over potential and possibilities for the season ahead. However, 2023 was a shake-up because of the building works and MotoGP arrived for the penultimate round instead. The timing found teams and riders reaching the limits of energy and patience for what was the fifth race in six weeks. Conflict flared up when Franco Morbidelli and Aleix Espargaró found each other on track during Saturday's FP2 session. Morbidelli, who had been gaining a reputation for cruising and interfering with flying lap attempts during the previous season, came a little too near to the Aprilia man in Turn 5 and closed the line to Turn 6. This draped a massive red flag across Espargaró's visor. Aleix gesticulated and vented – so far, so normal – but when Morbidelli throttled alongside him on the exit to the corner and reached out his right hand either to calm his rival or apologize he was met with a left jab to the side of his visor. By clubbing the Italian with his fist Aleix showed that relationships between MotoGP riders can be more about cordiality and avoidance of controversy rather than genuine friendship and bonhomie. The incident led to an exchange of spiteful personal barbs to the media that dominated the chat that day. Espargaró was dropped to sixteenth on the grid and fined 10,000 euros.

Exhaustion could have been fuelling the short tempers. Another Espargaró, Pol, two years Aleix's junior, got involved in some on-track bother with another Italian, Marco Bezzecchi, on the Friday. They cut each other up in the first sector then Bezzecchi shadowed the GASGAS rider and butted his rear wheel with his front Michelin six times when the pair stopped for practice starts. The onboard footage was both bizarre and damning of the VR46 rider's antics, as Espargaró gave the gesture as much attention as a barely noticeable insect.

Bezzecchi, with his jet-black, ringed hair, unshaven face and slightly disdainful look can also come across as mischievous. He repeatedly fidgets in press conferences – removing stickers, playing with his seat stool. In the post-race formality at Misano in 2023, he was subtly swigging from the large Prosecco bottle in between questions. In media debriefs he regularly swings on his rear chair legs, like a bored kid in class, and has developed an impressive knack of batting away the more mundane enquiries. At Mugello for the 2023 Gran Premio d'Italia, he looked blankly at a colleague who had asked, 'What happens if it rains?' 'If it rains … then we will get wet,' Bezzecchi deadpanned, to smirks among the other hacks. He grinned to himself at his wit and then appeared to feel bad, and gave a bit more riposte to the question about riding at the fearsome Mugello circuit in the damp.

On Saturday evening in Qatar 2023, Marco was extra playful while also being nonchalant about his fairly aggressive-seeming transgression. This had Espargaró piqued to the point where the Catalan said: 'I don't want to talk about this. There is nothing to gain talking about it or complaining. I think in these moments my age gives me knowledge to know when to talk about this.'

'I touched him, but he didn't turn around, I wanted him to turn around and say "hello", but at the end, he was maybe very angry.' Bezzecchi remarked. 'I already was smiling. But after I met him here, because I didn't have a chance to speak with him, I was smiling, and he was smiling as well. So, fortunately, nothing crazy. It was more dangerous what happened today with his brother …' MotoGP going mad.

Three months later, tempers had eased, and MotoGP was back at Lusail for the second and last pre-season test, two weeks before yet another return for round 1 of 2024. After a few attempts and some conversations with very helpful circuit staff, I had been granted a time slot with Lusail International Circuit President Abdulrahman bin Abdullatif Al-Mannai.

I was quickly ushered through the entrance to the main pitlane building opposite the media centre (with fifty large garages, it is the longest pit complex in the world). To my surprise, Abdulrahman's office was on the ground floor in the corner space at the beginning of the pitlane. I hoped that nobody gets out of shape as they throttle by. The large floor-to-ceiling glass windows must have been bulletproof thick in order to banish the noise. The interior was spotless and incredibly well ordered. We sat on the armchairs towards one corner, his permanent red pass and grid access token standing out against the pure white of his thobe.

I'd been briefed that he would not talk about the costs of Lusail's radical building works. Perhaps the total will only add to the gargantuan outlay that Qatar has made over the past ten years pursuing an image as a centre of elite sporting competition, no matter the discipline or the city-shaping investments required.

Abdulrahman is the power player at Lusail and has worked for seven years at the Qatar Motor and Motorcycle Federation (QMMF). 'We strongly believe that sports bring people together. We are a very small nation, but we have a very big ambition to be a centre for sporting events,' he understated.

Lusail resources to run MotoGP put almost any other grand prix in the shade. But with Qatar angling for a range of topflight sports where does motorcycle racing now rank? 'We are the only country in the region that has MotoGP and F1,' he countered. 'Formula One is not a new thing in Qatar. We had been talking to them for a long time and we never had a good timing for it until 2021. MotoGP has been here for twenty years and it's very important for the country. It is the season-opener. When I travel through Europe and I tell them I am from Qatar, "MotoGP" is usually the first connection they make. That is a clear sign of payback.'

For a younger generation, Qatar is synonymous with the 2022 FIFA World Cup. But it seems there is a compendium of other top events, from basketball, athletics, golf and tennis, to powerboating, equestrian and many more, happening frequently in the country. MotoGP is another grain in the desert now. I queried how the government decided on allocation or priorities for sports or fixtures and the investments necessary. 'For the last twenty years, the government puts a strategy together with different focuses,' Abdulrahman explained. 'Medicare was one, education another and sport was one. Since then, all the sport agencies, ministries and companies focus on delivering these specialties. Qatar focused on bringing the top sporting events, whether it was football, tennis, golf and motorsport like Formula One and MotoGP, and now we have the World Endurance Championship. These three are the pinnacle of motorsport, if you think about it. Nothing is simple, easy and quick but the events are world class and speak for themselves. They attract tourists and fans. It helps us to make better infrastructure and it motivates us.'

MotoGP was one of the first world championships to camp in Qatar and the deal signed with Dorna was the extra oomph the Qataris needed to get a shovel into the Lusail sand and rock in 2003. Tome Alfonso Ezpeleta, now FIM safety officer, was the man picked to help get Lusail built and up to spec for MotoGP in just eleven months. He lived in Doha for four years to enable that process and induction. 'It was like a hook because it was an amazing project and Qatar back then was nothing like it is now [for development and profile],' he told me from his office at the Grand Prix of Valencia in 2023. 'Two years beforehand, Bahrain had started construction on the F1 track, and having MotoGP in the region with a new circuit was something I wanted to be involved with. The government had been in contact with Dorna for a long time already so it was question of bringing everything together to make that first date of 2004. Everything went very fast.

'The first year was a learning experience of how to keep the circuit clean,' Tome continued. 'Grip is important! We also had to educate people about MotoGP; similar to the situation that F1 found when they went to Bahrain. We had to talk to authorities and border control, customs about freight, checks and deadlines. There are different rules and regulations for TV as well, and we wanted to do things in a different way. But the collaboration was there. It was a state project, so the will was there. It was more that we were explaining what we were trying to do rather than begging for things to happen. When a country like Qatar commits to something then you get their best efforts; like the World Cup, MotoGP 2004 was a deep project.'

Installing the lighting was a secondary phase but wasn't a straightforward operation of fitment and then pushing a button. 'In 2006, we did a test with three riders,' Tome recounted. 'We prepared Turns 1, 2 and 3 for the trial. The amount of light we were providing we considered acceptable and then they rode and we watched. We had a meeting afterwards and I remember them coming back saying, "It's not enough …" We got a bit nervous because the companies we were working with had a lot of experience but it was in different areas like a football stadium or hockey, or even NASCAR ovals, where it was different to what we needed, which was coverage on the run-off, the inside of turns and how that was managed. But we had specialist partners and we got the result finally.'

As a track, Lusail is a rapid, flowing test but the paddock was dated with rows of temporary cabins and huts and by no means sufficient for F1. Again, the government was able to throw their weight at a project. 'It was very challenging because we had a short time. We brought in Tilke [German circuit designers] and wanted the paddock and facility to be modern and warm,' said Abdulrahman. 'We wanted the teams and the riders and drivers to feel very at ease when they come here, so the whole design was based on that and then the question was: can we finish on time? With the help of government agencies, we were able to do it. I think we had 15,000 people here working at one point, over thirty companies and contractors to finish the project before Formula One. We had eight months. We pushed and pushed. Not all the offices are finished, the academy building also. We have another phase as well where we will work on the spectator areas. The implementation will come at different times because we have other events.'

In 2023, MotoGP breached virgin shores by heading to India for the first time.

The barrage started from the first minutes inside a Delhi taxi. It was late and dark – always the worst conditions to arrive at a new destination, but the utter lawlessness of Indian metropolitan streets was accompanied by the cacophony of horns from cars, buses, tuk-tuks, bikes, vans, all manner of four- and three-wheeled vehicles. Even the bicycles trying to fit their way into the major highway of chaos and peril must have had their own hooter of some kind. It would be the most aggressive transit scenario in the world if the continuous audio din wasn't used as a warning system. The trucks even had 'Beep to Pass!' lettering on the back. Forget mirrors and indicators. Beep, swing out and hope for the best.

I've driven in territories in southeast Asia where you have to forcefully relax all ideas of road discipline, but India is another level of disorder, stress and outright danger. I was virtually open-mouthed at the rally from my hotel in the southern central zone of the city out to the Buddh International Circuit the next morning, that takes forty-five minutes, while maintaining a stern grip on the rear passenger seat, and one hour forty-five back into town with the utter cluster of traffic that explodes Friday evening.

It seemed that even rental cars in Delhi come with a driver. I chose to pay for the service through my hotel at the Sheraton, in a district of Saket in New Delhi. I met Nagender; an incredibly patient man, finely dressed every day in a white uniform with blue and gold shoulder epaulets and apparently the right mild character for the madness of the roads we navigated. I felt a little guilty that we pulled into the Buddh International Circuit [BIC] every day around 8.30 and he then parked and waited until I was finished, 12–13 hours later. By Sunday, I was at the point of asking him to please return to his home or family, which I found out is only an hour away, but he insisted on being present in P1 parking for the duration. I did spot a cooler box in the boot by day three, however, so at least he was prepared.

MotoGP's incursion to India came about with a lot of strong will from local but ill-fated promoter FairStreet Sports, surrounded by 'will-it-won't-it?' speculation for months. Debates raged over issues such as the alleged state of the circuit, that had not seen world championship action for a decade, since the last F1 fixture in 2013, the situation for work visas, the customs fees, and the taxes and clearance process that had proved such a tough obstacle for the cars in their last stay.

The visa application and approval system was hit and miss, and created heightened off-track emotions in the media pack and paddock. There was no rhyme nor reason to it – some arrived reasonably early, others in the nick of time, others too late, forcing flights to be lost or rebooked and prompting a flood of panicky messages and anger in WhatsApp groups. A skeletal international media corps made the trip. HRC had to cancel an important promotional event in their biggest market where they were the second bestselling brand among 13.5 million bikes sold in 2022. Marc Márquez was held up. He arrived and went straight into the pre-event press conference, his face wearing the contours of a man who hadn't slept much on the plane.

Adversity was an ingredient of the event. It was accentuated by the desolation and the poverty so heartsinkingly found on almost every street corner. In contrast to the majority of teams that were camped in the Noida district closer to the circuit and within the Uttar Pradesh state where the track was based, my hotel in Saket meant I had the standard and security of international accommodation but at a greater distance. Part of the shuttle run was through the Okhla area, across the daunting, dense mass of the Yamuna river, until we got to the open expanses of the Delhi Noida Direct Flyway tollroad with its welcoming green shrubbery, low trees, and frequent advertising boards with a large image of Fabio Quartararo in action declaring that MotoGP was about.

The stint before traversing the Yamuna meant encountering the kind of urban decay and squalor that was jaw-dropping. 'Wreckage' is about the only suitable word I can use to describe the crumbling buildings, the precarious street wiring, roads disintegrating in broken slabs, and bricks protruding out of pavements and bridges. Precarious installations, remnants of vehicles and shelters and waste strewn everywhere. I could not tell if people were working, surviving or simply waiting for something. The sight of one man sat having a haircut in the street looking at a tiny, wonky, broken mirror hung on a factory wall while another person wielded a white sheet and scissors increased the sense of farce to my spoilt Western eyes. On Thursday, Friday and Saturday, my goal of working in the back of the car on the way to BIC was scuppered not only by the Nagender's battered suspension but also the panorama outside my passenger window. A fifteen-minute delay one morning was caused by the stubbornness of a huge, horned ox that decided to sit in the middle of the throughfare and would not budge, glancing at the traffic trying to squeeze by with a defiant air of disinterest.

There were bikes and bicycles everywhere. Weaving, accelerating, braking, swallowing every metre of space between overloaded buses and trucks. There didn't seem to be a limit on the passengers or what could be towed. There was also no dominant brand. All types, sizes, states and speeds. The rusty remains of expired motorcycles or those not so lucky with the traffic-dodging were left to rot with other refuse at the side of the streets. A gaze-inducing example of commuting was a family of three hurtling along on a small cylinder road bike; father in control, mother at the rear and a two- or three-year-old baby wedged in between, held in place while swigging from a bottle of milk.

Arriving at the BIC four days in a row left me in a ponderous mood each time. The feeling of upheaval was heaviest on the first day when we pulled up to the circuit to be confronted with a large group of people waving broomsticks in the air – apparently some form of protest by the cleaners. Resistance from the people in or around the grand prix would flare up again as practice sessions were delayed, allegedly due to marshals leaving their posts due to a lack of drinking water.

Socioeconomic echoes quietened the moment I stepped inside the MotoGP bubble, where we all found a surprisingly vibrant environment of friendly, enthusiastic people and innocently curious national media. 'Every person you bump into on the way into the paddock tells you about their bike and what they ride and where they ride … it's awesome,' surmised Brad Binder.

The strong warmth from the staff and some of the fans I saw was still nothing like the temperatures that seared in the mid-thirties. The short walk from P1 through the paddock and into the media centre was brutal – the kind of glare that instinctively makes you trot along pursuing the smallest jagged edges of shade. Perversely, the air conditioning in the press room chilled us to the bone and caused some technical difficulty for photographers with the sharp contrast fogging the lenses. The track itself had caused concern among the riders for the proximity of the walls, particularly at Turns 4 and 10, when they could make the first checks between warm rain showers on Thursday, but the prospect of tackling a new track prickled the curiosity. The vast main straight even provoked talk of a new top speed record (in the end, the figure in the race was 14kmph short). The daunting dive into the tight Turn 1 was deemed more of a challenge. The bend would test the braking skills of the entire fields in all three classes (Aleix Espargaró: 'Corner one is like ice …') and must have been one of the fieriest crash or error points on the 2023 calendar. India would head the crash stats for the year, tying with Le Mans for seventy-nine falls. Álex Márquez was the worst victim, with a set of broken ribs.

Although some way from Delhi's highest recorded temperature of 40.6 degrees for September, the IndianOil Grand Prix shed light on one of the rarely considered features of the purpose-built, prototype motorcycles and the way they are not built for rider comfort in mind. In sweltering climates the bikes can boil, but the way they distribute air around the machine is often the issue. In India, it was the Aprilia riders who were suffering the most and being clasped in the optimum tuck position out of the blast of air was unbearable. 'I don't know [for] the rest of the riders, but for us it's over the limit,' Espargaró exclaimed. 'The heat that the bike produces is crazy. We could not really breathe after eight–nine laps.'

'This is the one where I suffer most the heat,' admitted Maverick Viñales. 'We need to do something on the bike because it burns. Phwoah; really, really.'

The world champion, Pecco Bagnaia, was not immune. 'You start to feel that your throat is burning. Your legs are burning … and our bike normally is good for that. Malaysia is already hot, but not like this.'

The inauguration was marked by Bagnaia's crash and trudge back to the pitbox with his helmet visor firmly pulled down and by Jorge Martin's weird scenario in which he had to back off the throttle to zip up his suit and then collapsed in the pitlane and the Parc Ferme afterwards. Martin had won the Sprint on Saturday for the fourth time that season and would be the master of the shorter contest with nine wins all through the pilot year of the format scheme in 2023. 'I think I'm the best Jorge Martin that I've been so far in my career. I hope to keep improving,' he'd felt compelled to tell us after the checkered flag.

On Sunday, and after being victim to the Indian temperatures, he was a little humbler. 'You have to trust me when I say I gave my 100 per cent,' he gasped. 'I was dehydrated when it was eight laps to go. So, you know, was really difficult to finish …'

By the time of the Indian Grand Prix, the duel between Martin and Bagnaia was chasing the mercury up the gauge. Martin's crash in Indonesia and his wrath at Michelin in Qatar were to come, while Bagnaia would recover from his Buddh blunder to go on a six-race podium streak to the finale in Valencia. In

India, Pecco was asked to comment on Martin's presumed lack of fitness or conditioning. It was tricky to tell if the Italian was being sincere or pointed with his comments. At the time, there was a little bit of curry spice to his view that Martin's fade was 'something strange but is also very singular. I had the luck that I'm not suffering so much … I did many laps behind him and it was very hot. But I was not feeling any problems.' Perhaps there was a small hint of nettle. And perhaps Martin responded, because he promptly defeated his fellow Ducati rider by almost two seconds the following weekend in the rain-hit and cooler Motegi in Japan.

BIC had been dusted off for MotoGP but its dormant status (save for a few corporate events and other activities where the track had been used for running and bicycle races) meant it was a bit rough around the edges and in need of a deeper spring clean. The world championship's brief residence had also ruffled some of the wildlife. I was preparing documents early Sunday morning when my attention was drawn to the full-length windows to my right. A large macaque monkey was casually hovering outside, circling the bushes for any shavings of food. It could well have been Jack Miller's friend from Friday.

'I was sat watching the Moto3 session,' the Australian recalled of his experience inside the Red Bull KTM pitbox. 'The TV's quite high on the wall. I was just sat there chilling and there are cables going into a tray. I saw something out of the corner of my eye and, honestly, [I] thought it was a f**king dog. I thought, "What the f**k is a dog doing here?" But it was a monkey. And it was not a small monkey: it was a big monkey. I want to say almost like a baboon. I was waiting to see the pink butt. I said to the boys: "There's a monkey in the box!" We threw some bananas up there but he hasn't come back yet.

One of the boys had a coffee knocked over yesterday and they couldn't work out for the life of them what happened. I think we found the culprit.'

On race day, some photos of what looked like a large cobra in the grass in the infield circulated in the photographers' WhatsApp group; although it was a little too blurry to be substantiated.

Ticket prices to enter Buddh were rattling around the £30 mark for the general infield (the monthly minimum wage for a skilled worker in Delhi is allegedly just under 230 euros) with the price increasing for grandstand seats. Sadly, in 2024 the grand prix would falter; FairStreet went out of the picture to be replaced by a direct deal with the government but the stability of the grand prix melted into the heat haze. What next for Buddh and Bharat …? The possibility is there for a big fanbase. 'It was the first edition and the people wanted to see how was MotoGP,' said Fabio Quartararo. 'They could see the show was on.'

For the MotoGP 'show' then it doesn't get any better than at the best track of them all. I first went to Phillip Island in Australia in 2018, but it felt like I already knew every dip and curve. If there is one race to watch on TV each year then it's around the 2.7 mile trajectory that bends and flows with the contours of the land metres from the Bass Strait and almost Australia's deepest southern tip. For a European, it's a long way: usually two long-haul flights to reach Melbourne and then an hour-and-a-half drive from the city across the bridge and onto the island.

'PI' feels like a track in a nature reserve. Driving up to the entrance gives the impression of entering a park: green lawns, white fences, trees and a lack of the concrete and big grandstands that typify most circuits. The paddock and pitlane are small and antiquated but, somehow, it adds to the flavour.

In 2018, it was eye-opening to see how narrow and tight the Phillip Island asphalt is compared to the wide sweep of pace on TV. It was also staggering to consider that the track has one of the highest average speeds of the whole season, so much so that dialogue had already started in 2018 about MotoGP being too fast for the venue.

As many will know, the epic 1989 grand prix was the first in the country and at PI Gardner clocked an average of 103mph during that bright day in April. In 2022, Jorge Martin set a new lap record and beat it again to pole position in 2023: seven seconds quicker than the 500s were managing at the end of the 1980s. Alex Rins won the 2022 grand prix – one of the most memorable contests in the modern era of MotoGP as 0.8 of a second split the top seven finishers, at an average of 109mph. The race was one of three at Phillip Island to sit in the top ten all-time closest podium margins.

Strangely, Marc Márquez's 2013 race record still stood as the 2024 event approached and part of the reason involved one of the biggest drawbacks of the Australian Grand Prix. The alleged insistence by the Australian Grand Prix Corporation, who organize and promote both the Aus F1 and MotoGP fixtures, that the bikes have to run in October and a spring climate (the F1 takes place in the drift from summer to autumn in March) means the weather is viciously changeable from one day to the next. In 2018, t-shirt conditions shifted to the need for a jacket in the space of twenty-four hours. When I went back in 2023, the forecast for rain, wind and cold forced MotoGP to be swapped to a Saturday race for the first time since the Dutch TT in 2015 and was notable for Johann Zarco finally reaching the top step of the box. On Sunday and in the deluge, hardy Moto3 riders were complaining about numb hands as they completed their race distance. Moto2 was started, halted and eventually scrapped for half-points and the re-jigged MotoGP Sprint was also binned. Sitting in the media centre, it felt farcical. It was also frustrating to have come all that way and paid all that money to have the grand prix affected by circumstances that were avoidable. I guess the soaking and wind-battered fans that turned up thought the same. I wished I could have had some of the stoicism of Phillip Island Auto Racing Club's Warren Reid, who I'd interviewed on a sunny Friday. 'You just have to spread the events out and it depends on the calendars,' was all the capped septuagenarian could offer on what is evidently quite a political issue. 'We're used to it! It's part of the attraction and that you never know what you are going to get,' he smiled.

The timing of Phillip Island – one of *the* anticipated races of the year for the whole paddock – is an annual gripe. The year 2023 was an exaggerated case but it's generally accepted that the grand prix will be windy and brisk, so much so that Michelin bring a special tyre allocation to Victoria.

To emphasize the unpredictability, the climate was not an issue on the hot and bright Friday in 2023. I walked down the dip at the end of Gardner Strait and around Doohan Corner and as far as I could up to the southern loop. The view over the Bass waves and beaches was majestic. There is a purity to the setting and the surroundings that makes it even more of a spectacle. It looked very busy along the walkway already but the 'time warp' sensation and the prospect of the track in front of me added to the singularity of Phillip Island on the MotoGP trail. Saturday was cloudier and cooler as skies switched. It was still impressive watching the glide and braking into Lukey Heights, and nervy observing the drift out of Stoner and the hard braking for Miller and what used to be the problematic Turn 4.

'The major change to the layout was Turn 4 being shortened, and the circuit in total by about 400 metres to give some run-off into that corner,' Warren told me of the major upgrade undertaken by Bob Barnard and his crew during 1988 to convert Phillip Island from a dilapidated circuit into a reference. 'Originally, you could have been doing the same sort of speed as the main straight and there would have been nowhere to go if you tried to do this tight right hander and made a mistake.'

Phillip Island has a history for motorsport going back almost a hundred years, when cars used to race on a simplistic street circuit. The current grand prix course was created in the 1950s by the club. 'I was here in the 1970s, working on the track, and we ran a combined car and bike event here in January. It was used as a farm in between those races,' Reid recalled. 'The Lukey family owned the track and put it up for sale so they wouldn't give a lease and nobody was going to make the resurfacing that was needed. It was finally sold; Bob Barnard finally leased it and did all the track works to make it what it is now.'

'We also had confidence that Phillip Island would be a world-class track, now proven to be correct, and in our ability to stage an event such as they had never seen before,' Barnard wrote in his journal that became the self-published 2020 book *Seven Crazy Years*. His tome is an anguished account of the hassles, politics, pettiness and general chaos of trying to organize a grand prix, and quite a sobering tale of PI behind all the beauty.

'There was so much media,' Reid remembered of the landmark 1989 bike debut and Phillip Island rebirth. 'We had great motorcycle riders but we didn't have those high level events to attract large crowds of people. That event attracted a lot of attention and extra people for future years and helped the profile of motorcycle racing in Australia no end.'

The New South Wales government sniffed an opportunity to attract the grand prix to Eastern Creek and Phillip Island lost MotoGP until 1997 (while retaining solid WorldSBK links, a race that *does* happen at the right time of year). 'It is probably more corporate now than it ever was, that's just modern sport,' Reid said. 'I think it has gone from strength to strength and there are improvements made every year with safety. The whole of Turn 12 has been redone with gravel traps and run-off areas. Turn 1 the year before that. Also, the amount of attention that is given to making this event look good is quite spectacular. It is getting harder and harder to fit it in.'

The retro atmosphere of the grand prix and the less invasive commercial side of MotoGP are complemented by another absurd factor (or endearing, depending on your point of view) of sessions being halted for local wildlife that have invaded the track. It's a characteristic singular to Phillip Island but, in my opinion, also a bit amateurish at the same time. 'The fact that cars and bikes are roaring around the track doesn't seem to have any effect on the wildlife at all and they go about their business!' Warren laughed. OK then!

As it's a rider's course, it's little surprise to learn that Valentino Rossi, Casey Stoner and Marc Márquez have the highest number of wins there. '*Allora* … every circuit is very different so every weekend you need to work and make research of the year before together with [your] experience,' Rossi explained to us in 2018 and ahead of his 400th career start. 'When you arrive in Phillip Island, it is something big for sure. First of all, because you have to always keep great attention; the track is very fast and the conditions are always cold, sometimes it is wet. You have to be very careful. It is not easy to use the track.'

'Honestly, it scares the shit out of me but I love it at the same time,' Scott Redding said. 'There are not many tracks when you are coming out in fourth gear, hitting fifth and going over the crest with a sidewind that is lifting the front up and then you need to go into the fast corners like that. It is one of those tracks that has so much character. There are few places with the same charisma and you have to understand it to go through it.'

Marc Márquez's 2019 win was achieved by a massive eleven seconds after a tussle with Maverick Viñales ended with the latter on the floor. It was his fifty-fifth win and, appropriately, allowed him to jump over Mick Doohan as Honda's most decorated rider. 'Most of the riders, if you ask them which is your favourite circuit, which is your favourite corner, they will say a fast one, because we enjoy it more,' Márquez said. 'But it becomes more dangerous. This is one of my favourite circuits but a small mistake can become a big mistake.' Márquez had a massive moment the previous year when a collision with Zarco on the Gardner Straight sent the Frenchman into grass-cutting mode all the way down to Doohan, where he was unharmed. 'You just say: "Oh shit!"' Zarco explained of the contact that created one of the worst but luckiest crashes at PI.

Denial is extra helpful on the Island. Riders have their hands full as it is. Rossi banked five MotoGP wins at PI. Stoner was better, though, with six triumphs. 'He was so fast here,' Danilo Petrucci said in awe. 'I only met him on track in 2012 – my first year in MotoGP and his last – and I think it was the first time that a man really impressed me on the bike. I saw him doing exactly what he wanted at this track and he won the race easily. Unfortunately, I don't have his skill.'

Stoner in Stoner Corner is one of the iconic MotoGP sights and demonstrations of the otherworldly technique these racers have. He would pick up, manipulate the front end and point the

Ducati or Honda at a different angle to achieve the drift and the speed. Casey has chatted about the genesis and formation of his approach to the corner on podcasts. It is weird to hear something so precise and difficult (and dangerous) presented so easily. Watching riders copy the side-slip and direction change up close does make you fantasize about how it must be in the saddle.

———————

In March 2020, I had the first and, to date, most instructive 0.1 per cent level of insight into what motorcycle racing feels like. KTM's launch of their revamped 1290 SUPERDUKE R involved a presentation and ride in the Algarve: a morning spent on the lanes of southern Portugal and an afternoon lapping the Algarve International Circuit (AIC) to digest the speedy spirit of the punchy naked bike. The SUPERDUKE has 180hp and banks of torque. It is still one of the finest and most ludicrous motorcycles I've ridden on the road but Portimao, scene of MotoGP grands prix since 2020, represented a track 'debut'. Gulp. KTM had asked ambassadors Jeremy McWilliams (one of Britain's notable grand prix riders in the modern era and still the world's fastest racer in his sixties) and ex-AMA superbiker, Supermoto and dirt track ace Chris Fillmore to add some tuition. Even now, I can remember how I sat on the KTM in the AIC pitbox, fastened my gloves and took a large preparatory breath as I motored down pitlane following Jeremy and riding the track special SUPERDUKE with slick tyres and all the trimmings removed.

I'm a naturally cautious motorcyclist. I have very little trust in the people around me or my own ability to correct a major error, so I happily motor along in my comfort zone. Kicking the SUPERDUKE aggressively up a few quickshifted gears took a while but the batch of twenty-minute sessions quickly became one of the most exhilarating experiences I've had.

Initially, I found it hard to fully commit and lean into corners. The AIC is between ten and fifteen metres wide but it seems like 100; it was fiddly to know exactly where I should be and where I should be braking, tipping and aiming. At the same moment, it was utterly thrilling. The swoop into the downhill final turn that winds up to the main straight is like a g-out. The speed up to sixth gear made my head shake and my vision go blurry, and I held onto the SUPERDUKE with all the power in my arms and with the alarm that I might get sucked off the back. I was talking to and coaxing myself all the time.

Turn 1 was a quest and remained so for the entire day. The dip into the braking zone made my stomach roll and the apex of the right hander came alarmingly into view quicker than I'd have liked. Jeremy told me to brake when he braked, but I have no recollection of trusting my skills and courage that quick, that much. With more and more laps, I learned that the Brembos of the 1290 SUPERDUKE are pretty damn good and I slowly got a bit later, a bit harder and a bit closer, my knee lower and lower. I loved the exit of Turn 5 (scene of Bagnaia and Márquez's clash at the 2024 grand prix) and the full throttle run up 6 and into 7. Winding on the gas out of the long right Turn 14 got the KTM wobbling and working the traction control, which I managed to slowly dial down as the afternoon went on. It was a revelation how well the bike handles when it's pushed. You realize you are tasting only a little of what it (and you) can actually do with it on the road.

'I think I was fourteen years old when I hopped on my dad's Superbike at Grant Raceway in Michigan and everything was too fast and everything happens too quick. You don't feel comfortable, you don't trust the tyres: there are so many different things going on. It's foreign!' Fillmore said to me in one of the breaks. I'd known Chris for a while, since he'd raced for KTM and the old RC8 superbike model. I made a story about him and his predilection for action sports by heading to his shared flat at Newport Beach in California. Ray Archer took some cool photos of him in his leathers hanging from some rocky overhangs down on the sand.

'As a racer, you hone your skills on slicks with tyre warmers and we push the limits,' he added. 'We understand them. On a surface that is unpredictable then that is another thing. For a person coming from the street to the racetrack, there are a bunch of "red flags", and it was the same for me getting on a street bike where I wanted to be much more cautious: there was traffic, white lines, guard rails and the knowledge that the road surface could change at any time, or you didn't know what was around a corner. On a track you know, for the most part, it is in a certain condition and there are track marshals to let you know if there is something wrong. So, you start to turn off all those little signals in your head that might make you hold back a little bit.'

'What makes a good circuit rider? Somebody who is very consistent, very smooth and learns good throttle control,' said Jeremy, who has remarkable levels of tolerance. Later on, when I pulled the KTM across the track and 'attacked' Turn 15 from a line on the curb to get a solid thumbs-up from him, it felt like a gold star. 'A lot of things you won't learn for the road you must for the circuit, like brake management and how hard you can pull it and how hard you can push the front tyre into the turn, how much throttle you give when you are in the turn. A lot of guys will go into a road turn and open the throttle when they want to get out: that's not what we do and not how we go faster; it's the opposite actually, and our rolling speed is much higher than it would ever be on-road. It's another level.'

I ended my own track day eager for more, and knowing I could do more. I also know there were a few alarming 'moments' or twitches, so to have been able to ride quicker than I'd ever done and keep everything 'on the island' was part of the adrenaline bundle. I'm well aware that I was riding somebody else's bike and with minimal responsibility, but I went back to the hotel that night with the awkward feeling of really wanting another go, but also not wanting it. 'It is something that starts as a hobby and it can become an obsession,' Jeremy related. 'There are people I coach on track that I see becoming quite obsessed. I think it tests everything: your brain power, your physical shape. You have to use many "inputs" at the same time. It is not the easiest thing to learn in a short space of time and every time you come back then you can improve. The more you ride, the better you become.

'Why do we keep coming back?' he posed. 'Probably because we never really crack it.'

EIGHT

Riders

There are so many intricate and expensive moving parts to MotoGP, it's a small miracle how it spans the continents so easily and maintains a consistent level of entertainment and performance that stimulates a growing fanbase and batters lap records each season. The key fulcrum, that can justify the costs or cause a factory or team to fade away, is the guy who pulls down the visor as he strides out of the pitbox.

Consider the life of a MotoGP racer for a moment. To become the elite, they have been wrapped in their own practice since childhood. They have broken bones and crossed a hospital threshold many more times than you or me. They have been hyped and feted. If they have ridden for a factory team, then they have had a group of people analysing their every movement and gesture on the motorcycle, followed by a fleet of older, experienced professionals crowding around them offering guidance, opinions. They are in demand. They must excel at a risky activity with limited margin for error or misjudgement. Their best limit-pushing might be a blink of an eye too slow, thereby affecting results, confidence, morale in the environment around them, their reputations and their livelihood. They pant at 220mph and exist in a world of tenths.

Some are paid well. They wear the watches, choose their

cars, jet away to the tropics in the winter, flying first class or even private. They spend the hours between sessions on a multi-million-euro race machine training, thinking, plotting. Free time can be swallowed by commitments to sponsors and companies. They have to wear a baseball cap even though they compete in motorsport. They wince in the mornings and must find ways to treat skin burns. They have to diet. They have the adoration of fans, families and girls and guys. They appear on posters and FIM penalty PDFs. Thanks to social media, we know what they are 'really like'. Their words and actions are critiqued. Their motives evaluated and assessed. Their potential and attitude endlessly judged.

Sounds easy. Personally, I think the baseball cap is the worst part.

We want to know them because their desire to enter this lifestyle is unusual. Their essence is based on Shakespeare's 'we know what we are, but know not what we may be', and the biggest difference between us and them is the work and the commitment they apply to find out. Very few get to the root of how and why a person becomes one of twenty-two special sportsmen.

Writing the term 'men' makes me think about how the prospect of women joining MotoGP in the future might be closer than we think, with the WorldWCR finally firing into life in 2024. Who knows what the series could produce in the next decade? The gap to bridge in MotoGP might be easier than in MXGP. The Women's World Championship was formed in 2008 and produced real talent in the cases of Livia Lancelot, Kiara Fontanesi, Courtney Duncan and lately Lotte van Drunen, but the physicality of the sport is a divider, as has become clear when MXW riders have tried MX2 with the boys.

The partners of MotoGP riders often fill the role of the cliched 'rock' to their other half, as well as serving as humanized TV fodder when the director cuts to reactions in the pitbox. (Lucy Crutchlow once gave me the nicest, politest refusal for an interview – she understandably didn't want to talk about the privacy or perhaps the anxiety of accompanying her husband into an unpredictable and uncomfortable sporting vortex.)

Then comes the long-standing friend or friends who convert that relationship into employment as they travel the circuit. Uccio Salucci being perhaps the best and most famous example, but Marc Márquez also has Jose Luis, and Fabio Quartararo has long been part of a double act with Thomas Maubant.

'I met Fabio when he was fifteen,' Tom says. I'm back in Yamaha's 'microwave' in the Jerez paddock. We're sitting at Fabio's designated table, a '#20' sign propped next to us. Maubant is chatty and I get the feeling that an interview in English about his story might be a novelty for him. He recently turned thirty, so he's six years older than the Yamaha man. 'I was managing a beach near Nice that had jetskis, wakeboarding and other activities, and he was there every day. He was living in Spain at the time with his previous manager. It was the first year of him being part of the Estrella Galicia team. He was a kid and was like a little brother with a lot of energy.

'Fabio's dad was working in Nice. We became friends and, at the end of the year when the beach business closed, he asked me to go with Fabio to Japan and Malaysia. I started travelling with him and it was cool because we were friends spending time outside of Europe. In 2016, he was with Leopard [now Honda, then KTM] and we did the same, but then that year we started to work more professionally – I organized and sorted out the gear. He moved to Andorra when he was eighteen and only just had a driver's licence, so I went with him at first so he could adapt for six months and then we made a contract and worked properly in 2017.'

A fighter jet blasts over us. It feels like the ceiling shakes a little. Quartararo's first year in Moto2 was 2017. He didn't blend with the Kalex and was thirteenth in the championship. All the hype and the excitement from his two consecutive seasons of CEV title success as a fourteen-year-old (what is now effectively FIM JuniorGP) had started to subside. Riding the Speed-Up chassis in 2018, he earned his first win and gathered two podiums, but was plucked for MotoGP by the old Yamaha Petronas team after four seasons in which he had not scaled higher than tenth in any championship. A sticky period. But the combination of the 'friendly' Yamaha M1 in 2019 and low expectation for a rookie campaign allowed the breakthrough.

'Moto2 and Moto3 were difficult times. He knew he had the talent but could not exploit it,' Maubant remembers. 'We had two years of Moto2 and then MotoGP was a big step. It became more professional, more people around, and then another step was having the good results right away and the fame, big fame, because the French fans were looking for the next "one", as Johann had problems at KTM. There was a lot of attention, and then he started to earn big money. More and more people came to him for different reasons, and I was here to manage that. I don't know why but I am quite good at being able to quickly make an opinion about people … and Fabio was not trusting many – his family and me. He was friends with a lot of people but kept his distance.'

Quartararo had been managed by two people, the last being Eric Mahé, but then made a change of direction and asked

Maubant to step into the breach. 'Eric helped him a lot because he had experience in MotoGP with other riders and he was able to make the step, but in the end, they were two very different characters,' Tom says. 'The more Fabio grew, the more difficult it became. We talked about what to do. Fabio said he didn't want someone who had a very different lifestyle to him and he asked me, "Do you feel ready to do it?" I thought, "Why not?" It was the eighth year together and I knew everybody here and have good relationships.'

'He is one of the only people I trust 100 per cent, he is like a brother and it's always good to have someone close that you can have fun in the tough times and then also when you are 100 per cent,' Quartararo had told me.

Maubant oversaw the largest current contract in MotoGP at the beginning of 2024 but, contrary to Fabio's occasionally tough words about the motorcycle and his perceived criticism of Yamaha over the past two years, the deal was relatively straightforward. 'I see a lot of media stories saying, "Fabio is not happy with Yamaha," but nobody knows what happens inside,' he reveals. 'We have never had a problem with the team. Never. The atmosphere here is amazing and that is another reason why he decided to stay; there is not a single person that he would change. Even in the low times, the atmosphere was good. Sometimes people get another impression, and that is because of Fabio's words, and we tell him, "Maybe you shouldn't say this …" But he is honest and when he makes a comment or a [social media] post he doesn't always think. He just posts what he wants, but this is also good because he is not fake.'

Tom says the travelling to grands prix is both the bugbear and the benefit of liking and working with a worldclass rider. Tom has been in a relationship with Mathilde Poncharal for some time,

Tech3 Team Principal Herve Poncharal's daughter, who is a press officer for the squad, and that makes the constant movement easier. I can remember when I found the couple and Fabio in a Japanese restaurant on Monday afternoon after the final 2019 Grand Prix in Valencia (he had claimed fifth in the championship as a rookie and with seven podium appearances to announce his arrival), in the one-day reprieve before the Tuesday test. We were the only people in the place and Fabio was partially slumped in the booth, clearly hating a hangover.

'We have the kind of life that is difficult to explain to people that are not involved in this world,' Tom offers. 'Fabio is really famous in France and has famous friends. One day, we would be eating dinner with Neymar and the next day, I was having food with a friend in Nice: the balance is difficult to get. The people who don't know Fabio might think he's from another planet, he wears funny clothes, but if you really know him then he's the opposite of this.'

I ask Tom if he ever remembers seeing his friend under excessive stress. 'Once. In the overseas races in 2022,' he replies, firmly. 'Mid-season, he was seventy-eight points ahead but then the bike started to have some issues. Also, Fabio and the team made some mistakes. Bagnaia was coming back with all the Ducati "games" and they were doing what they could to help him. In the end, if there were eight Yamahas then it would be the same. I don't think I saw him under *a lot* of pressure ... but I think he learned and understood a lot about this world at the time. In 2019, 2020 and 2021 he was enjoying himself, but 2022 showed him some of the dark side. It can be good but also super-shit when you see the mindset of the Ducatis helping each other and Fabio was alone, no teammate. Difficult.

I question Tom further on Fabio's mentality. The talent is beyond doubt, but can he also lead a factory and develop a motorcycle? The response, unsurprisingly, is unequivocal. 'Mentally, he is one of the best, with maybe Marc also. He has taken Yamaha on his shoulders and this gave him a lot of confidence. He knows what he can do. He wanted to stay, improve the bike and come back with this brand. It could be one of the best comebacks in history. He is one of the youngest and he has time, plus he has achieved his dream already with the title.'

Tom and Fabio are the team within the team and have endured all the way from the beginning of Quartararo's grand prix story. That riders are in need of some sort of assistant is made clear by the fact that they all have one (they take care of the leathers, gear, passes, personal requests and other requirements, even down to being good company), but Maubant also believes he needs to keep his ward in touch with reality, to burst the MotoGP bubble and therefore help with overall focus.

'In MotoGP, you need someone, and I think the young riders in the smaller classes are starting to understand this. Firstly, there is pressure and their dream is to come to grand prix and then make the next steps and follow the next dream. At one point, you need someone with their feet on the ground. Many times in the past, after a bad result, I've had to say something like, "Hey, look! We're in Japan, eating sushi, you are doing what you love, getting paid for it! Yeah, you finished fifteenth. Do better next weekend!" I remember in Misano in 2021 before he won the title. We were in the truck and the office where he gets ready and does the warm-up. It is only him and I: he doesn't like to have people around. We were bullshitting. And he was sitting on the sofa being pessimistic because he was starting far back on the grid. I had to say to him, "Would you rather be here now or like two years ago when we were in the shit? Enjoy it." He thought about it, laughed and then said, "Yeah, it's true …" You need people to say things like that because young riders are just like this [puts hands to his eyes to mime tunnel-vision]; they just want to win, be first, be famous, earn money. They must remember that they have a privilege because there are many other people who work so hard every day just to pay the bills or buy things for their children. In the end, one race is one race. There are many races …'

Some riders have had an assistant in employ and treat them as such – handing gloves or helmets across almost like to a manservant. 'We laugh at this,' Maubant says. 'I said to Fabio, "You do this to me one day and I say 'f**k you' and I go home!" I am one of the only ones who can tell him the truth. If he does something badly, like a post or goes with strange people, then I can say, "What the f**k did you do?!" It's important to have guidance, and we see more and more young guys with family here. There are two systems: the Valentino way with twenty people around and then our way. On the professional side, there are more people, like a lawyer and an accountant, doctors, but on the other, we are two, with Maider [Bathe, Yamaha PR] taking care of the Yamaha side, the media, the personal sponsors, and the general assistance. In the box, I might be like the co-driver in a rally; I get all the information for him to see, and it has been that way since Moto3. He doesn't want to change it. Then I talk with the sponsors and the other crew.'

I wonder whether it helps that Tom doesn't have a racing background ('I knew absolutely nothing about it. I saw some races with my dad and knew the basics, like all kids, about Valentino. I was more into football'), and if that means the two can maintain a more rounded friendship. He nods. 'I never go into technical things because, first of all, I know nothing! It is not my job. There are 20–30 people in the pitbox for that. Since Moto3, [my job] is not about the riding or the lap-time but what is happening or has happened in the session. I make notes on the sectors about the others. I'm sure other riders have similar systems. I'll never say to Fabio, "Why didn't you take that line?" when I know nothing about the lines!'

The next level of collaboration for a rider comes through the crew chiefs. This is a specialized role. Again, there are only twenty-two of them qualified to do it. There are numerous precedents of link-ups: Jerry Burgess with both Mick Doohan and Valentino Rossi; Santi Hernandez with Marc Márquez; Cristian Gabarrini with Casey Stoner and Pecco Bagnaia; Ramon Forcada and Jorge Lorenzo; and many more that have burned bright, such as Christophe Bourguignon with Cal Crutchlow; Paul Trevathan with Pol Espargaró and now Pedro Acosta. The crew chief has to be a leader, manager and motivator, a jack of all trades with a wider understanding of the motorcycle, and then balance the politics of senior management's wishes, the requests of R&D departments and the goals of the rider. He must be the smoothest possible channel between the racer's demands and the possibilities of the crew and the equipment. He'll also need to be a pin cushion, a father figure in tough times and a psychologist when it comes to squeezing as much out of his already-motivated charge. The crew chief needs to harness the maximum of the bike and tyres and inflame the heart and soul of the person he sends out to steer it. He will need to stir a chemistry, and either stop the boat from sinking or maintain it skipping across the top of the waves.

On race day at Mugello in 2024, not long past 7.30am, I find Andres Madrid in the Red Bull Energy Station alone on a table for six. He's still eating breakfast. I raid the buffet window and sit next to him. The rest of his crew have obviously just left. I make small talk. Andres' football team, Real Madrid, won their fifteenth Champions League title last night and he is happy to mull over the victory. He says that his in-laws joke that the only thing they don't like about him is his allegiance to the *Meringues*. However, after a few minutes, his stare gets lost in the middle distance and he starts to reflect on Binder's lack of feeling with the bike and how the erosion began after round two in Portugal. He speaks about his rider's predicament like a grievance. The need to find a solution, a direction, is clearly preoccupying the Spaniard. 'It's not good to test at races,' he finally concludes.

I think back to our long interview in Catalunya in 2023. 'Life does get more complicated in terms of pressure,' he admitted then. Handling Binder is his first MotoGP crew chief assignment. 'You feel it on your shoulders, and you cannot compare it to any other level of job here. You get used to it in a way, but I have to say that every evening when you go to bed, you carry some of it with you and it can make for difficult nights. I don't know how it is for the other crew chiefs but you can read between the lines sometimes when you talk with them. You look at each other and you know, but it is something you don't say.'

Madrid never needs to go far to speak to Paul Trevathan. From 2025, the Kiwi will be back in the KTM box as opposed to the GASGAS red of Tech3. 'I think there is way more stress than fun in this job,' Trevathan said to me in 2024. 'And you feel it with the riders too. You get honest comments sometimes. Pol told me in Qatar this year that he did not miss the stress of it at all. Johann Zarco when he was at KTM said that each qualifying lap was like losing one of his lives. If a rider goes through to Q2 directly then they "save a life" every weekend. Those little moments when you're just sitting around the table and the comments come out really brings it home. They give all they have but know anything can happen at any moment and they are not in total control. It is an amazing part of the sport but also good to hear because it drills your focus even more as a crew chief on the safety side and making sure the bike is as good and as ready as we can. The mechanics are aware that they are playing "mini-gods", and if they are unsure then they should always stop me and ask for another minute. We can't take the risk of being unsure and sending him out there to hope all is OK: if they didn't hear the click of the tool or they have that "Did I do that?" feeling then they have to put their hands up. I'll never crucify someone for that. We have to respect it.

'The psychology. Some riders just need to be moved on to the right road. If you look at the Olympics, then athletes take years to train and build themselves up for that one shot. But these guys do it every other week.'

LCR Honda's Christophe 'Beefy' Bourguignon said that the personality of the rider is key. It can make the behind-the-scenes rhythm of MotoGP chime and is the bedrock of the work and the route to success. 'The energy that these charismatic riders can bring to a garage is crazy. You can feel it. Johann [Zarco] who we have now is the same. They have a way of pulling people with them – that's a leader. Without them, we are nothing. If they don't feel good or don't feel confident then it's easy for them to lose four tenths of a second, and when the bike is already behind, then …'

I asked Paul if he and the team could ever feel or forecast how a grand prix would go simply by the rider's mood and pallor at the start of the weekend. I recall an anecdote from a mechanic in MXGP who said the factory team could tell right away if they were going to have a good GP by the complexion and mood of his rider when he first walked into the awning. 'Yeah …' Trevathan started to concur, 'but what shocks you more is when you look at the guy and think, "Oh my god, we're really on it today." Sometimes in FP1, you see the yellow and red helmets popping up on the timing screens and you think, "We're going for it", and you concentrate on building from that. It can also be the way where the helmets are grey, and it's a case of "OK, this weekend we might be in a bit of trouble" and you have to really work to get a good result. Then you get these special athletes that just walk around the corner of the screen in the box and you go, "Wow …" You can feel it. Dani [Pedrosa] was one of those. He was phenomenal for that. It gave you goosebumps.'

How? 'It's a presence,' he replied. 'The thousand-yard stare or the way he'd look through something. Sometimes, even the way he walked around the box. You knew that he had something "in the pocket" and he was ready to show it.'

To me, Beefy's best insight was about the Crutchlow years. 'He was clever.' He smiled at the memory and of a term that is four years in the past. 'He never stopped thinking about what he wanted to achieve, about details, strategy. But when he trusts his people, then he does not lose any energy for jobs that he knows we can easily take care of. He focuses on his riding, looking at the video. He had a special way to look at his data on paper, whereas others use a computer. That was his method. He'd point at a corner and say, "Don't worry there, that's me, but on the next corner, we need to find something with the engine braking." He was able to separate out the performance. I had some riders that would talk about an important thing for fifteen minutes and then for another forty-five about little things like lever positions or the footrest position. Cal was not like that because he knew that it would not make him go any faster. Cal would say, "I don't like the feeling I have, but I know I can go fast with it and I will suffer through it." People loved him in the team.'

The nerviest time for the whole crew comes on the grid and that drawn-out period of waiting and formalities that forms such a crucial part of the show's rising anticipation. Watching how riders deal with this is revealing. Some hunker down behind glasses, headphones on, and block out the world, gesturing occasionally from fleeting words from their crew chiefs. Others chat and joke to dispel tension.

'I always tried to make it clear what we'd discussed about strategy, and what [mapping] switch when and why,' Beefy said. 'With some riders, like Cal, you could really plan a strategy; like when we put his name on the pitboard then that was the time to be careful and not over-use the rear tyre, or the word "Monster" would mean something else. We'd pass messages. He would then remember things like not to abuse the front tyre because we'd grained it. We also use the dashboard now.

'They all stress,' he added. 'Which is good, I think. Some people can hide it, some show it more. Once the bike goes off then they are in their bubble. The stress can have a cost sometimes and we see that those affected make an unusual mistake on the first two laps. They want to do too much too quick.'

'And also there's the fear factor. What you feel on the grid is fear,' stated Trevathan. 'I remember Dani Pedrosa telling us that the first time he went to a F1 race, he thought it was amazing being on the grid because there was no fear. He said there was a party feeling in the box with the music on and laughing and joking. They won't talk about it but it's there. Trust me. That first lap. I don't think they will look in the mirror and admit it but that tension is not only about the butterflies to go racing. It's something more.'

Perhaps it's part of that awkward drug of MotoGP: they don't always like it but then crave it at the same time. 'It's possible,' Paul said. 'But I think it is hard to get a very honest answer from a rider about this, especially when he is still racing. With the injury rate we have now, I see more riders talking about the danger. In the Safety Commission, I think they are talking about it more, and that's a good thing. For many other sports, you are not facing life and death, and it's a sad part of our sport that we do lose people now and again. It must be hard to keep it all in check.'

When the team departs from the grid and the riders breathe and set themselves for the sighting lap, then that's the moment when they are truly alone. It's a time when solidarity is scant. Are riders naturally lonely people? 'They must be,' Trevathan reckoned. 'In the end, they are the only ones who put the [race] helmet on. And trust me, nobody is friends here in the paddock. They have respect for each other, and some get on better than others, but I really think it is like going to war on Sundays.'

Going deeper into the psychological aspect, the extent of the demands on crew chiefs, including those amplified by the exaggerated emotions of their riders stemming from stress, is hard to judge. And how do these people restrain themselves and put the state of the team as priority one? Sometimes it requires a sub-strategy and some subtle manipulation.

Trevathan understands anger provoked by underperformance but has his principles. 'Don't get me wrong, if the guy did not come back and apologize then I'd say something, but I give them the room.' It works the other way. Manuel Cazeaux's annoyance with Alex Rins' crashes at Suzuki was taken out on his headset and captured by TV cameras. The passionate and experienced Argentine is one of the highest-rated crew chiefs in pitlane.

More extremities come when the session ends with a broken

bike in a trailer coming back to the pitbox and the rider doesn't arrive. 'I've visited a few medical centres ...' Trevathan hesitated. One of his worst experiences was Espargaró's crash in Portugal at the beginning of 2023 that led to a broken jaw among other fractures, hospitalization, an eight-race absence and the end of his full-time MotoGP career. 'Your job as a crew chief is to push the rider and to take these risks. When something like that happens then it's not a nice place to be because you also see how it affects the families. That part is not why I come to work, that I can tell you. When Pol crashed, I tried to understand why from the TV pictures we saw in the box but then I decided to get out of there. They wanted to follow, but I said no. I needed a bit of space and the guys were OK with that.'

Crew chiefs also evolve. Some follow riders to other squads or manufacturers; some are more ingrained in the team structure and will adopt a new racer as the cycle of MotoGP moves bi-annually or, in some cases, season upon season. 'With every rider, every group and every team, you always pick something up,' Frankie Carchedi told me in 2021, the year after he won the world championship with Joan Mir and Suzuki. 'It's not about being stubborn and thinking, "I'm the best at this" but about picking the strong points of others and effectively adding it to your arsenal, so that when you get a different rider, you can be more ready. Joan was very young and one of my specialties was working with young guys and bringing them on. I think that helped us a lot, especially in Joan's first year, because these guys now don't get three to four years to learn. They need to be showing podium potential in their first season. We finished 2019 always around the top five or six, and it was a progression we could see, so we knew going into 2020 that we were on the right level and we just needed that last step.'

The amount of trust and the confidence required between rider and crew chief, and the spectrum of emotion shared in countless hours of work (Binder visits the pitbox almost every evening of a grand prix to look at data with Madrid), means establishing a durable professional union and a friendship.

Though a complication comes when the partnership has to end. 'We might say we are "friends" but it's not a normal friendship in a way,' said Trevathan. 'It is a trust and "needs-based" friendship. It has to exist so the rider can come, perform, be himself, let off steam, rebuild, feel protected. Sometimes you get close. Me and Pedro get on fantastically, but if we met in a bar then a nineteen-year-old would not be hanging out with a fifty-four-year-old man! We're "forced" to bond and it's my job to make it happen as well as to ensure that his bond with the team is working. The people-management aspect of my job is massive. Even if I don't like some of the things that he does, then I will support my guy 100 per cent. There are some riders I've worked with who I would not like as a human being or to be dating my daughter! But I respect that this is his job and this is my job and we both have to do the best we can.'

Trevathan spoke quickly, warmly and with evident passion for his work and what it entails. At one point, during a pause in our conversation, he looked at me and said: 'It must be amazing to know the full mind of an elite racer. They are freaks, really, because to do what they do for as long as they do is quite crazy. It is something I admire … though there is a lot going on.'

A rider's sphere includes his rivals, naturally. Many of them have known and shared a track with each other since puberty. This was the case for 2023 and 2024 championship rivals Bagnaia and Martin. They had a relationship and casual friendship extending back to their first days in grand prix racing and this history prevented any real hatred or resentment forming as the pressure built to the final rounds – to the disappointment of onlookers who wanted more friction in their on-track disputes.

The hazards of racing establish a base level of respect among riders (this is easy to see just through the greetings and little off-the-cuff comments when they pass each other in the media centre). And in the baggage of being a MotoGP star, there is a shared acknowledgment of the trials and tribulations. They are all in The Beatles: trapped in a hotel room with people outside, waiting for the next gig on the list, trying to whip up a tune that will create a legacy and bounce them to the next step of what they are capable of.

Watching the riders 'cattle truck' parade on Sunday mornings – a decent idea for the fans and borrowed from F1 – is always a minor observation exercise. Their body language and the cliques and the friendships, who they draw to when they enter the trailer and who they steer clear of. It's a pack of people that, apart from the grid and the first corner of a race, only congregate like that once (maybe twice, if all attend the Friday Safety Commission meetings) per grand prix. When they enter the vehicle, it's a little like looking at a group entering a classroom. Some talk and joke, others find solace or distraction with a phone or a drink bottle. The Spaniards stay with the Spaniards; the VR46 mob and the Italians; teammates that actually like each other. Outliers like Taka Nakagami, Brad Binder, Miguel Oliveira and Jack Miller either make polite conversation or stare into the distance, wishing the whole exercise was over with.

Genuine friendships link Aleix Espargaró and Jorge Martin,

Binder and Miller, but then you also have the freaky mix of siblings pervading the posse as well. In 2022, there were two Márquezes, two Espargarós and two Binders on the MotoGP grid. Where does all this DNA flow from?! Among the competitiveness is also the comfort. A brother is one more person to race but one less to slice through. On the contrary, spats between riders whip up the fervour of the fans, and are poked by the more salacious media, but there is usually one dominant party and the umbrage fizzles out. Think of the inequality of Rossi and Sete Gibernau or the clash of personalities between Rossi and Stoner and Rossi and Lorenzo, which the Italian with his media charm was always going to win. This might be a reason why 2015 and the Rossi/ Márquez war still reverberates. It might be too soon for those two, but other rivalries have melted.

'*Bellisimo*,' Uccio told me, when I asked what life is like for Valentino in retirement from MotoGP, when the angst of hated opposition has paled. 'It all goes away. We are friends with Jorge [Lorenzo] and he comes to Tavullia to say *ciao* to Vale and we have a pizza together. Also, with Casey. He exchanges a lot of messages with Vale during the year about family and his daughters. I like this very much because in the moment on the track, these guys are f**king bastards, but after, when they stop, arrives the respect. They understand that it is not just about sport and the bike: there is life and respect. Vale has a lot of respect now for adversaries. Vale now is happy to get messages from Stoner … a few years ago it would not have been like that!'

Any sincere MotoGP conflict means cash. Sensationalism stokes a greater following and some of the grimier elements of tribalism. For the riders, it is another aspect that can suck willpower or prove a distraction.

Naturally, the best opinions on the heft of MotoGP carriage

come from those who have recently jumped off the wagon. Sometimes the incumbrance of being part of the elite, even for a brief period, is something that marks the psyche.

'I happy that I don't have it every weekend [now],' Pol Espargaró said at the Red Bull Ring in 2024. The Catalan was attempting his second wildcard from three that season, and the smiley, happy-go-lucky manner of the former racer – who now seemed much more relaxed with a microphone of the broadcaster DAZN – darkened. 'These guys who are every weekend riding, and here with you guys, with the media, with the pressure of all these people,' he said of riders who were his peers only ten months earlier, 'they don't realize how bad it feels in [their] bodies and brains. When you are outside – and you see it from outside – and you go inside again, you really feel it. My character really changes a lot. I'm with my wife this weekend and I can feel how [badly] I'm reacting to her every time.'

I looked over at Carlotta, who was waiting patiently to one side. Afterwards, I asked her how temperamental Pol had been that weekend. 'He can be so moody,' she said, rolling her eyes.

'The pressure to handle is very big,' Pol concluded. 'They don't realize because they are used to [it], but it's very big.'

Riders mutate, they grow, they deal with injury and immobility, inflexibility, aches and pains, scar tissue … but also the considerations of what is needed to be successful. To still have the gumption to work and pivot and search: it's nothing but admirable. 'You cannot afford to never be trying 100 per cent, which was different to years before, where you could have an average day but on the right machine you could still be eighth. Now you're eighteenth!' Simon Crafar said in the context of his own grand prix career, now able to appreciate it from a distance. 'To be honest, I don't envy the pressure they are under now. I'm no psychological expert, but I think there will be a necessity to help the riders more in that area of handling pressure because it is every lap of every session now. It was always important to do well but I feel it's ramped up because of the competitiveness of it.'

I couldn't resist nudging Simon to talk about how he dealt with the scrutiny of leading Yamaha's charge against the fortress of speed that was Mick Doohan and how he burned so bright but so briefly. 'Well, I remember a couple of things really clearly,' he began. 'When you had a good session then you couldn't go anywhere without people patting you on the back – fans but also other people from teams, mechanics, crew chiefs, managers, helmet guys, hospitality people. Then, as soon as you had an average session you became the invisible man. Literally. You could walk anywhere and people ignored you! It's a strange world and it's not other people's fault … more the fact that there's nothing to be said if you haven't done anything! You won't be congratulated, and nobody will say to you, "Well, that was a shit one!" It's really weird.

'I remember a time as well when I got to the grid a little bit early from the warm-up lap and I looked over to see my team on the wall,' he went on. 'I thought, "There are two semi-articulated trucks behind them, there's 14–15 staff, Dunlop. Öhlins, the Japanese …" and I started to feel that it was too much for me. I was anxious. My heart was going. It was the first time in my life where I had to make a conscious effort to push all of that away because I knew it wouldn't help and there was more chance of making a mistake. I was at a point where I could not handle the anxiety. The only way I could push it away at that moment was to say to myself: "I'm going to do my very best on every single lap so I know I couldn't have done any more … and if someone doesn't like it, then f*** 'em." Then I felt the weight come away from the shoulders and I could just go about my work. I wish that someone had helped me with that before, instead of the blunt way I did it.'

In 2024, I interviewed Jorge Martin at the British Grand Prix. Part of the story went into what was a short and aborted stint with *Autosport*. I met him in the Pramac hospitality, where we sat at a high table and I asked if he preferred speaking in English or Spanish. 'No, no, with you in English is fine.' We talked a bit about his elevated level of fame. The shoulder scraping, the incessant speed and weekly competitiveness, the contests with Bagnaia and the increasing interest in his life and activities. In 2023, Martin appeared on the zany popular Spanish chat show *El Hormiguero*, where he received flak for using a slang term that translates to 'gay boy' in a derogatory sense. He was being neither intentionally homophobic nor malicious, maybe just green. For all his brilliance on a motorcycle, he still needed to learn the knife-edge balance of good PR. He won the 2024 Spanish Grand Prix Sprint at Jerez but, as many noted in the media centre in the immediate aftermath, all the acclaim and the reverence from the Spanish fans seemed split between Pedro Acosta and Dani Pedrosa, who were also on the box. Throughout 2023 and 2024, the twenty-six-year-old was always on view, always judged. 'Look, you can see,' he said, raising a hand in gesture to the Dorna camera crew behind us, filming in Silverstone. 'I have one of those all day.'

After a while, I noticed a change in Martin. He'd had a weary aspect when we started chatting. I could almost see him bracing for yet another round of questioning about Ducati, Bagnaia, his decision to go to Aprilia. When we talked about other things, like his mental approach and some more personal areas, his eyebrows raised at a few questions and his voice quietened. At times I could detect his cogs whirring inside and thinking: 'Should I have said that?'

'I think I improved the mental side quite a lot because I did not understand how much I was pushing,' he outlined of his 2024 form. 'For sure, I am still learning and improving and there have been moments this season when I have crashed in the lead, so I still need to improve a lot. One thing I work on is refocusing, because sometimes you might lose concentration and you need to bring it back straightaway. This is really difficult and it's a thing I can do quite a lot. Maybe that's my strong point.'

I learned that Jorge cycles as a form of escape as much as a training tool. He enjoys watching true crime or police reality series and he reads about psychology and mental health. 'I can see a lot of sportsmen and athletes having issues with this now. When I read or perhaps learn about these stories in documentaries, I see that my situation can be similar. I don't feel the kind of pressure where, say, I'm unable to breathe … but if you don't work on it then you can arrive at that point. It's not easy and in the past, people didn't know so much but now some people are suffering. I want to be happy. I race motorcycles but I want to enjoy my life, and I want to do it as a job but also because it's my passion and a fun thing.'

To fully clinch the life of a MotoGP title contender and all it entails, Martin began meditation. 'I started this season and it helps me a lot to know about myself and get away from bad thinking,' he said, almost in a whisper. 'I mean … we all have problems and meditation helps me to realize that the problems are not always with me. I can put them away and solve them step by step and not get obsessed by a thought.

'I'm an energetic guy, I'm always doing something from 8am until 11pm,' he added. 'I never stop, so it's hard to stop even for fifteen minutes every day and think about myself, try to breathe and be conscious of my body. I think it is helping me and it is

80 per cent of the step I've made from past seasons to this one. It helps for concentration too.'

How does it make him feel? 'Really relaxed! Really good.' The tanned face and the light eyes sparkled as he smiled. 'Like exiting a sauna; you clean a little bit! It does not stop your problems or thoughts but it helps to understand the important ones or for putting priorities.'

The good looks, the jets and Andorra lifestyle, attractive girlfriend and otherworldly talent: Martin can attract jealousy and quick criticism. 'I don't show all what I have, but for sure, I have my things because I earned them! I worked every day and dedicated my mentality to it, to great performance. I make my money and I try to enjoy it, not only on myself but on my family and family of the future. I do it to enjoy my life. But these days … you cannot show anything or they kill you.'

He seemed the sensitive type and perhaps the online courts of opinion have hardened him in recent seasons. He revealed a lot about his personal story of humble beginnings and that crash in Portugal that led to multiple fractures during his debut MotoGP term in 2022 for Amazon's *Unlimited* series. 'It's very personal but wasn't difficult,' he told me of the exposition required. 'It depends on the guy you are speaking with, if you want to open up, but at the end of the day, they will know everything, so it is better to explain and the way I want people to know. Also, if you don't speak then they won't know you at all.

'My story is a bit different. I don't think much about it, but sometimes I do stop and want to be like the guy who used to go and do laps with a pocketbike. Now there is a lot of pressure, a lot of sponsors and it is complicated. For sure less fun. My story was difficult and I tried to get 100 per cent out of every opportunity I had because I did not know if the following year I'd still be racing.

I'm proud of that. The pressure was high when it was about winning or going home. Now it is winning or being fourth or third. It is a different kind of pressure.'

When we finished the fifteen-minute slot, Jorge said, 'OK, that was something different.'

I have always thought Jorge's nickname of 'The Martinator' was the wrong side of naff. I opened the story for *Autosport* by stating that the moniker is terrible. But, then again, the Spaniard did resemble the relentlessness of one of the near-indestructible movie cyborgs in 2024. I found out later that Jorge was slightly miffed, though the feature was very complimentary.

Eventually, like every rider, Martin will be replaced at the peak of MotoGP. Grand prix retirement can be injury related or it can involve burnout or the competitive urge subsides.

At the end of 2023, Sam Lowes was ending a ten-year stint in grand prix for a move to WorldSBK. He had been the UK's most prolific racer, with ten Moto2 wins, double that in pole positions, and nearly thirty podiums. He was not retiring, but he was pulling back from a long spell chasing a title and dealing with injury and setbacks. Sam came up to meet us in the Ricardo Tormo Media Centre in Valencia. 'It has hit home,' he told the assembled journalists. 'The end of ten years here. You always look back and think you could have been better, unless you are Vale or Marc! On the in-lap, I had a bit of a cry to myself but managed to hold it off when I got to the garage.'

Lowes' path to MotoGP was Crutchlow-esque. After a delayed start to racing, he didn't follow a talent cup route and leaped straight into Moto2 after winning the World Supersport series at the 'elderly' age of twenty-three. He won at least one GP in five of his ten seasons – that included a brief, harsh year with an uncompetitive Aprilia in MotoGP – right up until his final one. 'If somebody told me when I was nineteen and working down the quarry with my dad that I'd be a grand prix winner then I would have taken that!' he grinned at us. 'So, when I won in World Supersport and had the chance to come to grands prix … well, I took the punt and came across. It would have been easy for me to go to Superbike with a two-year deal and with triple the money compared to what I had here. I had some good advisors and people around me and I think it paid off. I achieved. I wanted to do more.'

Lowes believed that the growing prominence for the European Moto2 Championship would be a better fit for promising British riders who traditionally move into Supersport or straight to BSB. There are several names – Augusto Fernandez, Fermin Aldeguer and Senna Agius, to pick just three – who have elected to skip the Moto3 option due to opportunity or their physical size and have made decent career steps. A bigger bike and a fair shot, plus Dorna eager to stimulate the scene; any Brits eying MotoGP in their future first need to have the same thirst as their predecessors and the tank is quite dry at the moment.

'It's a lean spell,' Sam assessed. 'It's going to be a tough few years. For the ones that do arrive here, they need to take some risks. I've crashed too much in my career but … you have to be fast. If you are fast, then people keep you around. People say, "Lowes crashes a lot, but when he doesn't then he's on pole or he can win." I've beaten most of the guys in MotoGP now! It didn't happen very often … that's why they are there and I'm here! I was a match on my day and that's why I stayed. British riders need to go for it. Speed is the base of everything.'

The speed will slide, and riders who walk away from the track and into another area of the paddock can offer golden tickets for more insight, particularly if they join the media. They have the knowledge of the sport and – if they were decent at the PR side – know what press are after and how to tell a story. Then, having swapped a rubbery throttle grip for a metallic microphone, they can impart details and experience to make their position very tenable. If that delivery comes with personality and bravery to back opinions, then you have the best pundit.

It took ex-grand prix rider and World Superbike champion Neil Hodgson time to find his flow as a live broadcaster. He joined what is now the TNT Sports crew in 2014 and one of his first duties in the 2015 season was to bound after Cal Crutchlow when his Honda had stopped while exiting the pits at Lusail and ask what had happened. Cal, helmeted, irked and striding back to the box, didn't give too much rationale. In the wake of that spiky start, though, Neil has become an expert at being an expert. As with, say, Simon Crafar, his racing pedigree also gives instant gravitas to his perspective. He's very likeable and looks a decade younger than his fifty years (dammit).

Hodgy is able to understand what I'm digging for when I request a chat about his career. To turn the onus back onto him means, appropriately, talking on a Thursday at a grand prix. He's either recording TV links or onboard laps, or is in the commentary booth for the other three days. The Alpinestars hospitality in the Barcelona paddock is the venue of choice (again).

The first thing I throw into the air is whether he ever thought he was a bit odd to have been driven, ambitious and focused, racing 125cc grand prix as a British champion by the age of nineteen. 'I've always thought I'm odd!' he says self-deprecatingly. 'I think you have to be obsessed with a sport to become a professional and it becomes the norm in terms of a lifestyle. The crossroads comes when you're fifteen, sixteen and you discover alcohol and girls and proper distractions. It was then that I thought I was different. My brother was a fast motorcycle racer but he discovered those other things and was like, "I'm done." I thought I was different to my mates because anything that interfered with me being the best version of myself and a motorcycle racer was never an option.'

Neil had that paternal push that others, like Luca Marini, didn't have. 'I don't know where the ambition came from but my dad put me under a lot of pressure. I was always trying to please him and if you get the result then everything is happy at home. I don't know if it's the right or wrong way, but it worked for me because it motivated me. I also struggled at school because I was dyslexic and back then I was told I was thick, and that's a horrible feeling. I clung onto sport and motorcycle racing as my outlet.'

As a father to a twenty-one-year-old and a teenager himself, does he understand his dad's approach? 'Absolutely. I had a good relationship with my dad and I don't blame him for pushing me. We had some really tough times but it worked. If he had been nice to me then I wouldn't have been going as fast. I'm sat here now talking to you because of my dad. I needed a kick up the arse. A lot of people think I've come from money; I've had that a few times in my career and the "silver spoon" thing could not be further from the truth. My mum was a van driver for a local printer.'

Neil raced in grands prix and finished eleventh in the premier class in 1995 before he signed to be Carl Fogarty's replacement in the factory Ducati WorldSBK team for 1996 'which was the next best thing outside of GPs … and I wasn't ready for it because I had no idea how to ride a Superbike and I was thrown onto Michelins which I'd never ridden with. I was lost,' he admits. The way that Hodgson encountered and faced difficulty in a career that involved stints in BSB and AMA Superbike and that WorldSBK title in 2003 throws some light on the mental trauma motorcycle racers deal with. 'When you get to this level, you can have massive imposter syndrome because you are against the best riders in the world. Some people are born with it and some have to build and work at it. I was one of the builders and workers,' he opens up. 'I was on a 500 and going well, and then a Ducati and not going well, and the imposter syndrome strikes and it sticks around for years. The only way to get rid of it is by results and they go hand in hand.'

It sounds gruelling, strenuous. When riders habitually say that the fun goes out of racing when the professionalism comes in, it's easy to believe. Hodgson is very frank about his struggles and his comprehension of the whole rigmarole. 'When you have the spotlight then you have to perform,' he continues. 'This sport is 80, sometimes 90 per cent between the ears. How many times have we had good riders here who have never won or had a podium but then suddenly they make that breakthrough and then by the next round they have won again. They have not learned a new skill. Nothing has changed. Riding a bike is the same. It's their approach, mentally.

'When I changed my career around at world championship level and started winning, it was like the last piece of the jigsaw had been slotted in. It's so easy to say: "I believe in myself" and "I can beat this lot" and "I'm the best out here" – but to really believe it? You cannot lie to yourself. In interviews, I'd say, "I know I can beat them all" but I didn't believe it myself. That's why you can do one hundred grands prix and not win, and then you get one and realize "motherf**ker! This is my life and I can do it! It's my time and my opportunity."'

But how did he get to the point where it clicked? 'What comes first? The chicken or the egg? Unfortunately, you need the result to really believe what you are saying, but you cannot get the result until you believe! That's why this, MotoGP, is so f**king hard. We sit here and we discuss it, but I cannot tell you what the key is because I don't know.'

What did those moments of clarity and 'highs' feel like? 'Well, it's the magical part of "feel": what is it? Where is the limit? Is yours the same as mine? I won a race at Oulton Park from the back of the grid and it was one of my better ones. I rode with free abandon. I was fighting for a championship; I had qualified on the front row but was moved to the back and I felt really calm. I wasn't angry. It was like the pressure had been taken off me and I had nothing to lose. I thought, "They are getting it: I'm having everyone." I was Valentino Rossi for a day. I passed them all and checked out. But the magic had disappeared the next week.'

An illustrative picture of how expectation builds but then also brings a rider down comes through Hodgson's description of his eighteen-year pro-career culmination. It is a process of stopping and taking stock, then reflection. 'The day I retired was one of the best of my life,' he states. 'I crashed at Brands Hatch and as I was rolling down the road – and I'm not being theatrical – I was retired from that moment. And it was the best feeling, mixed with pain, as I went to the medical centre. My mum and dad came in and I said: "I'm done. I am f**king done." I never again wanted to have the pressure of that shit. But up until that point, I had worked so hard to get where I was. I wasn't the greatest but I had a decent career. We are in a paddock of gods now, Rossi, Márquez and Acosta, and it's another level. They have much more talent than I ever did and they have the ridiculous desire and determination.

'I'm very aware of where I sit in the rankings and I'm happy with it because it was all I had,' he summarizes. 'I say to younger riders – stating the obvious – "Give it everything", and by that I mean dedicate everything you have because it's a short window. The main reason to give that effort is so that when the day comes – and it might be decided for you – then you can sleep at night. I'm a really happy retired person because that was my lot. I was obsessed and I did all sorts of weird things, especially with food because that was my thing in the 1990s. I was racing 125s and I was a tall rider. I had to starve myself and f**ked my metabolism. I had bulimia and all sorts of shit that you don't talk about, and you certainly didn't back then. You do it because you want to be the best.'

Fans like riders for different reasons. They may support a MotoGP racer because they perceive them to be the best, or because of their personality, sense of fun or style. Sometimes it is even as basic as a piece of iconography. Whenever you speak to riders about fans, they usually say similar things: that the sport is nothing without them, that they wish they had more time for them and that their energy drives them on. All fair and consistent comments, but, as in society, there are all types. I know of motocross and supercross riders who stopped signing gear or attending to hangers-on with a folder of photographs because they knew the items would be floated on eBay within hours. MotoGP athletes can be protective of giveaways for the same reason.

In Aragon in 2024, I walked out of the media centre and the Pramac truck was parked next door. I turned the corner in the paddock to be confronted by Jorge Martin approaching on his electric scooter and watched him almost be pulled off the bike by a rabid fan even before he could get to the team area. There was no request. Jorge looked peeved but still parked beyond the dividing barrier and wandered back to satisfy the selfie demands.

For the absolute most part, MotoGP fans are the lifeblood of grands prix. I cannot efficiently describe how their persistence and excitement at places like Le Mans, Assen, Sachsenring, Jerez and more make the whole scene worthwhile and elevate the importance. Scenes before the 2024 Indonesian Grand Prix in Lombok were overwhelming, as the riders' trailer weaved through heaving, people-lined streets in Mataram for a public event. It was like a football team celebrating a league title. 'I have never seen anything like this in my life,' Martin said in the press conference later. 'It was incredible how the fans were cheering for us and that they were so passionate. It seemed like we are gods or superheroes or something.'

Fandom is thick and real in MotoGP and the prevalence of official apparel (even despite the absurdly high prices of the VR46 lines) is one of the clearest visual signs in local airports, supermarkets, restaurants and high streets that a grand prix is on. As a kid, I had t-shirts with the same design as Ron Haslam's Elf Honda and Barry Sheene's Suzuki leathers; I loved those things.

The appeal of a rider can be multifaceted and there are companies studying and analysing how professional athletes should be more likeable or marketable. Cracking the code for popularity is something Dorna is trying to decipher after Valentino Rossi carried the paddock and the sport for so long. Nagging the riders for improved English skills and more media training is one route but so is a more thorough approach to the sort of storytelling that Trackhouse is keen to explore. The candid 'behind the scenes' TV footage of riders prepping for the podium or sharing a car ride to the rostrum is part of this reworked fabric of how we digest and enjoy MotoGP. Martin's infamous camera buddy from Silverstone will be shadowing and shooting for most of the day when he's at a grand prix to present his profile away from the leathers, helmet and pitbox in some sort of featurette somewhere. Lifting the lid and getting more personal might be the ripest strategy in this Instagram and TikTok era, and as MotoGP balances on the precipice of the potential Liberty Media age.

At the 2024 Austrian Grand Prix, the excellent MotoGP 'Heroes Walk' concept was taking place at the entrance to the circuit. I looked down from the media centre to see hundreds of fans crowded at the fenced enclosure. Riders made their compulsory appearance and the one who stayed the longest and seemed the busiest was Jack Miller. The Australian worked his way along, signing, posing, chatting and smiling. In Aragon a few weeks later, I quizzed him about his status. 'I probably still haven't got my head around it yet!' he replied modestly. 'I can understand that some people enjoy what I do ... I still remember to this day the first time I was stopped in a public place that was not a racetrack. I was living in Tarragona at the time and it was not long after I'd won my first Moto3 race. Someone stopped me in the supermarket: you see them do the double take, they ask if you are who you are and you do the photo. It spun me out at first. It was surreal that they knew who I was. It still happens now [being spun out] a bit.'

On the way home from the 2024 Red Bull Grand Prix of the Americas, I was in Heathrow, squinting against the bright morning light flooding Terminal 5 early on the Tuesday morning. My attention was momentarily distracted by a tall, tattooed lady to my left. I realized it was Ruby Miller, Jack's wife, passing by, with the Red Bull KTM rider following behind with a black travel pushchair containing their smiley and impossibly cute seven-month-old daughter Pip.

We talked and then the Millers sat two rows in front of me on the plane to Barcelona, just a young family on the move, dealing with the logistical complexity of international movement with a baby. At COTA, Miller was one of the main draws, unable to walk anywhere around the circuit without stopping for someone or something, which the Australian obliges with his usual cheery disposition. There was an abundance of 'Miller 43' merch on display.

I first met Jack in 2012 at the Grand Prix of Valencia. He, along with fellow Australian Damian Cudlin, was part of a group that included good friend Gavin Emmett grabbing some dinner at the Bonaire shopping centre, adjacent to the main motorway from the circuit to the city centre. Miller was another youngster trying to claw through Moto3, though with a bizarre cropped red Mohican, his wacky character or individualism was already evident.

We did numerous interviews as he shone for Red Bull KTM in 2014 and came so close to the Moto3 world championship. One media opportunity involved some riding shots at the motocross track at the Circuit de Barcelona-Catalunya, now the impressive Rocco's Ranch. KTM Spain didn't have any SX-F motocross bikes to spare so loaned us an EXC-F enduro bike instead. Watching a nineteen-year-old Miller attacking the motocross jumps with glee with a headlighted and ill-fit for purpose dirtbike gave me sweaty palms and I spent an hour flinching and praying that he wouldn't come a cropper.

At Valencia in 2014, having won the Moto3 grand prix for KTM, he entered the press conference room – sparsely populated at that moment – sat down with Isaac Viñales and Álex Márquez, who had also been on the podium, and immediately grasped the results papers that someone from the team had handed him. 'Two f**king points …' was the audible comment as he stared down at the list of final championship standings and where he missed out by the narrowest margin.

It was tough to watch a fruitless campaign with KTM ten years later in the premier class almost curb his ten-year MotoGP career. But, to this day, Jack is the bright and entertaining rider who gives us the biggest laughs. How can you not want to listen to a racer that drops words like 'prevalent' next to a self-deprecating 'f**king idiot' in his debriefs? His emotional grand prix win for Ducati at Jerez in 2021 and antics such as his hilarious grid predicament at Argentina in 2018 when everyone else peeled off to change tyres ('It was like I had farted and everyone disappeared') or waving at former teammate Bagnaia while tapped out down Mugello's main straight at the start of the 2023 race have only made him more well-liked.

I asked him if the Hero Walk and signing sessions mean fans just blend into one fleshy wall of arms and expressions. 'No, I see the faces and I try to interact,' he insisted. 'Maybe I'm more genuine than some others? I genuinely enjoy seeing people and how happy they are, getting a kick from their programme or their hat being signed. I grew up seeing some athletes who were good with fans and others who weren't and just walked by. I can understand that it gets a bit much sometimes … but it doesn't take much out of your day to give a bit back. Without them, we're nothing.

'I think we put a lot of ourselves out there,' he said. 'The way we interact with people and other riders. You see people getting very excited, some even get tattoos and I say to them, "You don't have to do that!"'

What about the stereotypical elevated fandom in Japan and

the tendency for personal gifts? He laughed at a memory. 'Cal was always really popular in Japan. I think it's because he had that cartoon face about him. I remember his room being full of stuff and thinking it was pretty cool.'

Conscious of his wife and daughter, I prefaced the question about MotoGP 'groupies' with the provision he could tell any stories off the record, but we didn't get that far. But, still, his job description cannot have harmed his pick-up prospects in his bachelor days. 'It's not what people think ...' He turned a little bashful. 'At the end of the day, we're dirty motorcycle riders, not rock stars. It depends what you're chasing!'

The subject does lead on to the theme of how he 'explains' himself outside of the MotoGP world. I'm surprised by his response. 'I had a negative connotation of being a motorcycle racer when I was younger. I did not want to say what I did because it felt like I was bragging, but as I've become older and realize that racing motorcycles is what I do, it's been OK. I used to tell people I was a student. But I love my job and I'm proud of it. I guess I'm too old now to say I'm a student ...'

Aren't MotoGP riders supposed to be mental lions? 'For some people, being here [in the paddock] is their whole being and when they move on to the next chapter in their life, they get a bit lost. I've aways had that understanding that I am a motorcycle racer but I also have a life outside of racing. It does not define who I am. And I don't want it to be my whole persona.'

Jack pondered this further. 'I thought this shit would be over a long time ago because I never thought I was good enough,' he reflected. 'You always think that. Sometimes, I do wish I could be more blasé or delusional. Some people are so sure of themselves or what they can do on a motorcycle that they do get delusional about how good they are. Whereas I feel that I am on the other end of the scale. That's a good and bad thing, I suppose. I think I was more [cocky] in my younger years, signing up for MotoGP [straight from Moto3] and all that. I was delusional then: I knew my talent and my ability, and I knew I could get by with it, but when you're at the top and you are doing well there is doubt that comes into your mind. From what I can see from the outside, maybe other people deal with that better because they are so assured. The chest is pumped out so far.'

As our interview time was running out, a question flashed to mind. I told Jack a little about this book and asked him what he thought fans or readers would like to know about him and his peers through the contents of these pages.

He paused: 'I think what makes us tick,' he said. 'As a fan, that was always what I was curious about: to see what makes them do what they do and be the person they are.'

The underlying allure of MotoGP always comes back to the blatant presence of the extraordinary. The speed and the physics of the machinery, the synchronization with the athlete, the stories that sprout from the sport and the will of the people involved. Motorcycle racing always has a magical madness, and for this reason it fosters addiction.

It's impossible to imagine this changing.

By watching bikes, riders and speed, we might spark the hidden or deep strain inside us to do something equally special. Surely, there is no better feeling in life than being inspired. OK, maybe sliding the rear end of a factory prototype at 150, perfectly balanced, poised, controlling what can snap out of control in a moment … That must be pure zen for the zany.

Acknowledgements

I t feels like this book has been written in many countries and in many places. Snatching moments where possible, whether on the floor of airport terminals, the back of taxis or in an endless sequence of coffee shops. When the keyboard hasn't been active then the brain has been ticking, so for the stints of distraction or diminished energy, I'd like to thank my amazing wife and busy and understanding family, both in Barcelona and back in England. And sorry for the missing phone calls.

I guess it's the case with many books, but there was so much here I wanted to include and couldn't. There is still plenty more ground to cover.

Working in MotoGP would be a harder without the moments of levity and help from a special bunch of friends and colleagues. David, Neil and Steve for all the laughs and weekly banter on the *Paddock Pass Podcast*: thanks for letting me add my weirdness to your weirdness, and for all the people who like to listen or read what we churn out. To Rob Gray for his exceptional work ethic and for trying to make a creative difference in a tough industry and profession. Never change and don't tire with the individualism. The same for Cormac Ryan-Meenan (and cohort Sienna) – very much his own man and amazingly talented with a camera lens, but also a big softie with a very large heart. Pete McClaren might be the most underrated journalist in the sport and the best kind of 'egg'.

Thanks to Chris Hillard for being the kindest person and the best kind of person. To Matthew and Gavin for the friendship for so long and people like Michael Scott, Mat Oxley, Oriol, Birty and the TV comms crew, the excellent Steve Day and Nick Harris. There are other colleagues who have formed part of the journey: sometimes it is hard to put down the headphones and have a proper conversation – gripe-free – at MotoGP, so to those that always have the pleasantness to say 'hello' or offer a smile I also convey gratitude.

Thanks to all those in the 'MotoGP Book Club': you know who you are. The MotoGP football gang as well. Thursdays just aren't the same without a kickabout these days. Elsewhere, the influence and friendship of souls like Ray Archer, Juan Pablo Acevedo, Pascal Haudiquert, Lorenzo Resta and Stefano Taglioni plus the forces of energy that are Lewis Phillips, Steve Matthes, Jason Weigandt and Mike Emery, Simon Cudby and James Lissimore.

At Dorna, there are some amazingly efficient, tolerant and serene people, so thank you to Carlos, Dan, Carles, Sergi, Fran, Frine, Sandra, Ruben, Pilar, Phaedra and all the TV guys that posit an 'hola'.

This book would not have been possible without the good grace and the assistance of the hard-working press and PR staff for the teams in the paddock. Sarah Kinrade, Lia Sissis and Seb Kuhn at KTM, as well as Mathilde Poncharal. Artur Vilalta and Julie Giovanola at Ducati Corse; Carola Bagnaia, and Sara Falzolgher at Ducati UK. Pol Bertran and Laura Beretta at VR46, Cris Massa for his best efforts at Gresini, Lucia Gabani at Pramac, Maider Barthe at Yamaha, Ana Granado at HRC and, of course, the irrepressible and permanently under-appreciated Harry Lloyd. Victoria Ortega and 'Boss' at Aprilia, Irene Aneas and Elisa Pavan at LCR Honda, Maria Pohlmann and Jeremy Appleton at Trackhouse. Karina and Susi at IntactGP and Vicente Vila and

Majo at Aspar: thanks for the Spanish corrections and I'm still waiting for a decent coffee.

The entire Red Bull KTM team for letting me get in the way. Sandra, Riaan and Sarah from the House of Brands.

Also, Alison Hill at Silverstone, Montse Sogues at the Circuit de Barcelona-Catalunya, Simon, Chris and Jimmy at Monster Energy. Bob at 6D and Jason Thomas at Fly Racing; thanks for having my back, JT.

Those who kindly gave up their time to be interviewed (I wish I could have included more of your excellent insight): Tome Alfonso, Abdulrahman bin Abdullatif Al-Mannai, Lorenzo Baldassarri, Beefy, Davide Brivio, Lucio Cecchinello, Mitch Covington, Simon Crafar, Freddie Spencer, Neil Hodgson, Heinz Kinigadner, Michael Laverty, Tom Maubant, Justin Marks, Gabriele Mazzarolo, Bob Moore, Oriol Puigdemont, Florian Pruestel, Warren Reid, Uccio Salucci, the MotoGP Health Centre crew, Paul Trevathan, Paul Williamson, Wilco Zeelenberg. And all the riders.

A major thanks to David Luxton and those at David Luxton Associates for all the phone calls, the endless forbearance and for being the major guiding light (also for the empathy over poor football). To Louise Dixon for standing in my corner. Liz Marvin for the big help with editing. To Ross Hamilton for the initial belief in the project.

A special mention to 'Zam' and the brotherhood of being the last to exit quiet and echoey media centres.

As usual, I've abused my word limit all through this project, so the final gesture goes to those I may have neglected here but do appreciate.

Index

A

bin Abdullatif Al-Mannai, Abdurahman 271–3, 275
Acosta, Pedro 91, 121, 155, 169, 175, 182, 205, 241, 256, 300, 312, 320
Agostini, Giacomo 82, 106
airbags 128–35, 137
Ajo, Aki 164–6, 173
  see also Red Bull KTM Ajo
Aldama, Enrique 232–3
Alfonso Ezpeleta, Tome 244, 273–4
Algarve International Circuit, Portugal 15, 36, 288
Alpinestars 125–6, 128–9, 147–55, 265
Amazon documentaries 119, 122, 314
Ambrogio Racing 163
American Motorcycle Association (AMA), Supercross 100, 173, 186, 188, 245
Americas, Grand Prix of the 110, 179, 225, 267
Andalucian Grand Prix 80, 133–4
  see also Circuito de Jerez – Ángel Nieto, Andalucia
Andorra 156–7, 158, 261, 295
Aprilia 53, 58–60, 61, 64, 157, 168, 174, 194, 200, 204–7, 279, 312, 316
Aragon Grand Prix 81, 86–7, 120, 166–7, 177
  see also MotorLand, Aragon
Argentinian Grand Prix 88, 255, 325
Asia Talent Cup 206, 222
Aspar team 76–7
Assen TT, Netherlands 77, 83, 93, 117, 133
  see also Dutch Grand Prix
Australian Grand Prix 86, 282–8
  see also Phillip Island circuit, Australia

Austrian Grand Prix 155, 170, 191, 251, 323
  see also Red Bull Ring, Austria
author's experiences (Adam Wheeler)
  career in sports journalism 42–7
  childhood and motorcycle racing 37–42
  KTM 1290 SUPERDUKE track experience 288–91
Autosport 312, 315

B

Bagnaia, Pecco 9, 62–3, 64, 65–92, 101, 111, 120, 124, 144–5, 178–9, 198, 260, 269, 280–1, 297, 308, 312, 325
Baldassarri, Lorenzo 75–7, 78, 82, 91
Barnard, Bob 285
Barry Sheene – Daytona 1975 ITV documentary 124
Bastianini, Enea 86, 87, 175
Bayle, Jean Michel 100–1
Beirer, Pit 172–3
Bezzecchi, Marco 257, 270–1
Biaggi, Max 127
Binder, Brad 16, 19, 22–3, 25, 29, 88, 157–8, 160–8, 170–2, 175, 180–1, 182–3, 184, 260, 279, 301, 307, 308, 309
Birt, Matt 250, 254
Bourguignon, Christophe 'Beefy' 300, 302, 303–4
Bradl, Stefan 11, 128, 195
Brands Hatch, UK 37–8, 320
British Grand Prix 39, 41–2, 44, 100, 104, 215, 238, 312
British Superbike (BSB) 33, 215, 316
British Superbike Superteens series 161–2

British Talent Cup, Moto3 211, 213
Brivio, Davide 201, 203–4, 205, 206–7, 208, 209–10
Brno Circuit, Czech Republic 158, 170, 240
   see also Czech Republic Grand Prix
Buddh International Circuit, India 276, 282
   see also Indian Grand Prix
Bulgarian Grand Prix, MX 172–3

C

cameras, onboard 127, 221
Carchedi, Frankie 306
Casabianca, Carlo 71, 72, 78
Catalan Grand Prix 44, 138, 187, 189, 190–3, 204, 259
   see also Circuit de Barcelona-Catalunya, Spain
Cazeaux, Manuel 305
Cecchinello, Lucio 194–9
CEV Championship 69, 295
CFMOTO 145–6, 215
Charte, Dr Angel 139–40
Ciabatti, Paolo 61, 62
Circuit de Barcelona-Catalunya, Spain 11, 88–9, 190–3
   see also Catalan Grand Prix
Circuito de Jerez – Ángel Nieto, Andalucia 52, 82, 95, 98, 133–4, 165, 166, 170, 171, 249, 251, 264, 312, 322, 325
   see also Andalucian Grand Prix
Clinica Mobile 137–8
Costa, Dr Claudio 138
de Coster, Roger 150, 151
Covington, Mitch 186–9
Covington, Tom 186–7
Crafar, Simon 104–5, 107, 110–11, 115, 250, 310–11
crew chief role 300–307
Crutchlow, Cal 108–9, 190, 194–5, 255, 262–5, 294, 300, 303–4, 317
Cycle News 45
Czech Republic Grand Prix 80, 157, 170, 189, 240
   see also Brno Circuit, Czech Republic

D

Daily Express 42, 255
Daily Telegraph 45, 50, 108, 255
Dainese 127–8, 154
Dall'Igna, Luigi 49, 53–4, 57–64, 85
data collection/tracking tech 127
Di Giannantonio, Fabio 166, 254–5, 269
Domenicali, Claudio 49–55, 59–60, 62
Donington Park Circuit, UK 41, 96, 126
Doohan, Mick 41, 43, 85, 151, 210, 287, 300, 311
Dorna Sports 14, 17, 36, 37, 43–4, 52, 89, 95, 105, 127, 135–6, 137–8, 142, 146, 176, 178, 185, 191, 192–4, 198, 199, 200, 203, 205, 206, 213–14, 218–48, 250, 252, 255, 273, 312, 316, 322
   see also Ezpeleta, Carlos; Ezpeleta, Carmelo; Rossomondo, Dan
Dovizioso, Andrea 18, 61, 107, 191, 194
Ducati 9, 16, 18, 48–92, 117, 119, 122, 126, 133, 137, 171, 174, 179, 184, 195, 196, 198, 235, 257, 265, 281, 287–8, 297, 312, 318–19, 325
   see also Bagnaia, Pecco; Domenicali, Claudio; Márquez, Marc; Rossi, Valentino
Dunlop, Michael 115–16
Dupasquier, Jason 89, 143–7
Dutch Grand Prix 77, 83, 93, 117
   see also Assen TT, Netherlands

E

Edwards, Colin 46–7, 108, 136–7
Ekerold, Jon 166
Elias, Toni 201
Emmett, David 46, 50
Emmett, Gavin 44, 324
Espargaró, Aleix 124, 198, 270, 279, 308–9
Espargaró, Pol 173–4, 270, 300, 301–2, 306, 310
Everts, Stefan 122
Eyre, John 20, 23, 26–7
Ezpeleta, Ana 222
Ezpeleta, Carlos 138, 212, 223–4, 226–9
Ezpeleta, Carmelo 52, 220, 226, 227

F

FairStreet Sports 276, 282
fans 95, 321–3, 325–6
fatalities 89, 100, 136–7, 143–7
Fédération Internationale de
  l'Automobile (FIA) 193, 244
Fédération Internationale de
  Motocyclisme (FIM) 9, 43, 52, 99,
  100, 103, 128, 135, 157, 180, 193, 220,
  242–8, 293, 295
  see also Viegas, Jorge
Feld, Kenneth 245
Fenati, Romano 72–3
Fernandez, Augusto 169, 260, 316
Fernandez, Raul 168, 184, 200, 204, 260
Fillmore, Chris 288, 289–90
Fly Racing 135
Fogarty, Carl 41, 318
French Grand Prix 33, 82–3, 177, 253
  see also Le Mans, France

G

Gardner, Remy 168–9
Gardner, Wayne 283, 284
German Grand Prix 83, 117, 134, 204,
  224, 241
  see also Sachsenring, Germany
Gilera 99–100
Gobmeier, Bernard 60
Goubert, Nicolas 235
Graham, Les 99–100
Gresini 117, 194, 196
Guidotti, Francesco 19

H

Hailwood, Mike 91
Hayden, Nicky 32, 46–7, 128
helmets 134–5, 246
Herlings, Jeffrey 102, 122
Hodgson, Neil 116, 140, 317–21
homologation programme, FIM 128,
  177, 246
Honda 20, 22, 26, 35, 43, 57, 73, 79, 90,
  97, 111–12, 114–15, 116–17, 129,
  132, 136, 178, 194–9, 205, 210, 212,
  215–16, 257, 259, 262, 287, 288, 294,
  317, 322
  see also Márquez, Marc

I

independent 'satellite' teams 176,
  193–210
Indian Grand Prix 90, 275–82
  see also Buddh International Circuit,
  India
Indonesian Grand Prix 117, 129, 280,
  322
International Race Teams Association
  (IRTA) 14, 33, 36, 135, 193–4, 220,
  221
Ippolito, Vito 242, 243
Isle of Man TT 20, 100, 115
Italian Grand Prix 102, 132, 138
  see also Misano World Circuit Marco
  Simoncelli, Italy; Mugello Circuit,
  Italy; San Marino Grand Prix, Italy

J

Japanese Grand Prix 43, 57, 85, 90, 137
  see also Suzuka Circuit, Japan

K

Kato, Daijiro 136–7
Kinigadner, Heinz 172
KTM 19–29, 46, 49, 143–83, 189, 194,
  204, 212, 216, 288–91, 295, 301, 324–5
  see also Binder, Brad; Red Bull KTM

L

Laguna Seca Raceway, USA 97, 189
Latorre, Paco 218
Laverty, Michael 33, 211–13
Lawson, Eddie 106
Le Mans, France 15, 177, 249, 279, 322
leathers and protection 124–55, 235, 246
Leatt 135, 136
Lloyd, Mark 22–4, 26–7, 29, 31–2
Lorenzo, Jorge 11, 68, 75, 77, 82, 99, 125,
  136, 156–7, 191, 198, 219, 260, 300,
  309
Lowes, Sam 217, 265, 315–16
Lucio Cecchinello Racing (LCR) 194–9
Lusail International Circuit, Qatar 15,
  18, 21, 86, 176, 229, 252, 263, 267–9,
  271–5, 317
  see also Qatar Grand Prix

M

McRae, Colin 152–3
McWilliams, Jeremy 288, 289–90, 291
Madonna di Campiglio, Italy 55–6
Madrid, Andres 24, 165, 170, 300–301, 307
Mahé, Eric 295–6
Mahindra 76, 77, 164
Malaysian Grand Prix 85–6, 136–7
  see also Sepang International Circuit, Malaysia
Mandalika International Street Circuit, Indonesia 129
Marini, Luca 107, 120, 257–62, 318
Marks, Justin 200–203, 206–208
Márquez, Álex 73, 195, 260, 279, 309, 324
Márquez, Marc 67, 69, 84, 85, 90, 91, 94–5, 99, 101, 107, 116–23, 126, 129, 131, 134, 136, 177, 178–9, 182, 191, 198, 204–5, 219, 260, 266, 277, 283, 286, 287, 289, 294, 300, 309
Marsh, Simon 211
Martin, Jorge 9, 85, 88, 107, 111, 120, 126, 198, 241, 260, 269, 280–1, 308, 313–15, 321–2, 323
Maubant, Thomas 294–300
Mazzarolo, Gabriele 148–55
Mazzarolo, Sante 148, 149–52
Michelin 14, 16, 36, 80, 89, 94, 110, 198, 235, 270, 280, 284, 318
Miller, Jack 16, 28, 29–30, 81, 91, 101, 130–1, 284, 308–9, 324
Mips system, crash helmet 135, 136
Mir, Joan 120, 166, 208, 306
Misano World Circuit Marco Simoncelli, Italy 9, 10, 11–12, 69, 76, 81, 83, 89, 120–1, 224, 251, 253, 270–1, 298
MLav Racing 32–4, 214–17
Monster Energy 9, 45–6, 66–7, 132, 186–9, 223, 265, 266
Moore, Bob 180–5
Morbidelli, Franco 71–2, 79, 133, 270
Moto2 24, 25, 32, 75–9, 80, 81, 108, 111, 140, 143, 158, 162, 167–70, 174, 180, 181, 204–5, 212, 217, 257, 284, 295, 315–16

Moto3 32–4, 70, 75, 77, 89, 114, 138, 140, 143, 146, 147, 158, 162–8, 170, 173, 174, 180, 189, 210–16, 281, 283, 295, 316, 323, 324, 327
motocross/MX 44, 46, 102–5, 116, 118, 122, 143, 149, 186–7, 190, 241–2, 245, 302–3
MotoE 51, 235
MotoGP 13–19, 35–7, 44–6, 235, 267
  annual cost of rider participation 13
  control of excessive expenditure 176–7
  crew chiefs' role 300–7
  the fans 95, 321–3, 325–6
  Health Centre 137–42
  race weekends
    arriving at the circuit 249–50
    behind the scenes/paddocks and pitboxes 13–32, 35–7
    media coverage 250–1, 252–4, 258
  rider weight limit 107
  Saturday 'Sprints' 25, 88, 108, 120, 121, 131, 140, 171, 177, 197, 204, 222, 239, 280, 284, 312
  sponsorship 185–9, 196–7
  Sunday 'cattle truck' parades 308
  see also Dorna Sports; Fédération Internationale de Motocyclisme (FIM); leathers and protection; individual Grand Prix by country and track names; individual riders by name
MotoGP: Unlimited Amazon TV documentary 157, 314
motogp.com 43–4, 77, 98, 218
MotorLand, Aragon 120, 249
Mugello Circuit, Italy 29, 59, 73, 83, 88, 89, 90, 93, 94, 116, 131, 132, 138–9, 143–6, 185, 249, 251, 253, 256, 264, 271, 325
  see also Italian Grand Prix

N

Nakagami, Taka 195, 205, 308
NASCAR 200, 201, 202, 207
Nations Grand Prix 100
NBA, USA 83, 228, 231
Nolan 135

O

Ogura, Ai 205–6
Oliveira, Miguel 79, 133, 170, 174, 200, 204, 205, 260, 308
On-Track Off-Road 45

P

Paddock Pass Podcast 46, 50, 200
Pedrosa, Dani 99, 107, 135, 136, 144, 219, 303, 304, 312
Pérez (aka Pitbull), Armando Christian 200
Petrucci, Danilo 107, 256–7, 287
Philip Morris International 56
Phillip Island Circuit, Australia 15, 80, 97, 249, 266, 282–8
physical fitness, riders 107–9
Piaggio Group 60
Pierer Mobility AG 174
Pierer, Stefan 172
Pirelli 36
Poncharal, Herve 173, 194, 297
Portuguese Grand Prix 169, 170, 306, 314
Prado, Jorge 102–4, 172
Pramac 53, 79, 81, 196, 204, 256, 312, 321
Pro Circuit 188
Pruestel, Florian 143–6
Pruestel racing team 143–6
Puigdemont, Uri 178–80

Q

Qatar 273–4
    Grand Prix 15, 208, 240, 254–5, (*see also* Lusail International Circuit, Qatar)
Quartararo, Fabio 9–12, 77, 81, 82, 84, 85, 86, 87, 101, 108, 126, 133, 145, 177–9, 186, 277, 282, 294–8

R

Rainey, Wayne 110, 200
Rea, Jonathan 147, 182
Red Bull 173, 187, 189
    Grand Prix of the Americas 110, 179, 225, 267
    KTM Ajo 164–5, 168
    KTM Factory Racing 15–16, 19–32, 122, 143, 182, 189, 323–4
    MotoGP Rookies Cup 143, 160, 161–2, 174
    see also KTM
Red Bull Ring, Austria 15, 132–3, 171, 174, 200, 201, 251–2, 310
Redding, Scott 107, 108, 217, 287
Reid, Warren 284, 285–6
riders'
    celebrity and popularity 84–5, 95–6, 310–14, 319–23
    characteristics 302–5
        mental aptitude and intuition 105–7, 108–9, 112–13
        motocross/MX 102–4
        physicality and breath control 107–9
        technical innovations and rider confidence 109–10
        see also individuals by name
    pressure and scrutiny 310–14, 319–21
    relationships 293–4
        competitor friendships and rivalries 308–9
        crew chiefs 300–7
        Fabio Quartararo and Tom Maubant 294–300
        the fans 321–3, 325–6
        parental support 160–1, 162–3, 259–61, 318
        Rossi and Márquez clash 94–5, 99, 136, 255, 309
        siblings 309
Rins, Alex 73, 128–9, 131–2, 157, 191, 195, 198, 208, 283, 305
RNF Racing 53, 200, 202
Roberts, Joe 194, 200, 204–5, 206
Roberts, Kenny 39, 111, 112,
Roberts, Matthew 44
Rodman, Dennis 83
Rossi, Graziano 94, 96
Rossi, Valentino 9, 43, 52–3, 59, 64, 65, 67, 68, 70, 93–9, 125, 128, 133, 136, 137, 154, 188, 203, 219, 255, 257, 286, 287, 300, 309, 320, 322
    see also VR46 Academy; VR46 team
Rossomondo, Dan 222, 223–6, 228, 229–33, 237, 238–9, 241

S

Sachsenring, Germany 86, 133, 134, 224, 252, 322

Safety Commission, Dorna Sports 135–6, 235, 305

salaries and contracts, riders 177–83, 212

Salucci, Uccio 65, 71–5, 76, 78, 96–7, 99, 137, 257, 294, 309

San Marino Grand Prix, Italy 121, 148

Santamaria, Josep Lluis 191–3

Sepang International Circuit, Malaysia 86, 89, 108, 137, 204, 255, 257, 264

Sevlievo Motocross Track, Bulgaria 172–3

Sheene, Barry 38, 39, 94, 124, 322

Silverstone, UK 15, 39, 124, 135, 191, 193, 241, 249–50, 266, 312

Simoncelli, Marco 136–7, 145

Smith, Bradley 108, 217, 241, 255

social media presence, riders 157, 183–4, 189, 296

Spa-Francorchamps, Belgium 111

Spanish Grand Prix 80, 95, 165–6, 171, 312

   see Andalucian Grand Prix; Aragon Grand Prix; Catalan Grand Prix; Valencian Community Grand Prix

Spencer, Freddie 111–15

Stigefelt, Johan 212

Stoner, Casey 52, 91, 97, 99, 106–7, 125, 128, 135, 194, 195, 284, 286, 287, 300, 309

Suarez, Miguel 138, 139, 141–2

Suzuka Circuit, Japan 43, 136–7

Suzuki 46, 115, 203–4, 208, 209, 305, 306, 322

T

Tardozzi, Davide 57, 61, 62, 85, 144

Tech3 Racing 169, 174, 182, 194, 196, 265, 297

Thailand Grand Prix 86, 117

TNT Sports 238, 317

Trackhouse Racing 194, 200–10, 322

Trevathan, Paul 300, 301, 303, 304–6

Trimby, Mike 135

Triumph 32

Trunkenpolz, Hubert 175

V

Valencia Grand Prix 26, 44, 46, 83, 87, 88, 90, 116, 117, 162–3, 174, 251, 280, 297, 324–5

Viegas, Jorge 242–7

Viñales, Maverick 88, 101, 107, 108, 132–3, 134, 156–7, 175, 198, 205, 208, 280, 287, 324–5

VisionTrack 211, 214

Volkswagen Group 49

VR46 64–5

   Academy 65, 70–9, 93, 188, 261

   team 65, 70, 79, 87, 196, 255, 270 *see also* Bagnaia, Pecco; Rossi, Valentino

Wasserman Media Group 180–1, 185

Wheeler, Nuria 44, 219, 222

Williamson, Paul 32–5

Wilson, Jeremy 20–2, 31

WorldSBK 41, 44, 50, 52, 56, 59, 104, 136, 147, 182, 211, 265, 286, 315, 318, 319

Y

Yamaha 9, 10, 11, 20, 37, 46, 49, 53, 68, 84, 93, 97, 114, 115, 126, 133, 136, 157, 177–80, 186, 189, 194, 196, 203–4, 209, 223, 263, 266, 294–9, 311

   see also Quartararo, Fabio

Z

Zarco, Johann 29, 133, 283, 287, 301, 302

Zeelenberg, Wilco 200, 204–6

Zerbi, Francesco 52, 243